Nisha Katona

The secret
to amazing
homemade
curries

EBURY
PRESS

To my roots and my branches
Maa, Monmon, India, Tia, Shona,
Mirren and Nayan.

CONTENTS

Preface   11
The Spice Tree   14
How to Use the Spice Tree   16
Introduction   20
    The Indian Spice Kit   24
    Spice Traditions   24
    The Trinity of Spices   26
    Headnote Spices   27
    Tried-and-Tested Flavours   27
    Starter Buttons   29
    Headnote Combos   29
    Finishing Flavours   31
    Seasoning   36
    The Naming Game   38
    The Treatment of Spices   38
    How Indians Eat   39
The Spice Rack   40

Brassicas   **55**
Green Vegetables   **73**
Root Vegetables   **93**
Squashes   **113**
Light Lentils and Dahls   **137**
Heavy Pulses and Grains   **157**
Fish and Shellfish   **179**
Red Meat, Game and Offal   **201**
The Chicken and the Egg   **231**

Index   249
Acknowledgements   255

Preface

It is a little known truth that many of the Indians who left for the West came from homes that hired chefs. By virtue of the fact that one could afford a ticket to the West, it often followed that one had enough money for a phalanx of servants. Many first-generation Indians that came to the UK did not have the cooking skills of their ancestors. It is also a sad truth that the mothers and grandmothers who started our lives with their spice formulas and kitchen secrets will take many of those culinary arts to their graves.

These two points, in part, led me to write this book. I, too, will pass and there is little I can leave for my daughters of their ancient heritage. However, the Indian kitchen spice formula is one thing that I can articulate and enshrine in written form. This is something that they can open like a book of spells, or prayers, and conjure the taste of their mother's love, the smell of their grandmother's kitchen, the ferocity of flavour of nights around the home fires.

My attempts to articulate the spice formula, in a way that makes sense to anyone wanting to cook like an Indian, grew into the infographic at the heart of this book, the Spice Tree. It is a kind of flow chart that maps the neural pathways of an Indian cook.

The main aim of this book, for any reader, is to become a go-to, kitchen shelf, spice Sherpa. It is not a recipe book that slavishly shackles one to the written word, but rather aims to liberate by revealing the ancient, tried-and-tested spice formulas that are second nature to billions.

This book will help anyone master spices and understand why they work with some ingredients and not others; to create the perfect authentic curry every time; and also to apply the spice formula to everyday ingredients to tease different and exciting dimensions out of the ordinary.

The aim of the Spice Tree is to be a quick reminder of the formulas always at play in the Indian kitchen; to lay out the systematic routes you should always take.

The spices and finishing flavours used in Indian cuisine are not unusual. They will be familiar to you. Many of the ingredients that you need will already be lurking, untroubled for months, in your cupboards. This book will breathe new life into those ingredients, those that you might want to cook, but are afraid to approach.

What I find so wonderful about the Indian spice formula is the way that the most humble and lacklustre ingredients become the most exciting and flavourful dishes in minutes. Never again will you look at a packet of lentils or chickpeas and sigh the lament of the unworthy. You will understand why ingredients like the meagre Savoy cabbage become king in the Indian kitchen. Indian spice formulas draw magic out of these robust, deep, chlorophyll-rich jewels of the vegetable garden.

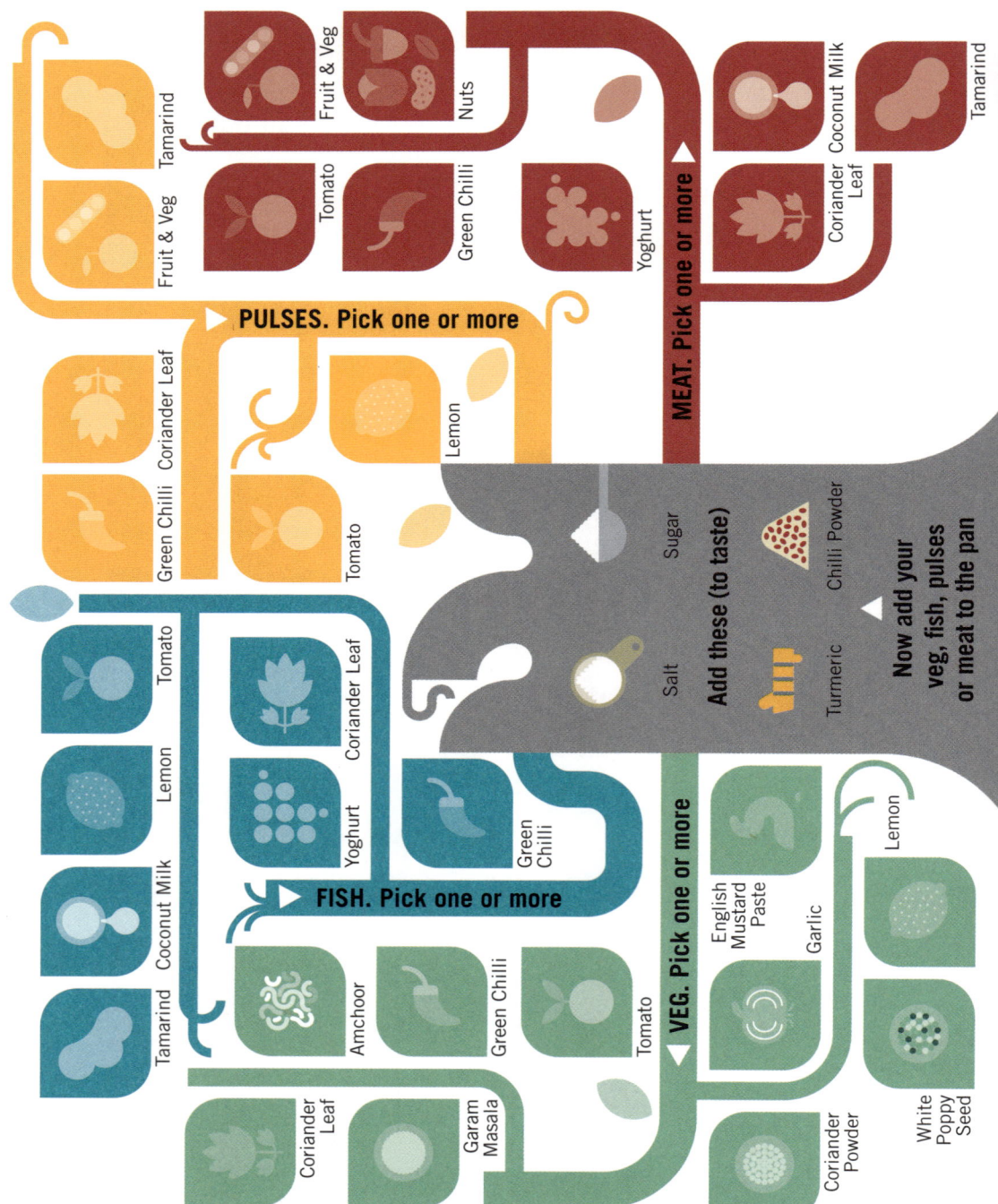

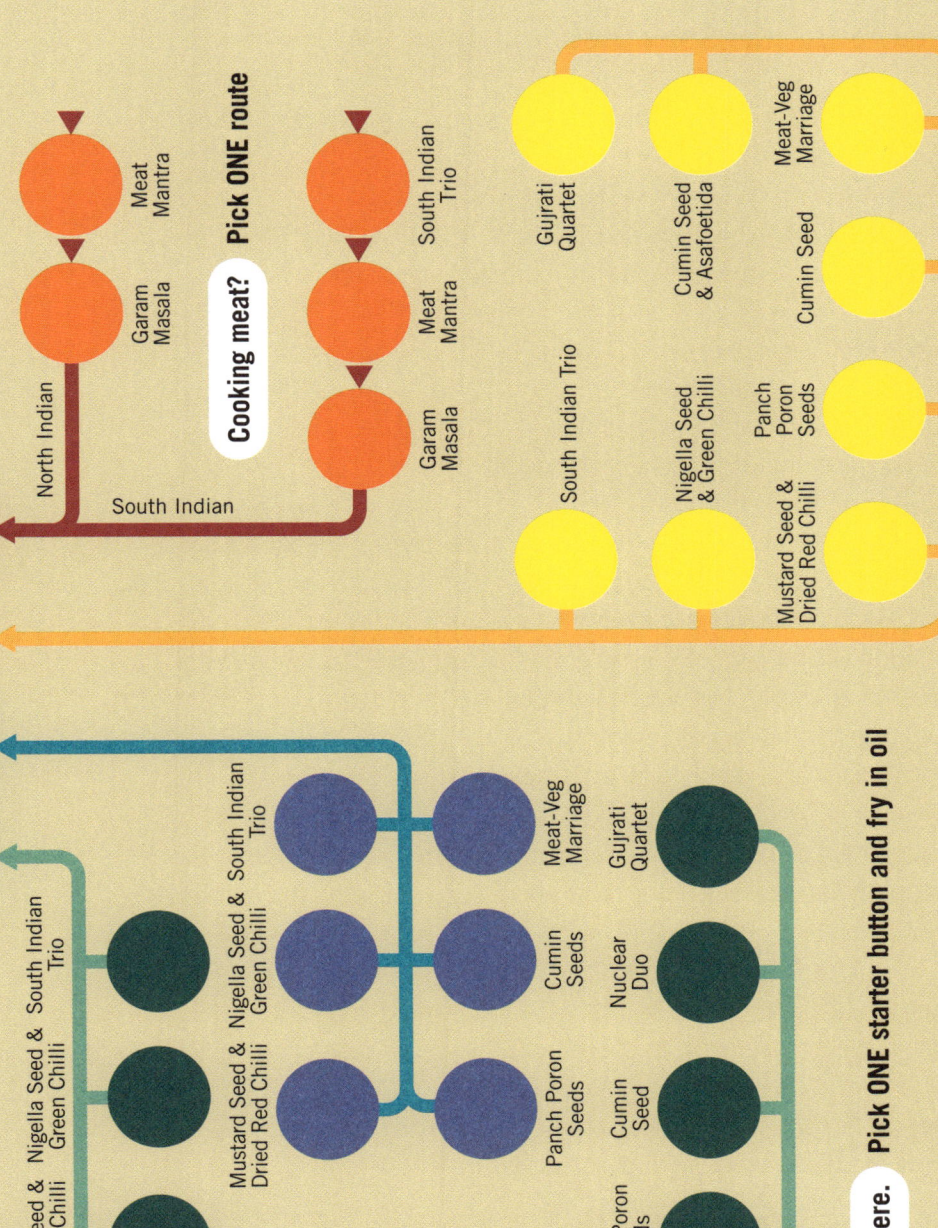

How to Use the Spice Tree

The Spice Tree maps out the ingredients you generally need to cook all Indian cuisine.

What are you cooking? Potatoes? Trout? Lentils? Chicken? Locate the colour coded root system appropriate to your main ingredient.

Green = all vegetables
Blue = fish and shellfish
Yellow = pulses (both light and heavy)
Red = meat (including poultry and eggs)

The starter root balls are your options for the 'base' or headnote flavour for the dish. In the trunk you'll find turmeric, chilli powder, salt and sugar – all essential additions to every dish you cook and which should always be added according to your taste. As you reach the branches you find the range of appropriate 'finishing flavours'. It is here that you can dream up your own combinations, adding as many as you like, working within tried-and-tested parameters, to tailor the finished curry to your taste.

Follow the 4 steps shown on the Spice Tree whenever you want to cook like an Indian, starting at the roots and flowing up through the tree to the leaves.

Step 1: Pick ONE starter ball from the root system and fry it awake in a pan with a little oil. See opposite for a key to the starter balls.

Step 2: Add your main ingredient – the veg, fish, pulses or meat – and toss it into the pan with the fried base spices.

Step 3: Now travel up the trunk and add turmeric and chilli, the mother and father of all curry. Season with salt and sugar to taste.

Step 4: Follow the branch, sticking with the same colour. Choose one or more of the ingredients in the leaves to finish your dish. Play around and have fun – this is how you personalise your curry.

At the start of each chapter, you'll find a simplified version of the tree for that kind of main ingredient to act as a concise reminder wherever you are in the book.

A key to the starter balls

The starter balls are tried-and-tested age-old combinations. For example, South Indians always start with a certain combo, or meat dishes are always started with onion, ginger and garlic (see more about this on page 18). I have given these combinations nicknames on the Spice Tree and throughout the book with the aim of making them easier to remember. When you see these names, they always call for the following ingredients to be fried together in a little oil.

Gujrati Quartet:
Mustard Seed, Dried Red Chilli, Cumin Seed and Asafoetida (to vitalise vegetarian dishes)

Nuclear Duo:
Fenugreek Seed and Asafoetida (when cooking lacklustre vegetables)

South Indian Trio:
Mustard Seed, Dried Red Chilli and Curry Leaf

Meat Mantra:
Onion, Ginger, Garlic (as much as you can be bothered to chop, then fry into a golden sweet mass)

Meat-Veg Marriage:
Any fried seed spice followed by Onion, Ginger, Garlic (for main ingredients considered to be a hybrid of meat and vegetable, e.g. chickpeas, kidney beans or all fish)

Two Ancient Alliances:

Nigella Seed & Green Chilli (pierce the green chilli and fry whole with nigella seed. Green chilli is the fresh antidote to earthy nigella)

Mustard Seed & Dried Red Chilli (the umami flavour added by frying dried red chilli complements the nutty warmth of the fried mustard seed)

Introduction

It is said of Bengali Indians that they are only concerned with three things in life: food, books and educating their children. As distant as I thought I was from this maxim, the older I get, the more I find the joys of my life have in fact distilled down to those three clichéd comforts.

My parents came to Britain in the 1960s as doctors and it was into a working class, gritty, northern town that I was born and raised. Some of my earliest memories are of bricks through windows and racist graffiti. My mother tells of being taunted in the streets by the very people she would then see as patients.

It strikes me that Indians are rather a humble sort. They just want to be liked; they want to feed. I correct myself, they want to be liked SO THAT they can feed. We are feeders above all else. The overwhelming cadence of Indian social interaction is that 'guest is God'. The foundation of Hindu religious ceremony is the cooking of astonishing delights to 'feed' the deities. The bible, too, speaks of such food offerings. Ever was it the ancient human yearning, to show love and reverence through food.

This way, the love and consideration one pours from one's heart into the dish, is really consumed by and internalised by the muse. It is reminiscent of that feeling of loving someone so much that you just want to eat them.

It seems that as we move away from this homespun craft of food-making to the sterile culture of ready meals, in so doing we lose one of the languages of love; a language that is based around the home fires, family, kitchen-table therapy and the fruits of our local, good tilled earth.

Back to the concrete cul-de-sacs of my childhood, we Indians didn't have much to offer. The anxious immigrant frugality of my parents meant we were still Choppers when everyone else was BMX, we were brown, hand-me-down knitwear when the street went Adidas. But what we had was a mother with a spice formula. Like every Indian mother before her she had an ability to create simple but immensely exotic food. This food invoked scents that floated down the drive and snagged on the unwilling salivary ducts of our neighbours; it awoke new senses and haunted them to seek the next fix; these were flavours that marauded across the tongue and splashed around in the endorphins.

For us, curry was the greatest force for race relations we could have known; korma became the Kofi Annan of Skelmersdale. My mother would return from surgery in the evening and within half an hour, would have conjured up a kaleidoscope of dishes. This alchemy turned our kitchen, quickly, into the teen commune that our uncool personalities and fragile charm could never have founded.

The creation of Indian food is not just a random dance of spices. It is far simpler and more structured than that crafted by a thousand years of Ayurvedic practice, which is at the heart of all Indian cuisine.

The precept is simple: we use turmeric and chilli powder plus one 'headnote' defining spice that changes depending on the type of ingredient we are cooking.

Too long has curry making been seen as a DNA borne dark art, shrouded in an ancestral holy of holies. Indian children by the age of eight know the spice formula in the way that Western children know their food partnerships: sausage goes with beans, chips go with fish, toast is buttered. The Indian child's neural pathways are no different. It just has not been spelt out in a book before.

The spice formula does away with the long, mindless lists of traditional Indian cookbook ingredients, blindly clung to by those who brave the high temple of curry making. It empowers, liberates and, most importantly, it openly maps curry DNA for those amongst whom I live and love.

The Indian Spice Kit

Across the Indian subcontinent, from Bangladesh to Sri Lanka, it is normal for people to have a container of about six spices that they transport with them whenever they travel, rather like a make-up bag to those of us in the West. Generally, the kit would contain turmeric, chilli, cumin and coriander. Different regions of the subcontinent then have certain beloved spices. Bengalis would carry their 5-spice blend, Gujratis would add mustard seed, Punjabis would have their Punjabi garam masala, while Sri Lankans favour fennel and cinnamon.

They will know those spices as well as they know their social group; they will know who gets on with who, who turns bitter when the heat turns up and who is utterly reliable.

They will carry them on their journey because the aroma of those spices invokes the familiar, just as a phone call to a loved one or a university food package invokes home comfort. Indians have a need to hear domestic spices speak into their dishes. They carry with them the defining scent of their home.

It is to this level of intimacy and understanding that I want to transport the readers of this book. So that as you look at an ingredient, your fingers will know for which spice you should be reaching before your brain has time to compute.

Spice Traditions

The crucible of Indian food is an ancient kitchen with one hob, one pan and scant 20 minutes of fuel. It is the simplest, fastest and most systematic way of cooking. These cooks do not conduct a random dance of complex spices.

My great grandmother's kitchen was essentially a cow-manure-fuel stoked portable fire stove on a small veranda. My grandparents would shop for local fresh ingredients in the morning and by noon the more perishable ingredient would have to be cooked. I recall many a Varanasi 5 a.m. where my grandmother would drag us, bleary-eyed, to the River Ganges for her morning bathe and prayers. It was then straight to the bustling, and often terrifying, fish market. This was a dizzying spectacle of bright-eyed shoals laid out like shiny fruit; buckets of writhing, onyx black koi; fat, pink, sweet steaks of river fish; prize, shiny-eyed heads arrayed like baubles of delicious promise.

In the heat of the Indian sun, perishable fish often featured at lunchtime. It is from this act of husbandry that the breakfasts of the British Empire came to include *kitchuri* (traditionally an entirely vegan rice and lentil dish) furnished with fish. The kitchen needed to use up the fish while it was fresh in the morning, so it was thrown into the humble lentil dish. *Kitchuri* became kedgeree and thus an Indian peasant dish became an aristocratic Memsahib's bubble and squeak.

I recall many a shopping morning of Lucknow roadside vegetable sellers, sitting cross-legged with their red potatoes, small green gourds and bright hallelujah cauliflowers arrayed and displayed on the pavement. Haggling and pleading led to a deal being sealed on a rusty Asterix-of-Gaul-looking set of scales to weigh out the winnings.

This assault on the senses is what makes ingredients all the more precious to Indians. Daily, one sees the fish, vegetables and fruit hand-selected for their prowess, bargained for and fought over for a humble home dining table. These are ingredients to be savoured, to be treated delicately and properly. Never would this precious fruit of the earth and sea be cling filmed and forgotten behind the hummus at the back of a fridge; condemned by the walk-to-the-bin sniff test.

As the buying process is marked by bustle and frenetic energy, so is the cooking process. Indian families are large and hungry. The men, historically, were banned from the kitchen and only women who were not breastfeeding, menstruating or looking after children could enter. This was a place of focused industry and economic genius. With limited fuel and limited pots and pans, time was not to be wasted pondering, mulling and reinventing the culinary wheel. The cauliflower was hurled down the tried-and-tested brassica spice route: mustard seed, turmeric, chilli. The fish was treated as all fish is treated: rubbed with turmeric and salt, fried and then dressed in a sauce based on either nigella seed or mustard seed. These spice formulas have not been broken, or dented, for millennia.

These spice routes provide a simple, quiet, quick consistency across the home-cooked dishes of India. Certain ingredients are paired with certain spices. The battle between mother-in-law and daughter-in-law will span only the distance between two spices, not two cooking cultures. Aunty Geeta's chicken will differ from aunty Krishna's chicken only in the type of virtuosity imparted by the different headnote spice. One is not looking at the chasm between Vesta and Vivek Singh.

The Trinity of Spices

So every Indian dish is based on a three-spice formula. Even simpler, two of those spices never change. Turmeric powder and chilli powder are the mother and father of all curries and at the heart of the trinity of spices.

Turmeric is a ground root with an earthy flavour. It invokes the very taste of golden, sun-baked Indian earth. This produces a foundational deep layer to the building of a curry. It is the defining Indian spice. The addition of turmeric is, in my view, the point at which any dish becomes a curry. Chilli is a fascinating, multifaced spice. In its powder form, it goes into all curries, not to produce heat, but to produce the second layer of flavour –

one of smoke and warmth. When one fries chilli powder in butter, it releases a most unexpected scent; that of roasted meats, of caramel warmth, of golden chicken skin. This is the warmth of which I speak: a fired-earth umami. Indians wanting a raw blistering heat can simply add more. Prior to that tipping point, chilli is an absolute gentleman, full of gentle culinary chivalry.

Headnote Spices

The third spice you select will depend on the ingredient in hand. That third spice will define the flavour of that dish in the way that a 'headnote' ingredient, such as rose or vanilla, will define a perfume. Creation of Indian food is like the creation of a perfume. It has a defining 'headnote' scent. It is this third spice that changes depending, generally, on the type of ingredient that you want to transform. For instance, mustard seed is paired with brassicas, cumin seed with root vegetables and nigella seed with fish.

It might not seem like it, but there are only a small number of headnote spices used in Indian cooking: mustard seed, nigella seed, cumin seed, panch poron seed, fenugreek, asafoetida, garam masala and curry leaf. That's pretty much it – for ALL Indian cooking.

Tried-and-Tested Flavours

Indian hands over the ages have gone to the same couplings time and time again. Some come from regional headnote preferences, some distilled from thousands of years of experimentation. This list is just a smash-and-grab general guide for you to remember. When you are experimenting, bear these marriages in mind. Start with them if you want to make a regional dish and then you can add layers of flavour on top of them.

SOUTH INDIAN DISHES
Use headnotes of mustard seed and curry leaf and tend to be hot with dried red chilli.

GUJRATI DISHES
Use headnotes of mustard seed, cumin seed and asafoetida and sugar, which is often used to create sweeter curries than in other areas in India.

BENGALI DISHES
Often start with a headnote of panch poron and Bengalis love the unique finishing flavour combination of tomato and mustard paste.

There are also a couple of flavour-marriages, forged over aeons, that just work. For instance, nigella seed is always fried hand-in-hand with a pierced fresh green chilli. Mustard seed is always fried hand-in-hand with a dried red chilli. So whenever you use nigella seed or mustard seed, don't forget to add their partners, the fresh green chilli and dried red chilli for that authentic oomph.

Also:
- Mustard seed and dried red chilli always go together in vegetable dishes.
- Nigella or cumin seed and green chilli are paired in vegetable, pulse and fish dishes.
- Onion, ginger, garlic and garam masala are the backbone to all meat dishes.
- Bay leaves are used in non-meat dishes to mimic the flavour of garam masala so you rarely need both.
- English mustard paste is used to emulate onion and garlic and so you don't need both.

Starter Buttons

Building on the flavour-marriage foundations opposite, in the Indian mind there are certain 'starter buttons' – big obvious starting points whether you are cooking veg, fish, pulses or meat.

Very often that starter button is one headnote spice: So, you're cooking potato? Choose cumin seed, fry it to wake it up, add the turmeric, chilli powder, season to taste with salt and sugar, then choose from one or more finishing flavours.

Now if you want to get to a higher level of curry making there are some flavour pairings and trios, headnote combos, that make up the more nuanced, regional starter buttons.

Certain areas of India always start by frying the same, beloved headnote combos. I have given these spice alliances nicknames, here, to hopefully make them easier to learn. You will then know that to cook like a South Indian, for example, you need to start with a certain headnote combo.

Headnote Combos

THE SOUTH INDIAN TRIO:
Mustard seed, dry red chilli and curry leaf are always fried together to give that verdant fragrance to South Indian curries, meat, fish or vegetable.

THE NUCLEAR DUO:
Ingredients like squash, that release lots of liquid during the cooking process, will inevitably water down your flavours, and your enthusiasm. They require a certain kind of bullying in the pan. Fenugreek seed and asafoetida are fried together to act like a couple of ferocious sheep dogs, herding flavour back into the pan.

THE GUJRATI QUARTET:
The Gujratis are the kings of the vegan kitchen. They know how to draw all manner of hidden beauty out of the most eager vegetable. They start by frying cumin seed, mustard seed, dry red chilli and asafoetida together.

THE MEAT MANTRA:
Just learn it 'onion-ginger-garlic'. They are THE meat starter button. Every meat dish is based on these three foundation flavours. These are not even considered spices by Indians. They are water, sand and cement. You just have to get used to starting every meat curry by peeling and chopping as much as you can be bothered to, and I mean that. As much or as little as your eyes and hands can take. Blitz and freeze prepped garlic and ginger in ice-cube trays. Every little helps. More onion means the thicker the sauce.

MEAT-VEG MARRIAGE:
Some ingredients, such as heavy pulses and fish, are treated as a meat-vegetable hybrid during the cooking process, as they are protein-rich (more on this on pages 160 and 182). We nod to their vegetable nature by starting the dish with a fried headnote seed spice. We then add The Meat Mantra (onion, ginger and garlic) to take them firmly into richer ground.

Got it? Once the headnote starters have been fried, and turmeric, chilli powder, salt and sugar have been added to taste, an Indian cook considers their armoury of 'finishing flavours': ingredients that are added to the finishing stages of curry creation.

Finishing Flavours

In the West, we believe that the tongue has four areas of flavour: salt, sweet, sour, bitter. In the East, we believe that there are an additional two areas that detect astringency and pungency.

Opposite: Finishing flavours for veg

The 'finishing flavours' correspond to those six different areas of the tongue that all demand stimulation. Indians reach for certain ingredients to 'tick the six tongue boxes'. This armoury of finishing flavours includes tomato, green chilli, fresh coriander, coriander powder, amchoor, garlic, white poppy seed, natural yoghurt, coconut milk, tamarind, lemon, English mustard paste, garam masala, tamarind, fruit, vegetables and ground nuts.

Certain combinations and permutations of these finishing flavours have been shown, through the centuries, to work with certain ingredients. For instance:

VEGETABLES

The finishing flavours in vegetable dishes correspond most strictly to the six areas of flavour on the tongue in accordance with Indian understanding (see page 31). Tomato, lemon and amchoor (dried green mango) bring a touch of tang and sourness to dishes. Mustard paste and garam masala bring a gentle and pleasing pungency and punch, while coriander leaf and powder are the equivalent of a parsley finish of freshness. White poppy seeds are often added in two forms – either ground into a paste and fried with your headnote spice, or simply fried and added in at the end of a dish. Both methods add texture and a wonderful nutty aroma.

VEG FINISHING FLAVOURS: tomato, lemon, amchoor, English mustard paste, fresh coriander, coriander powder and garam masala, green chilli, garlic and white poppy seed

PULSES AND LENTILS

These are, at heart, vegetables and so they follow the vegetable starting points of fried seed headnote spices and also the simple vegetarian finishing flavours (see above). We tend not to add nuts and dairy into our

Opposite: Finishing flavours for fish

lentils as they are naturally creamy and rich in texture. We do add tomatoes in with the lentils while they simmer, as the acids they bring tenderise and speed up the cooking process.

PULSES FINISHING FLAVOURS: tomato, lemon, fresh coriander, tamarind, green chilli, fruit (dried apricots, dried prunes, for instance) and vegetables like spinach leaves, carrot, potato, leftover peas from your roast – really whatever you fancy

FISH

Fish sit in an interesting hybrid intersection between meat and vegetables. Hindu priests, when banning meat, could not bear to part with fish and so considered them 'fruit' of the sea. Hence fish curries are cooked like vegetables and started with the vegetable headnote spices in recognition of their hybrid nature. They are also often cooked with onion, ginger and garlic as a nod to their affiliation with meat. They share in the finishing flavours of both ingredients.

FISH FINISHING FLAVOURS: tomato, natural yoghurt/coconut milk, tamarind, lemon, English mustard paste, fresh coriander, green chilli and tamarind

MEAT

There are three shades of meat curry, as you will well know from your take away. The spectrum runs from brown, through red, to cream-coloured dishes. To achieve this is simple. The brown dishes are finished with tomatoes for the simmer. The cream dishes are made with a finish of natural yoghurt or coconut milk. The red dishes are finished with both tomatoes and dairy or coconut milk. Often ground almonds or even cashews are used to add a luxurious weight to dairy or coconut milk sauces. Feel free to experiment with whole nuts, pine nuts and dried fruits in every kind of sauce. Dried apricots, raisins and prunes are all great

---

Opposite: Finishing flavours for pulses

additions. I add banana and cashew to the odd korma to scare my mother. I love the mischief.

MEAT FINISHING FLAVOURS: tomato, natural yoghurt/coconut milk, tamarind, ground nuts and dried fruit (dried apricots, prunes, for instance), green chilli, fresh coriander and vegetables (as with meat, whatever you fancy/have leftover).

Seasoning

Seasoning in the context of this book refers to tasting and adjusting the salt and sweet edges of your curry. Indian seasoning is different to the mainstays of Western seasoning. Where the West defaults to salt and pepper, Indians reach for salt and granulated sugar. Some areas of India, such as the Gujrat, like a sweeter edge to their dishes.

You can omit or you can add as little or as much as you like, but you really need, need, need to be tasting for both as you cook. Very often it is the under-salting or under-sweetening of curry that leaves you feeling underwhelmed. Whatever your thoughts are on salt and sugar in the forum of Western cuisine, please clear your mind and just have them to hand. Always revisit the taste of the overall dish at the end of the cook and think about both. Then tweak up the sweet or the salt as you like. A little tip if you have over-salted your curry is to simmer some finely chopped potatoes or small lumps of basic dough into the sauce as they absorb some of the saline.

What we don't, however, need in every dish is the additional dark glow of black pepper. We have already ensured the warmth and heat in every dish with chilli powder. Black pepper does not rank as a meagre seasoning, but has a headnote role in the Indian kitchen. Before chillies were introduced to

Opposite: Finishing flavours for meat

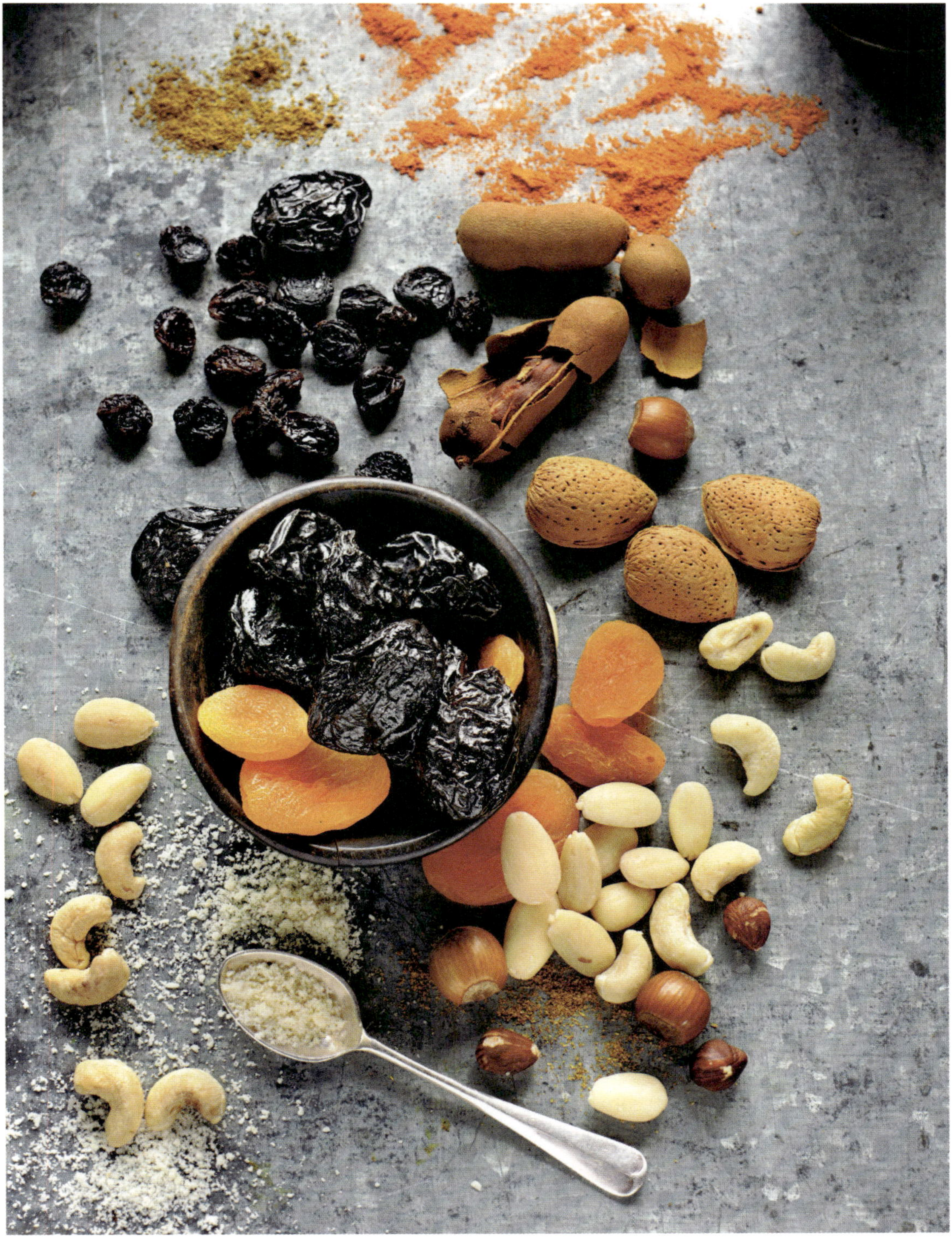

India, many areas around India used a long, black pepper-like catkin called the *pippali*, a Tamil word from which the word 'pepper' is derived. Thus, black pepper is a beloved and centre stage ingredient in some curries like the Pakistani national dish *nihari*, a bone marrow and brain curry. You will see that black pepper features in this book, but it is just one of the garam masala spices that you can isolate out and elevate by adding more to make it a feature flavour in a dish.

The Naming Game

Many of the names given to curries on British curry house menus are kind constructs, invented by Indians to make an English audience feel less intimidated by a ten-page, wipe-easy, myriad menu. Balti simply means bucket, and tikka masala was invented when a Glaswegian bus driver sent his dry chicken back to the kitchen for some gravy. This was begrudgingly thrown together with a tin of tomato soup and a touch of cream and a nation's darling was born.

The way Indians actually describe their dishes goes to the heart of the curry formula. They cite the headnote and they cite the finishing flavours. For instance, they would say, 'Tonight I'm making green beans with cumin and tomato,' or 'How do you fancy potato with nigella and poppy seed?' The word curry does not exist.

The Treatment of Spices

Each spice is rather like an expensive scented candle. Only when it is heated does it exhale and permeate through a dish. In their dry form, the spices' aromatic oils are locked in and dormant. Once fried or roasted, that potential is awakened and the defining scent is released. In this way, the Indian kitchen is cleverly stocked with dried, long-life ingredients that can be hailed to splendour, from a standstill, in a matter of seconds.

We, therefore, don't use raw spices. Roasting spices intensifies their flavour and so when they are ground, the strength of the powder goes further, and works harder. We roast spices when we want to grind them – to use in highly perfumed dishes like meat dishes and some of the heavier pulses like chickpeas. This aromatic powder can better infiltrate the terse fibres of unhung, un-tenderised meat, as much of the meat is in the East.

For more delicate ingredients, like vegetables and fish, we use a light-handed technique, frying whole dried spices in a little oil to release the perfumed oils from within the shell of the seed into the cooking oil.

How Indians Eat

The general rules of the Spice Tree will show you that vegetables are cooked with gentle seed spices and generally without onion, ginger and garlic. Meat dishes are cooked with dynamic and massive flavours, like garam masala spices and onion, ginger and garlic. Indians start their meals with vegetable dishes that are eaten with flat roti breads. You approach these dishes with an untainted palate. Then we eat the meat and fish dishes with rice. The lentils and pulses are eaten with both rice and meat, because dahls are often a meal in themselves. On this note, a typical quick meal for a busy Indian will be dahl, with rice or roti bread, with a portion of vegetables that has been fried with turmeric.

My mum, I kid you not, would often have rice, dahl and a bag of ready-salted crisps and slices of red onion, mashed in with her fingers. Try it, and forever change the shape of your munchies.

The Spice Rack

These brief discourses on the spices of an Indian kitchen will not focus on the myriad health benefits they may have. That is a whole different book. Here, I tell you where and when to use them in cooking, whether they are a headnote or finishing flavour, and how to draw the best flavours out of them.

AJWAIN
Also known as carom, this is one of the rare seed spices that tastes of herb rather than perfume. Because of its gentle nature, it is also one of the few seeds that does not need to be fried before use. It has the scent of thyme or marjoram. Used more as a finishing flavour, it features as a topping on flat breads. It's most commonly used tossed into gram flour batter for bhajis or in the stuffing for aubergines or bitter gourds, where it can bring only fragrance and do no acrid harm.

AMCHOOR
Amchoor is dried green mango powder. In India, limes and lemons are used in salads, but in the heat of the East, they are slightly drier and less fleshy than their Western comparables. Hence, it is very common to use sour green mango as a sharpening agent. Wherever we use sweeter flavours in a dish, we can balance it with the tang of amchoor.

ASAFOETIDA
Known as *hing* in Indian and as 'devil's dung' in the West, its Latin name even has the word 'foetid' buried within it. It is often paired with fenugreek seeds as a nuclear duo, to start vegetable dishes with an instant flavour hit. This is a genius spice that smells like Satan's own grandmother, but fries to give a buttery aroma. The tamers of this turbulent spice were Hindu widows, who used to be forbidden the 'passion-giving' ingredients of onion and garlic. They proved to be the most

resourceful trailblazers in their isolated kitchens, discovering this resin from a rhizome that, when dried, crushed and fried, emulated exactly the scent and flavour of butter-sautéed garlic and onion. Win, win, win. Because its role is to emulate onion and garlic, we don't use it in meat dishes, which are always on an actual onion-ginger-garlic base. Parts of India, like the Gujrat and the south, use it prolifically to start vegetable dishes.

BAY LEAVES

These are fascinating leaves. My mother and I studied them extensively. Lid on, shake, sniff, lid off and repeat ad nauseam. Why do we use them? What do they bring? Is it a herb-like fragrance? Is it delicacy? We found it is far from both. Bay brings pure punch. Indian bay leaves are longer and more grey than their Western counterparts and have a stronger flavour. So here is the secret of when to use bay. The smell is one of complex spice; it emulates the strong, woody spices in garam masala. Hence we use it in dishes where garam masala is NOT used. That means you throw them into vegetable dishes and pulses where you want a bit of spice punch. This would usually be humble, understated ingredients like courgette and white cabbage rather than delicate, fragrant beans and spinach. It is the wolf in sheep's clothing of the spice rack.

BLACK PEPPERCORN

Before India had chilli, many areas were using a type of long black pepper called *pippali* to add heat to their food. Hence, black pepper has a role in Indian cooking, but not as a seasoning. When we use black pepper it is used as a main feature in a dish. It is often ground up as part of garam masala as the heat-giving element, but also dishes like black pepper chicken are basically a chicken curry with the black pepper element elevated.

BLACK SALT

This is a high-content sulphur salt and is actually pink in colour. Do not confuse it with Himalayan pink salt, which simply tastes like normal salt. Black salt is commonly used to dress salads, fruit and cold snacks. Indians often have their fruit with black salt and I sometimes sprinkle apples and tart fruit with it and this makes them less tart. Try it, it has an addictive charm. Remember, Indians believe that the tongue has six areas of flavour, and that pungency legitimately corresponds to one important part. Black salt reaches for the part of your palate that appreciates blue cheese and boiled eggs. Buy some and sprinkle your salad with it along with a touch of lemon. It's one of those ingredients found in the heart of the Indian home kitchen, but that is rarely unleashed on delicate non-Indian visitors.

CARDAMOM, BLACK/PODS

This is a little understood spice that has a medicinal aroma and the unfortunate look of a cockroach. Understandably this may be why so many shy away from using it. Aside from being a common ingredient in garam masala mixes for meat dishes, there is something synergistic about black cardamom and rice. It's a big factor in biriyanis and fried rice dishes. Fry it to bring it alive, then toss in your raw rice and add water.

CARDAMOM, GREEN/GROUND

This love-it-or-hate-it spice is generally allowed to strut its stuff in heavy, sweet Indian desserts that can deal with its highly perfumed ego. We use it as a ground spice in garam masala where the cacophony of fellow A-list spices tames it a little. Always remember, you can add more to your garam masala to bring it out if you're a fan. My mother's garam masala contains just cloves, cinnamon and green cardamom.

CHILLI, DRIED RED

It's an interesting fact that Indians don't want the flavour of smoke in their dishes. One of the evocative yet inescapable charms of life in an Indian home is the all-pervading smell of smoke. If it's in your hair and also in your mattress, it kind of loses its charm and you really don't want it in your food, too. The only nod to that layer of smoke in dishes (apart from the

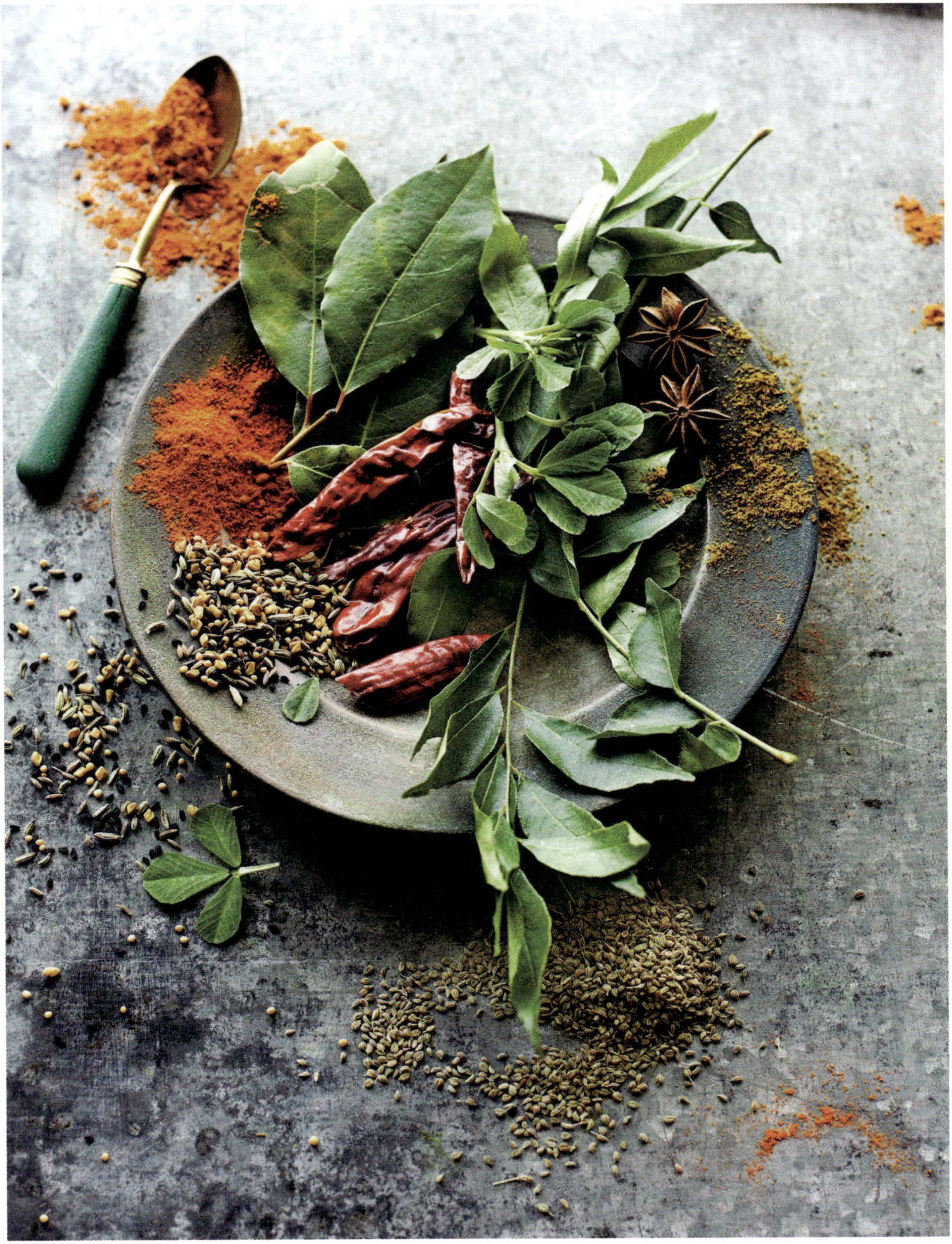

all out, know what you're getting tandoor) comes from frying red chilli, in its many forms, in hot oil. Dry red chillies come in a few forms and are used to bring a gentle smoked heat. The most commonly used are the small dried red chillies that have more heat than smoke. These go hand in hand with vegetable dishes started with mustard seed. The long dried red chillies bring more smoke than heat. Both are fried at the beginning of vegetable dishes for a subtle and nuanced fire.

CHILLI, FRESH GREEN
This is used not primarily to bring heat to a dish but to bring that green, chlorophyll freshness. Usually with vegetable dishes, we simply pierce them and throw them in with the seed spices. This way they release the flavour of 'greenery' but not so much heat. If you slice them and add them in, it gives heat and freshness. To reduce the heat in the green chilli, remove the white pith and seeds. The general rule is the thinner the chilli, the hotter it is. We tend to use green finger chillies, which give the right amount of zing and heat. The big banana chillies are great for a very mild and lovely 'green' hit, but long-cooked in meat dishes, they lose much of this green zing so you need to add heaps to get that hit. In vegetable dishes, wherever there is nigella or cumin, there must be green chilli. This marriage sweeps the dustiness of the spice awake through an open window and onto green chilli pastures.

CINNAMON
Perfumed, dominating spices like this are paired with meat. Cinnamon is found in the meat mother spice, garam masala, and if you are a fan, feel free to add either cinnamon powder or sticks of cassia bark during the cooking process. I'm not a fan of adding whole spices into meat dishes, as they can assault the senses and won't penetrate the meaty fibres as well as powdered spices, but cinnamon is slow releasing and big enough to dodge.

CLOVES
Although relegated to the pudding

kitchen in Europe, cloves form an integral part of garam masala, the meat mother spice. They are strong and medicinal in flavour, but almost 'open the pores' on the tongue, priming your palate for all the other garam masala flavours. Believed to be a breath freshener, many Indians chew them or hold them in their mouths. If you are a fan, grind the round buds at the top of the clove and add in a little more to a simmering meat curry.

CORIANDER LEAF

There are two finishing flavours that Indians use to give a fresh edge to absolutely any dish. In the way the West uses lemon and parsley, we reach for green chilli and coriander leaf. Both are optional, yes, and both are without boundaries. Coriander leaf is not generally cooked with, as it denatures at high heats and loses its potency. Toss chopped coriander through dishes once they are off the heat – and don't be afraid of using the stalks, please. We use the lot. I freeze whole bunches of the stuff and, moments before I'm serving, I bang the frozen bag over the pan. This cascade of coriander shrapnel does the trick if you can't get your hands on fresh.

CORIANDER POWDER

Coriander powder has a delicate, herby, floral flavour and is used in two ways. It is used as a finishing flavour in vegetable dishes, rather in the way that thyme or oregano would be used to brighten a salad or the end moments of a casserole. It is also elevated in mild meat dishes with garam masala to make for a herbier curry.

CUMIN SEED

A cornerstone of Indian cooking that embodies the flavour of strong 'curry'. Because of the dark depth of cumin seed, we often pair it with the fresh awakening zing of green chilli. The most common way to use cumin seeds is to fry them as a headnote spice, when they become citrus and pleasantly woody. Now throw in a pierced green chilli to balance the grunt and thud they produce. They start vegetables, lentil dishes and fish. Raw, they smell acrid, taste bitter and carry top notes of tom cat, in my view. They are the epitome of the scented candle theory behind spice treatment. They only come alive when you light them.

CUMIN POWDER

Cumin powder comes in two forms that have very different uses. The stuff you buy in shops is ground raw cumin seed. It is gentler and is used to embolden garam masala in meat dishes. If you are looking for more punch in your curry, don't reach for the chilli as many do, reach for a teaspoon of cumin powder.

CUMIN POWDER, ROASTED

Dry-roasted cumin releases a very powerful, toasted nutty spice kick when ground. It is used as a garnish on salads and many yoghurt-based street food snacks, where it awakens and sharpens. It is often paired with amchoor – sharp dried green mango powder. Ever wondered what the rainbow of tangy powders on Indian salads are? Well, these two compounds combined, often with black salt, are the iconic flavourings of Indian snacks and salads. Try them tossed into peanuts, roasted chickpeas or popcorn for a snack with a difference.

The general rule with cumin powder and coriander powder is as follows: more cumin powder for more curry oomph; more coriander powder for more fragrance.

CURRY LEAVES

Curry leaves are one of the iconic flavours of south Indian dishes. They invariably go hand in hand with mustard seed and often asafoetida, too. The curry leaf is best fresh, added in once the mustard seeds have popped. The leaves can also be used towards the end of a dish to add even more of their distinctive moss-green fragrance. Be careful: they need to be washed very carefully as raw they have been known to carry E. coli. They are also hard to get your hands on in fresh form so when you do find some, freeze them in bags and throw them in towards the end of your cooking. They freeze well, but the dried leaf is fine if you can't get fresh.

FENUGREEK SEED

Known as *methi* in Indian, fenugreek is the most overpowering bad boy of the spice rack. We often pair it with its Bonnie and Clyde twin, asafoetida, to awaken quiet vegetables like squashes.

The seeds are fried as a headnote spice at the beginning of vegetable dishes – and burn very easily, so beware. It will turn bitter if too brown.

Using it in any form will give a dish that instant curry house hit. It contains a potent compound called sotolone, which is also found in molasses and aged rum and is used in maple syrup flavourings. Sotolone passes through the body undigested, as it does with your soft furnishings, leaving your life smelling of 'curry' and your armpits of waffles.

FENUGREEK LEAF

The dried leaf is cooked in with the onion-ginger-garlic trinity for meat dishes to produce that instant 'tikka masala' *je ne sais quoi*. The fresh leaves are also cooked like spinach, often with potatoes for bulk, and are used to stuff flat bread parathas.

FENUGREEK POWDER

The powdered *methi* is great for meat rubs, but I also love to rub my chips with it before I fry them.

GARAM MASALA

This is THE meat spice and is a blend of numerous ground, aromatic, highly perfumed spices. If you scan the recipes in many Indian cookbooks, you will see an exhausting and demoralisingly long list of spices. I'm going to encourage you to be brazen and in place of all those, simply read 'garam masala' and go in heavy: two dessertspoons. Pull back next time if it's too overpowering.

I describe garam masala as an orchestra of spices of which you are the conductor. The garam masala spices generally include black pepper, nutmeg, cloves, cardamom, cinnamon, mace, bay, cumin, coriander, fennel. Now, when you see a list that looks like that and feel faint, own your curry, ignore it and go with heaps of garam masala instead.

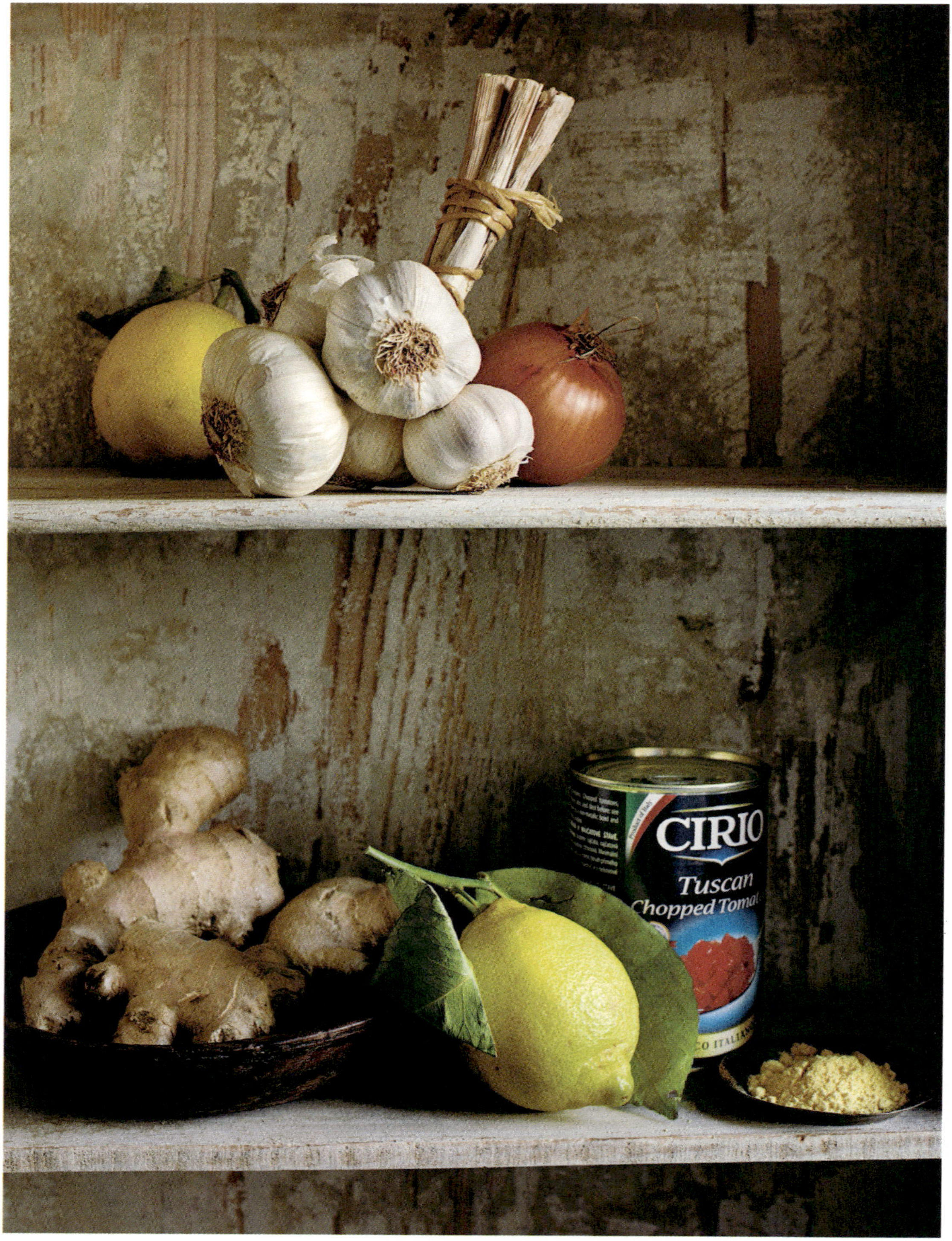
CIRIO
Tuscan
Chopped Tomat

Use garam masala as a base refrain and then elevate the spices you want to enjoy more. Add more cumin powder for curry oomph; add coriander powder for herby femininity; cinnamon or anise make for a mulled chorus. Where the recipes in this book include garam masala, I have sometimes suggested underneath which spices could be elevated to enhance the flavours in the dish.

Different homes have different blends: my mother's Rolls-Royce mixture is cloves, green cardamom and cinnamon. Most Indians buy it in big bags and meddle over the pan in the way I describe. Look for the deep red-brown blends as opposed to the grey dusty-coloured ones. The latter are full of cheap coriander powder and not the more expensive spices, such as cloves, cinnamon and anise.

Garam masala also has another role. It is used as a finishing flavour, along with ghee, in some vegetable dishes like the genre of Bengali *dalnlas*. It's a mouthful and a headful but understand, what garam masala gives you is punch. Try tossing a little ghee and garam masala into quiet vegetable dishes.

GHEE

Ghee is clarified butter. It is also one of those ingredients that besmirch the reputation of curry by making it unhealthy and heavy. There is no need whatsoever to cook with ghee. Use any oil of your choice instead, perhaps only avoiding extra virgin olive oil, which brings a skewing flavour. Ghee is something I only use to start light pulses. It adds a really warming, savoury dimension if you use it to either fry the headnote spice or add a teaspoon at the end. Truth is, you can go half oil and half ghee and just whisper a bit of richness into the dish. Many Indians love a simple dish of hot rice, ghee, salt and perhaps some boiled mooli or boiled egg as a light supper. Mash it up with your hands and taste and feel what it is to be a tired Indian pensioner dining alone in front of the television. It is buttered toast, it is honeyed porridge, it is very well loved, you can use it everywhere and nowhere, and hence you won't find it on the Spice Tree.

GINGER, FRESH
One of the meat curry trinity, it locks fingers with garlic and onion and is fried at the start of any meat curry. It is seen as a cooling ingredient according to Ayurvedic principles, and so is also permitted in vegetable dishes, where it is often used as a finishing flavour to help bring a fresh zing to ingredients like heavy lentils and cloying squashes. Use it peeled, blended, grated or chopped. I blitz huge amounts and freeze the pulp in an ice-cube tray.

MACE
Known in Indian as *javentry*, mace is the doily-like outside of the nutmeg. It's an expensive ingredient in India and so it is used sparingly. It has a woody pungency that adds a quality of 'old furniture' to dishes. It, like black cardamom, has two roles. One as part of garam masala, and also as a key ingredient in rice dishes like biriyani.

MUSTARD PASTE (English)
Also known as English mustard paste. Before chillies were introduced to India by the Portugese in the sixteenth century, Indians were using mustard paste and a type of black pepper to heat their dishes. Mustard is a very common Bengali ingredient and it is used in lieu of onions, ginger and garlic to bring that zing. Hence, we use it in vegetable and fish, not meat, dishes for an instant and fantastic kick. Please, please try to use ready made, good quality, English mustard paste. The powder watered down is just too hot and strong.

MUSTARD SEED
This is one of India's favourite headnote spices. Raw, mustard seeds betray no scent. Once fried, however, these little balls of joy release a toasted, nutty popcorn flavour. They are often used as a gentle headnote spice for brassicas and fish. Fried mustard seed paired with curry leaf are the defining flavours of south Indian dishes. Gujratis use mustard seed and cumin as a headnote duo, often with asafoetida for extra punch. Wherever you use mustard seed, you must fry her alongside

her sister spice, whole dried red chilli, while green chill is often used as a freshening finishing flavour.

NIGELLA SEED

Nigella has a dusty, earthy fragrance. It is THE fish headnote spice and also very important as a starting point for earthy vegetables and pulses. My theory is that the black, almost soil-like richness brought by nigella gives fish a pair of 'land legs', removing any overly fishiness it may have and that tug of the sea. When paired with root vegetables like potato or beetroot, it deepens the earthiness and makes them fuller in flavour. Nigella always goes hand in hand with one pierced fresh green chilli.

PANCH PORON (5-SPICE BLEND)

This translates as 'five spice' and is the Indian kitchen's best kept secret. It, for me, is the ultimate headnote spice for vegetables and is particularly loved by the Bengalis. Massive, nuanced and virtuosic, it is a heady blend of other spices, and each one of those voices corresponds to a very different area of the tongue: nutty mustard seed, citrussy cumin, heady fenugreek, perfumed fennel and the earthy foundation of nigella. Note: you need to be so careful when you fry the spices to awaken them. The tricksy brown nuggets of fenugreek will burn very easily and then their maple sweetness becomes bitter gall. As soon as they turn golden, remove from the heat and in with your vegetable.

STAR ANISE – POWDER AND SEED HEAD

One of the garam masala spices, so elevate it in your meat dishes if you are a fan. I use it in my lamb and plum curry, as it shines brightest in combination with sweeter ingredients. The truth is, although it is a common background noise in garam masala, it tends not to have a major role in the Indian kitchen where sweet curries are few and far between. Hence you will find it more often in the Chinese kitchen, where sweet-savoury dishes are celebrated.

TANDOORI MASALA

This is a blend of red and highly perfumed spices courtesy of cheeky additions such as fenugreek powder, an instant heavyweight, and often onion powder, which gives a shameless welly of flavour. Buy a big bag from your Asian grocer for buttons. For the ultimate barbecue tandoori meat, simply marinate your cuts with tandoori masala, garlic purée, vegetable oil, salt and natural yoghurt. For a quick and always impressive meal, I often cook a whole roast chicken or drumsticks using this paste with zero time to marinate. It's rub and go stuff.

TURMERIC, GROUND

The mother of all curry, it goes into everything. We use it in powder form. Its role has nothing to do with colour (apart from giving your fingers an edgy forty-fags-a-day look) and has everything to do with flavour. With every curry you aim to build layers of flavour and turmeric gives a deep foundation note of 'earthiness'. It is a ground root and in my view is the defining spice of Indian food. Adding turmeric turns any dish into a curry, almost bringing the very flavour of the sunshine golden-baked earth of India into our grey kitchens.

WHITE POPPY SEED

Grind these and use as a finishing flavour. They will keep in a sealed jar for a few months. They are a favourite Bengali ingredient and often paired with mustard in vegetable dishes. They thicken, but more importantly, they give a remarkable nutty, toasted flavour that makes any dish full-bodied. Add them into the oil after your headnote spice, as this slight frying activates the aromatic oils within the seeds.

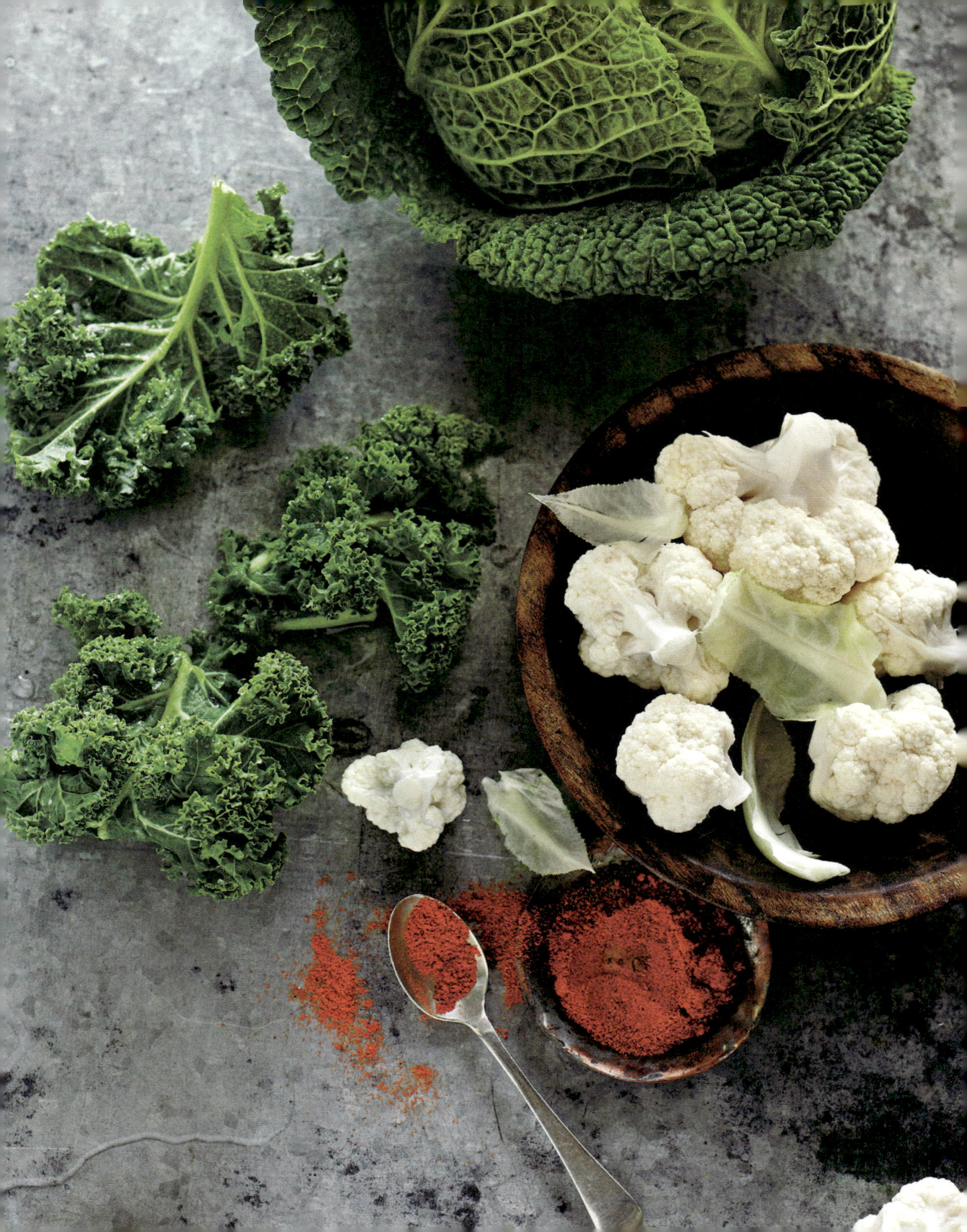

BRASSICAS

①

Pick ONE starter ball from the root system and fry the spice in a pan with a drizzle of oil.

②

Add your brassica to the pan.

③

Now travel up the trunk, adding turmeric and chilli powder. Add salt and sugar, to taste.

④

From the leaves, choose one or more of the ingredients to finish your dish. Play around and have fun – this is how you personalise your curry.

KEY

● = Mustard Seed, Dried Red Chilli and Curry Leaf
SOUTH INDIAN TRIO

● = Mustard Seed, Dried Red Chilli, Cumin Seed and Asafoetida
GUJRATI QUARTET

The Brassicas Tree

Garam Masala

English Mustard Paste

Garlic

Lemon

Amchoor

Tomato

Sugar

Salt

Turmeric

Chilli powder

South Indian Trio

Mustard Seed & Dried Red Chilli

Gujrati Quartet

Cumin Seed

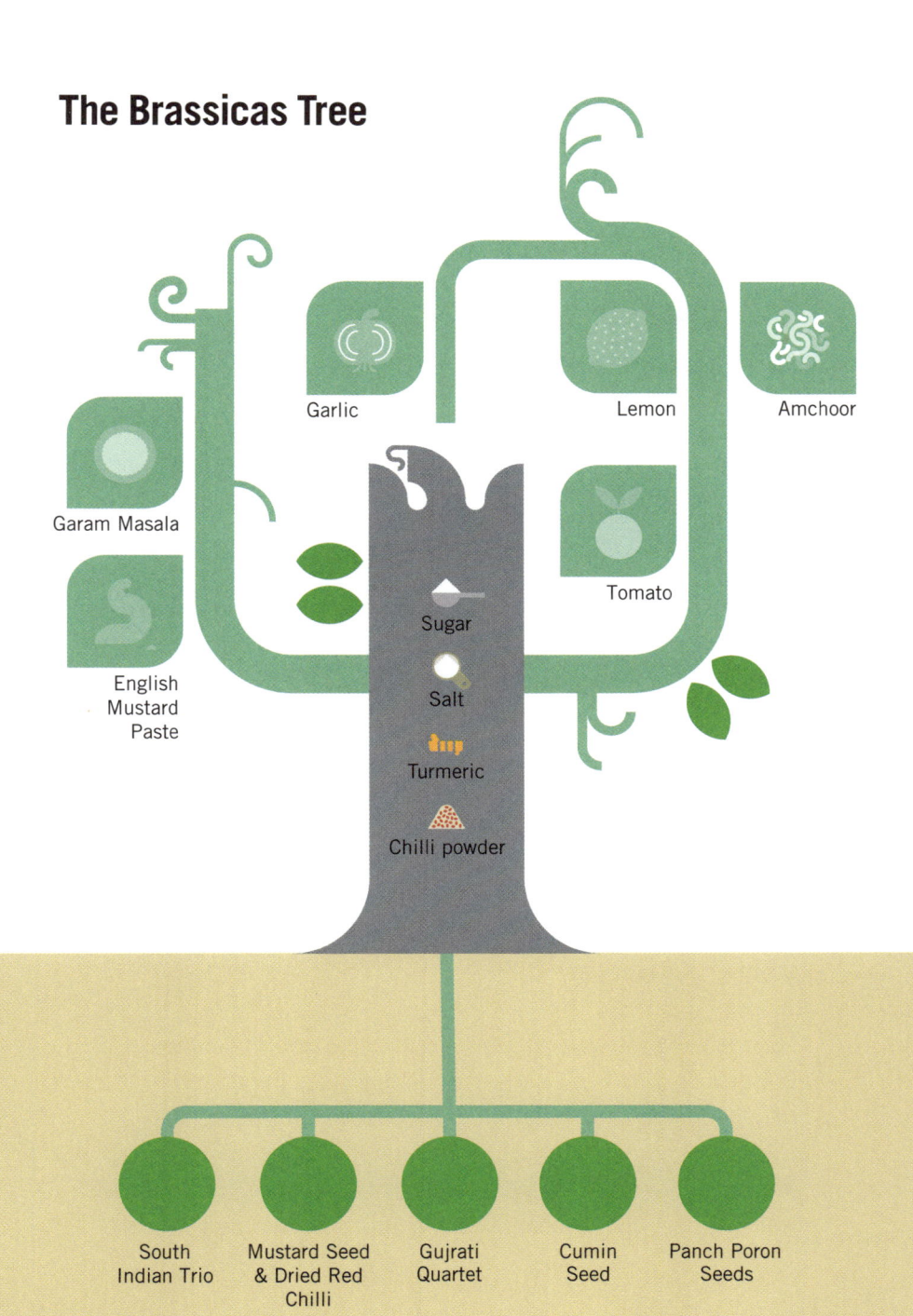

Panch Poron Seeds

Strange word isn't it, 'brassica'? An unhelpful word and one that does nothing to describe the members of its family. We all know, though, that it is their stench that defines this clan, poor sods.

Cauliflowers, cabbages, kale, kohlrabi, sprouts and broccoli are often taken for granted – gnarled, green, unglamorous leafy layers full of sulphurous compounds that become more and more unpleasant as they are heated. But brassicas are the vegetables that most spark my unashamed curry evangelism. What Indians can do with a geriatric cabbage is nothing short of virtuosic, and at the heart of this alchemy is the need to embrace the pungent.

In rural India, every meal will have brassica greens as a centrepiece, served with rice, lentils and roti. Hence the brassica aisle in the greengrocers is the one that snags most sharply on our nostalgia, and it is not an exaggeration to say that houses are chosen for their proximity to a good greengrocer. Toddlers are taught from an early age to inhale appreciatively at a grand moon of an extra-large cauliflower, and few Indians can walk past the dewy, emerald folds of the Savoy's crinkled robe without touching, as if for healing, the hem of his cloth. Winters in India are loaded with veg – baubles of brassica, garlands of greens, and this is the time Indians are happiest in their kitchens. The sulphurous notes are our mulled scent of Christmas joy.

Indians wield the word 'brassica' with sweet reverence: the brassica, in their view, is the mother of all good things and in naming the family there is sweet descriptive personification.

The word for brassica is *ghobi*. Kohlrabi is *gat ghobi*, meaning 'the Knotted One'. Tightly bound white or drumhead cabbage is called *bund ghobi*, 'the Tightly Bound One', while the cauliflower is *phool ghobi*, 'the Flower One'. Just holding that splendid bouquet of a white, peony-like cauliflower and then imagining her boiled to an undignified mass gives me feelings of guilt. We need to understand better how to elevate these humble staples.

Every part of brassicas is used in Indian cooking. Stalks and stems are prized above all, chopped into batons, lightly fried then added to simple dahls. This provides sweet nuggets of crunch but also adds a comforting pea soup rankness to the dish. And the stalks of a cauliflower make the finest and most surprising curry.

In the West, brassicas are often paired with salty ingredients, used to dull their powerful flavour: bacon and Brussels sprouts or strong, salty Cheddar cheese with cauliflower, for example. In contrast, Indian cooking techniques for these uncompromising vegetables are based around celebrating that sulphurous pungency. We believe, very much, in not masking the stench, but deepening it.

The headnote spice and finishing flavours best suited to these tricky vegetables are both mustard-based. Mustard seeds start the dish with a headnote of toasted nuttiness. To supercharge the dish, garlic often features as an additional headnote flavour – a small amount chopped and thrown in to fry after the seeds. To end, brassicas work monstrously well with mustard paste as a finishing flavour, along with a final 'wake me up' squeeze of lemon.

Panch poron, mustard or cumin seed are the choice of the Bengalis. Cumin seed alongside mustard seed will indicate a likely Gujrati chef. And, if you sense the nuclear weaponry of the power trio of onion, ginger and garlic, then you're probably dining in a Punjabi kitchen.

A note on veg and garlic: garlic is one of the ingredients forbidden in strict Hindu vegetarian Ayurvedic kitchens, as it is seen as passion- or heat-giving. The truth is, it is overpowering and so drowns out the delicacy of vegetables. It is always used with onion and ginger to start meat dishes (see page 209), but in the vegetable kitchen I highly recommend adding a little to the starting moments of brassica and squash dishes. There is no escaping the pungency of cabbage and so adding garlic simply celebrates this heady potency. With squashes, they release a lot of water and can become quite flaccid during the cooking process. Garlic props up the dish against any lost and evaporated flavour.

BASIC WHITE CABBAGE

The hard, round green cabbage that is too frequently the unimaginative subject of coleslaw or nursing home cabbage is nothing short of King in the Eastern kitchen. Over 4000 years ago, this vegetable spawned every subsequent form of brassica, from kohlrabi to cauliflower and for this we love him.

RED CABBAGE AND KALE

These are not seen in India generally. They work brilliantly with the Spice Tree formula, but my mother had never seen these until she came to Europe.

KOHLRABI

This is a popular vegetable in India known as 'the knotted cauli' or *gat ghobi*. They are often grated and formed into koftas, where they are mixed with gram flour, spices and ginger and fried into crisp soft balls that are added to curry or eaten fresh.

SAVOY CABBAGE

Our Lord's own brassica. Muscular, robust, chloropyll-rich, it takes a good beating in the pan and keeps its structure and flavour magnanimously. It works best in its simplest form. Just fry a headnote of mustard seed, add in a little garlic and use lemon and mustard paste to finish.

BROCCOLI
Something of a loveable upstart, Indians are not set a flutter at the sight of these handsome hulk fists. For them, broccoli was a Western construct that was only introduced to the East in the twentieth century. It is, in the Indian's view, the attention-seeking teen of the brassica world. Pungency and depth are here replaced by an inoffensive crunch. Try tossing broccoli into a fried mustard seed and garlic headnote and simply finish with a squeeze of lemon.

CAULIFLOWER
As Mark Twain said, 'A cauliflower is a cabbage with a college education'. Cauliflower is the most beloved of the brassicas. Sweet, nutty and texturally intriguing, they are the standard bearer of what our tongues want from our brassicas.

In India, cauliflowers are piled high on wooden market stalls in the rude midday heat. They are bought slightly limp, slightly dehydrated, a tired yellow and hence intensified in their sweet nuttiness. This is a far cry from the crisp, strutting cauliflowers of high street vegetable aisles. I have conducted numerous taste tests and I find the older the cauliflower – jaundiced and exhausted – the sweeter and deeper the flavour.

The most iconic cauliflower dish is *aloo ghobi*, which is actually one of the easiest dishes in the Indian kitchen. *Aloo ghobi* translates neatly as 'potato cauliflower'. There are not many lessons in Indian language that are required to understand the Spice Tree. However, the words '*aloo*' and '*ghobi*' are as important to Indian home cooks as the words 'litmus' and 'paper' to a chemist. This is the dish by which we judgmental Indians judge a chef's ability. *Aloo ghobi* (and the roundness and thinness of roti breads) tell you everything you need to know about the skill of an Indian cook. Its simplicity means there is nowhere to hide.

It is all about basic cooking techniques – and then stepping away, and letting it cook on low heat and being patient. Start with a headnote seed spice of your choice and generally you don't even need a finishing flavour, but experiment, please do, and show your Indian friends what your made of.

MOOLI
A beloved Indian vegetable, this is technically a member of the cabbage family, but looks like a root vegetable: majestic, glowing white and tusk-like. On first sight it can confound even the most accomplished chef. It is often given the same treatment as its more traditionally rooted radish cousins in the kitchen, but shares the sulphuric kick of its brassica siblings.

It is the embodiment of pungent – that boiled egg kind of kick – but has a wonderful sweet afterglow. It is a very common addition to mixed vegetable curries and here it serves the purpose of ticking that oh-so-important pungency box amongst the sweet carrots and stolid potatoes.

Many a simple supper will consist simply of boiled mooli mashed with rice, salt and possibly mustard oil if you're a Bengali. This saltiness and punchy aroma with the comfort of the musky white rice is replicated in many Eastern cultures – for instance the 1000-year-old-egg dishes in China, pickled mooli and rice in Japan and kimchi and rice in Korea. We also love the chiaroscuro of virgin white rice with the overpowering and uncompromising. There are few other flavours going on in these suppers other than the enormously pleasing flavour dissonance.

Pan-fried sprouts with mustard, lemon and cashew nuts

As much as I love bacon, it really is a sledgehammer method to drag the poor sprout into the echelons of the edible. Is the addition of unctuous smoked animal fat really what it takes to make sprouts sparkle? NO! I promise you, it is pure Santa's workshop magic what mustard seed, garlic and lemon can do to this most vilified of vegetables.

Prep Time: 10 mins
Cook Time: 15 mins
Serves: 4

Cashew nuts, 75 g
Pinch of salt
Vegetable oil, 4 tbsp
Mustard seeds, 1 tsp
1 dried red chilli
2 garlic cloves, peeled and minced
Brussels sprouts, 500 g, halved
Ground turmeric, ¼ tsp
Chilli powder, ⅛ tsp
Salt, 1 tsp
Sugar, 1 tsp
English mustard paste, 1 tbsp, loosened with a little water
Juice of ½ lemon

In a small, dry frying pan set over a high heat, toast the cashew nuts with a pinch of salt until they turn a deep golden brown, then set aside.

Put the vegetable oil in a large non-stick frying pan and set over a medium-high heat. When hot, add the mustard seeds and fry until they fizz, pop and turn grey, then turn the heat down to low, add the dried red chilli and minced garlic and fry for 10 seconds, taking care not to burn.

Add the halved sprouts, ground turmeric, chilli powder and salt and toss everything together, then partially cover and cook on low for 12 minutes or until the sprouts are tender but still a bright and vibrant green.

Add the sugar and mustard paste, stirring in the lemon juice just before serving. Finish with the toasted cashew nuts.

White cabbage with cumin and tomato

It is not necessary nor usual to use clarified butter, ghee, in vegetable dishes. They, and your arteries, just don't need it. However, the finishing slick of ghee used here with the surprising combination of ginger and coriander powder are the best of pals in a genre called *dalnlas*. You don't need to pronounce it, just get on and enjoy the silky luxury of it.

Prep Time: 15 mins
Cook Time: 35 mins
Serves: 4–6

Vegetable oil, 4 tbsp
Cumin seeds, 1 tsp
2 large bay leaves
5 cm piece of fresh ginger, 20 g, peeled and grated
1 large potato, 200 g, peeled and cut into 2 cm chunks
Ground turmeric, ½ tsp
Chilli powder, ⅛ tsp
Tinned chopped tomatoes, 200 g
1 small white cabbage, 700 g, outer leaves removed, cut in half and finely shredded
Water, 150 ml
Frozen peas, 100 g
Garam masala, 2 tsp
Salt, 1 tsp
Sugar, 1½ tsp
Coriander powder, 1½ tsp
Ghee, 2 tbsp

Put the vegetable oil in a large heavy-based pan and set over a medium-high heat. When hot, add the cumin seeds and fry until they turn dark brown and become fragrant, then add the bay leaves and ginger and fry for a further 10 seconds. When the bay leaves start to colour, add the potato, ground turmeric and chilli powder and toss until everything is well mixed.

Turn the heat down to low and add the chopped tomatoes, shredded white cabbage and water and stir until all the spices are mixed well into the cabbage. Cover and cook gently for 25 minutes, stirring occasionally. Add the frozen peas and garam masala and continue to cook for a further 5 minutes until the cabbage is completely soft and tender.

Finish with the salt, sugar and coriander powder, stirring in the ghee just before serving.

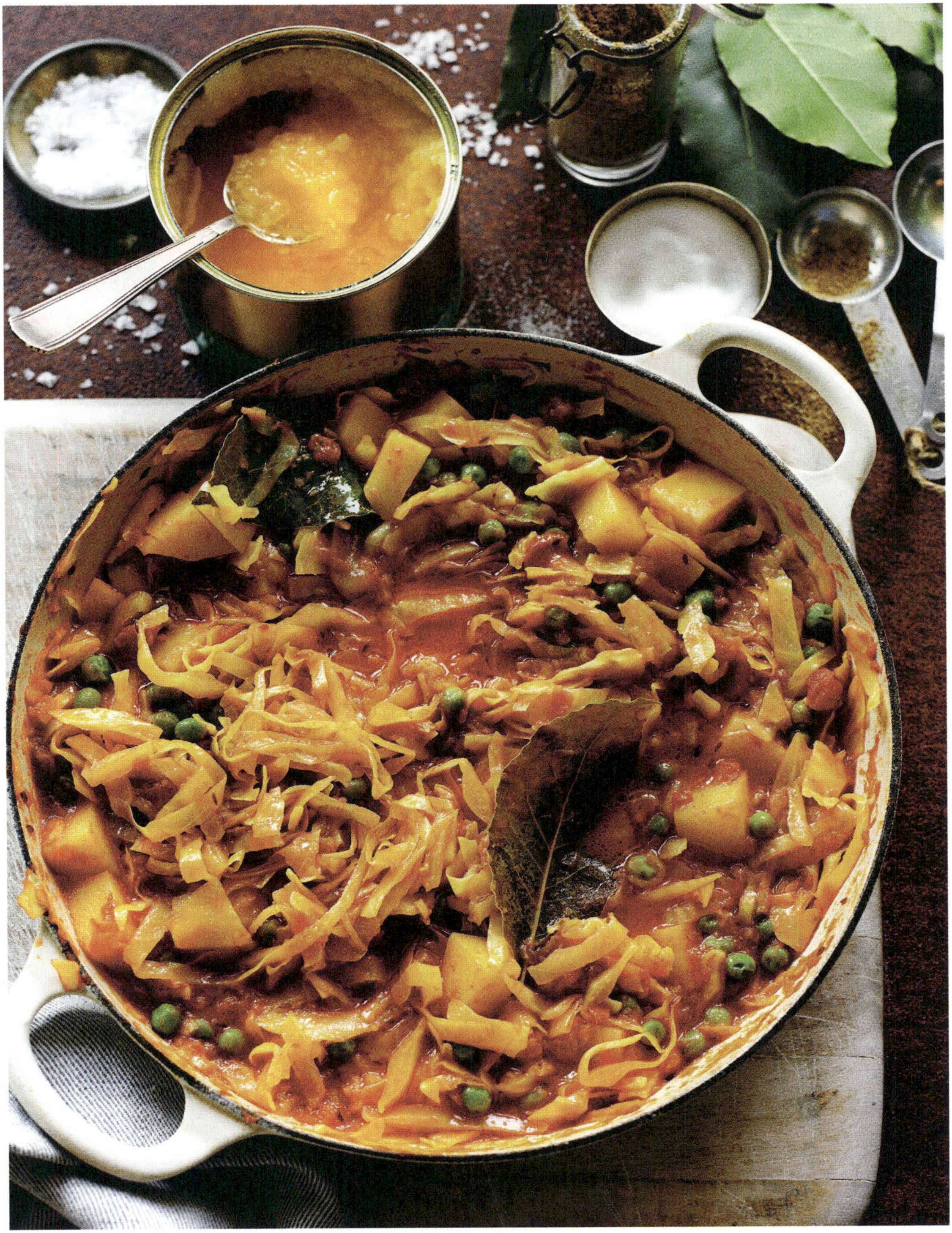

Gujrati kohlrabi

I love the Indian translation of kohlrabi, 'the knotted one'. Gentle and nutty, it works so well with the typical Gujrati opening trio of asafoetida, cumin and mustard.

Prep Time: 10 mins
Cook Time: 40 mins
Serves: 4

Vegetable oil, 4 tbsp
Mustard seeds, 1 tsp
Cumin seeds, 1½ tsp
1 large green chilli, deseeded and cut into 5 mm slices
1 dried red chilli
Asafoetida, 1 tsp
1 small potato, 150 g, peeled and cut into 2 cm chunks
2 large kohlrabi, 650 g, peeled and cut into 3 cm chunks
Ground turmeric, ¼ tsp
Chilli powder, ⅛ tsp
Water, 250 ml
Salt, 1 tsp
Sugar, 1 tsp
Coriander powder, ½ tsp
Obligatory backup jug of water, to loosen the dish to your taste

Put the vegetable oil in a large heavy-based saucepan and set over a medium-high heat. When hot, add the mustard and cumin seeds and fry until the mustard seeds fizz, pop and turn grey. Add the sliced green chilli, dried red chilli and asafoetida and fry for around 10 seconds until the asafoetida turns a rich brown and releases that telltale musky aroma.

Add the potato, kohlrabi, ground turmeric and chilli powder and mix together. Turn the heat down to low and add the water, then cover with a lid and simmer gently for 25–30 minutes, stirring occasionally and adding more water if necessary, until the kohlrabi is juicy and tender.

Remove the lid and continue to cook for a further 5 mins or until the water has reduced to a rich sauce coating the kohlrabi. Finish by seasoning with the salt and sugar and stirring the coriander powder through just before serving.

Kale with mustard and garlic

Gosh, I so love this dish. It very poignantly celebrates the synergy of combining simple, iconic Indian spices with the darkest and most over-wintered of British produce. I must make this at least once a week. The most basic of spice pairings – mustard and garlic – works magically with any brassica. Tie it to your apron and write it on your lintel, as it's your gateway to endlessly great greens. I'm getting evangelical I know, but give it a go...

Prep Time: 10 mins
Cook Time: 20 mins
Serves: 4 as a side

Vegetable oil, 4 tbsp
Mustard seeds, 2 tsp
1 dried red chilli
2 garlic cloves, peeled and minced
Kale, 600g, stalks removed, leaves finely shredded
Water, 200 ml
Ground turmeric, ¼ tsp
Chilli powder, ⅛ tsp
Salt, 2 tsp
Sugar, 1 tsp
English mustard paste, 1½ tbsp, loosened with a little water
Juice of ½ lemon

Put the vegetable oil in a large heavy-based saucepan and set over a medium-high heat. When hot, add the mustard seeds and fry until they fizz, pop and turn grey, then turn the heat down to low and add the dried red chilli and minced garlic and fry for 10 seconds, taking care not to burn.

Next add the shredded kale and toss everything together, then add the water, ground turmeric, chilli powder and salt, stir together and cover. Cook gently for 15 minutes or until the kale has completely wilted down and is tender.

Finish by adding the sugar and mustard paste, stirring in the lemon juice just before serving.

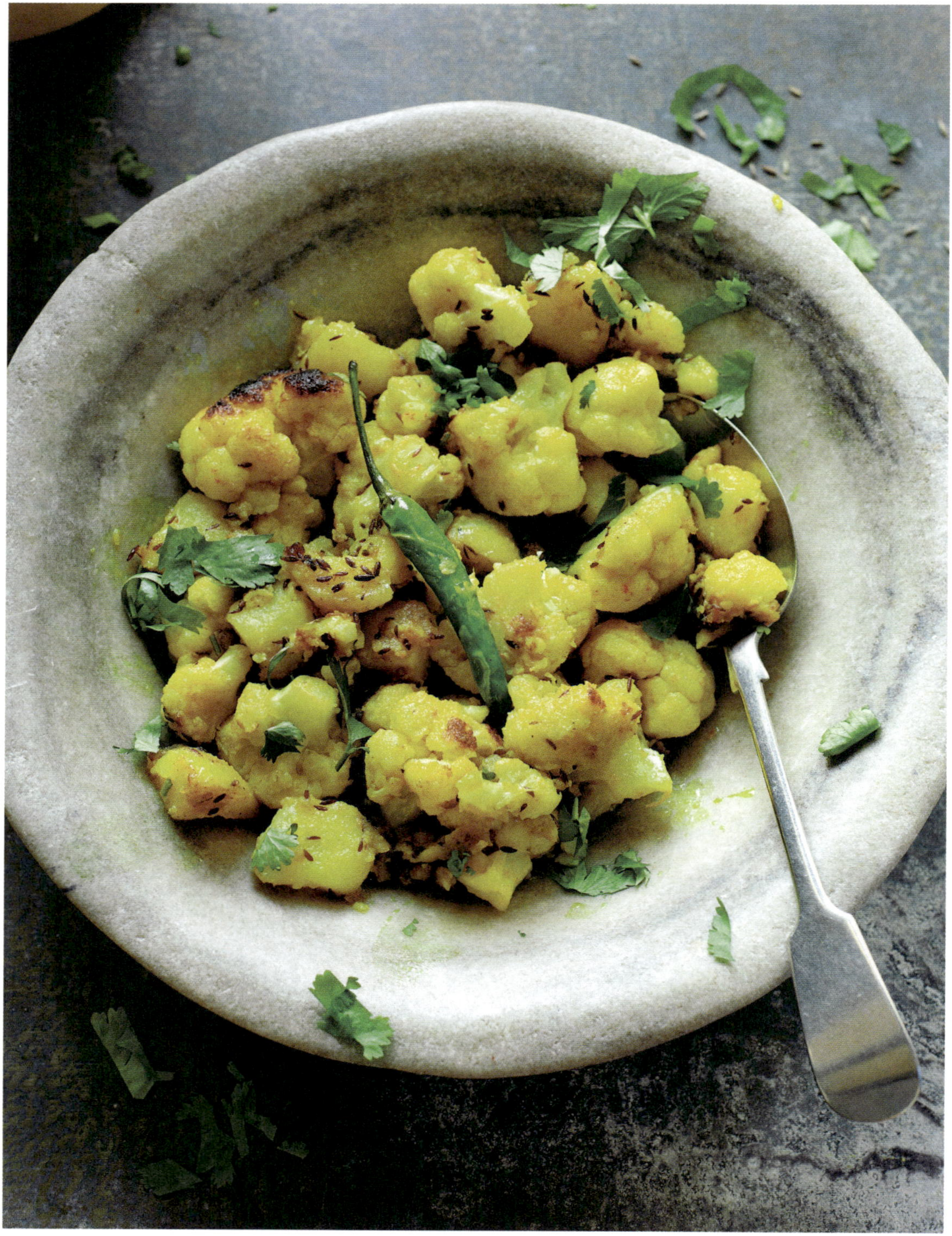

Aloo ghobi

It would be a lie to say that Indians do not judge people by how they cook, and this dish is the ultimate and most ruthless barometer. My aunty says, 'You can taste the chef's hand best in an aloo ghobi'. In this dish there is nowhere to hide, with such simple spicings and the most-humble of vegetables – but hold your nerve! Don't over-meddle or overheat. This is the dish for which my mother is best known and when we call round for a brew, it's straight to her hob to frantically lift every pan lid, on the hunt for her *aloo ghobi*.

Prep Time: 5 mins
Cook Time: 30 mins
Serves: 4

Vegetable oil, 4 tbsp
Cumin seeds, 1 tsp
1 large green chilli, pierced
1 large potato, 200 g, peeled and cut into 2 cm chunks
1 large cauliflower, 500 g, cut into florets
Ground turmeric, ¼ tsp
Chilli powder, ⅛ tsp
Salt, 1 tsp
Sugar, 1 tsp
Obligatory backup jug of water, to loosen the dish to your taste
Handful of fresh coriander leaves

Put the vegetable oil in a large heavy-based saucepan and set over a medium-high heat. When hot, add the cumin seeds and green chilli and fry until the cumin seeds turn a deep golden brown and become fragrant. Turn the heat down to low and add the cubed potato, cooking gently for 8 minutes until it starts to soften at the edges.

Add the cauliflower florets, ground turmeric, chilli powder, salt and sugar and give everything a good mix together until the cauliflower is fully coated with the spices.

Cover with a lid and cook gently for 15–20 minutes, adding a splash of water only if absolutely necessary and stirring occasionally, until the cauliflower is tender and cooked through. Stir through the chopped coriander leaves, then serve.

Braised red cabbage with mustard and bay

This is an exciting alternative to the usual red wine and apple braising. Truth be told, you *could* throw apples into this and they would work up an additional mulled warmth with the bay leaves.

Prep Time: 15 mins
Cook Time: 1 hour
Serves: 4–6

Vegetable oil, 4 tbsp
Mustard seeds, 1 tsp
1 dried red chilli
2 large bay leaves
1 small red cabbage, 600 g, outer leaves removed, cut in half and finely shredded
1 small turnip, 200 g, peeled and cut into 2 cm chunks
Ground turmeric, ¼ tsp
Chilli powder, ⅛ tsp
Salt, 1 tsp
Sugar, 1 tsp
Water, 500 ml
Juice of ½ lemon
Obligatory backup jug of water, to loosen the dish to your taste

Put the vegetable oil in a large heavy-based saucepan and set over a medium-high heat. When hot, add the mustard seeds and fry until they fizz, pop and turn grey, then add the dried red chilli and bay leaves and fry for 10 seconds until they start to colour slightly.

With the heat still on medium-high, add the cabbage, turnip, ground turmeric, chilli powder, salt and sugar and mix together. Turn the heat down to low and add the water, then cover and simmer gently for 45–50 minutes, stirring occasionally and adding more water if necessary, until the cabbage is completely soft and tender. Finish with the fresh lemon juice just before serving.

Broccoli with mustard and lemon

Broccoli is not a traditional Indian vegetable, but the brassica formula of mustard seed, garlic and lemon works a stunning treat alongside this flamboyant green veg. I highly recommend Tenderstem broccoli, as we really do find more sweetness locked in their stems than in the open, air-dried florets.

Prep Time: 5 mins
Cook Time: 15 mins
Serves: 4

Vegetable oil, 4 tbsp
Mustard seeds, 1½ tsp
Tenderstem broccoli, 300 g, stalks removed and cut into batons, leaving the florets whole
1 large dried red chilli
Ground turmeric, ¼ tsp
Chilli powder, ⅛ tsp
Salt, 1 tsp
Sugar, 1 tsp
Juice of ½ lemon

Put the vegetable oil in a large non-stick frying pan and set over a medium-high heat. When hot, add the mustard seeds and fry until they fizz, pop and turn grey. Turn the heat down to medium and add the broccoli stalks, dried red chilli, ground turmeric and chilli powder and fry for 2 minutes until the stalks just start to soften.

Add the broccoli florets, salt and sugar and cook over a medium heat for 10 minutes or until the broccoli is tender and vibrant green. Finish with the lemon juice just before serving.

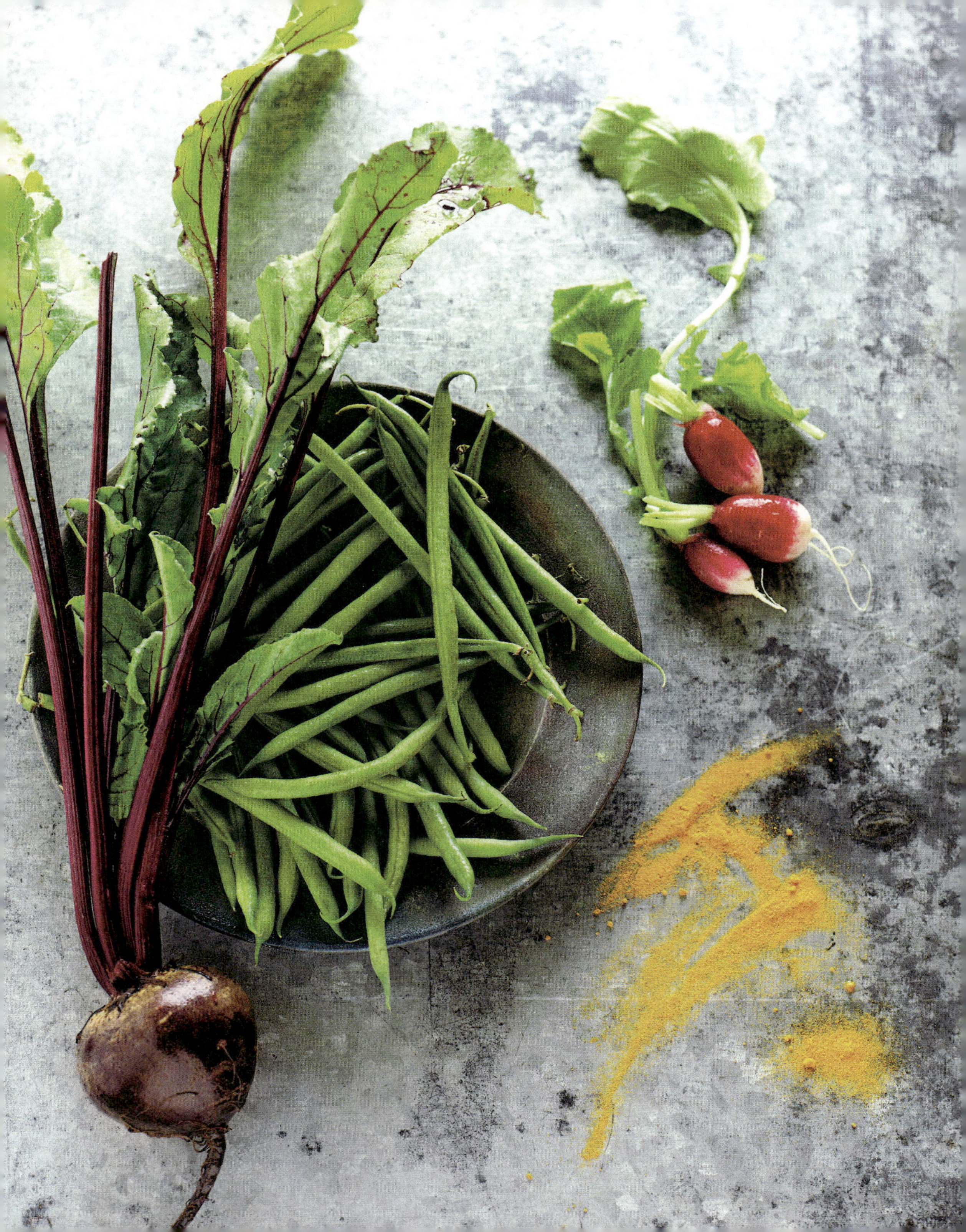

Green Vegetables

1

Pick ONE starter ball from the root system and fry the spice in a pan with a drizzle of oil.

2

Add your green veg to the pan.

3

Now travel up the trunk, adding turmeric and chilli powder. Add salt and sugar, to taste.

4

From the leaves, choose one or more of the ingredients to finish your dish. Play around and have fun – this is how you personalise your curry.

KEY

● = Mustard Seed, Dried Red Chilli and Curry Leaf

SOUTH INDIAN TRIO

● = Mustard Seed, Dried Red Chilli, Cumin Seed and Asafoetida

GUJRATI QUARTET

The Green Veg Tree

Amchoor

Lemon

Coriander Powder

Tomato

White Poppy Seed

English Mustard Paste

Sugar

Salt

Turmeric

Chilli powder

South Indian Trio | Mustard Seed & Dried Red Chilli | Gujrati Quartet | Cumin Seed | Panch Poron Seeds

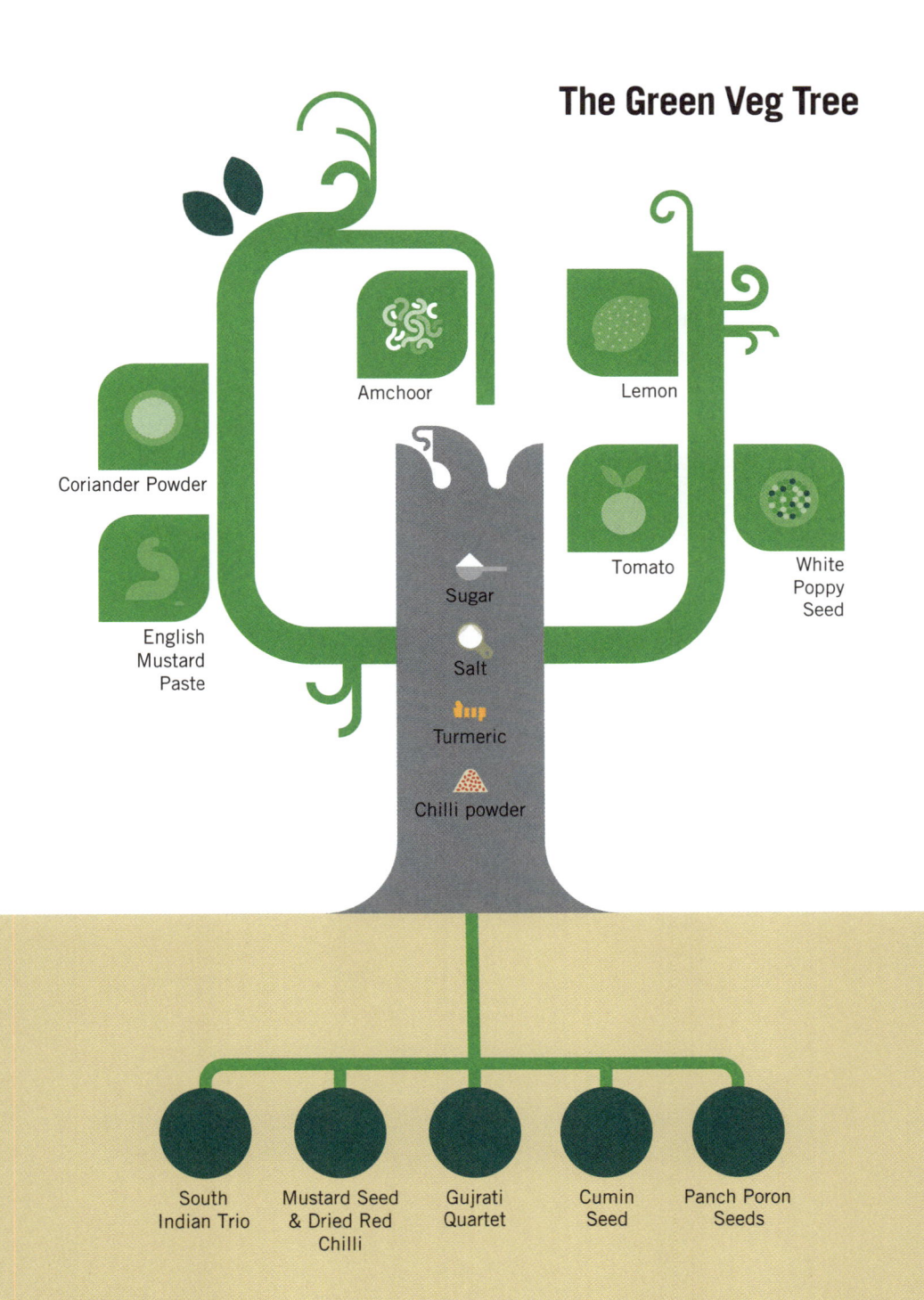

Green veg to my family are what handbags and shoes are to the Kardashians. The prospect of a retirement ferreting around in market boxes full of firm beans and velvet spinach is what motivates us to keep our hips and knees in shape. One of the reasons, I'm convinced, that living with the extended family is preferable to spending our latter years in nursing homes is that nursing homes don't conduct day trips to greengrocers for chlorophyll therapy. Within the family, however, there will always be a fellow okra prodder.

Green veg for me includes the simple, home-grown types of veg. Beans, spinaches, chillies, okra, radish pods, peas and their pods, courgette stalks, beetroot tops... OK, you see here that the list grows weirder and more desperate (I'm scanning my mother's Lancashire vegetable patch and greenhouse as I write). Not only are the vegetables in this chapter humble in their ability to be grown anywhere, they are also undemanding and flexible in their cooking methods. This means they are a great blank canvas for you to play with any three-spice formula. It is this ability to transform the creeping, prolific and unbidden into the exotic that most impresses me about spices.

So here is your simple rule: if you can grow it or if you spot it, unidentifiable, in a far-flung holiday market, chalk it up to a green veg and go to town on it with your tree formula and flair.

In my cooking lessons, I always start the day with a demonstration using green veg. I start by frying the different headnote spices – cumin seed, mustard seed, nigella seed and panch poron. You can play fast and loose with finishing flavours too and they will always, always work out. Bear in mind always though that green veg are delicate. Usually delicate in its structure as well as its flavour.

Hence, try to avoid the overpowering ingredients like garlic and onion which are more at home with meat. Also, try to use only small amounts of tomato in the finishing of the dish to avoid drowning out sweet subtlety with acidic tang.

Mustard paste is great as a go-to finishing flavour. It is so very savoury that it greatly enhances natural vegetable sugars. Just to ensure these can really sing out, a pinch of sugar to taste with green vegetables works a treat.

An Oral Culture

A kitchen table secret that my family and others are loathe to share is the love for chewing the fibrous. Some vegetables are selected for their indigestible rather than denture-friendly qualities. Freud would probably suggest that most Indians are stuck in the oral stage and I would agree. We have a culture of jaws going non-stop and many are addicted to the recreational chewing of *paan*, a betel nut leaf wrap. Indians are convinced that a good deal of challenging chewing strengthens the teeth. I vividly remember my mother handing me a long lean ribbon of bacon rind to exercise my teeth on while I watched her in the kitchen. OK, granted, it also stopped me talking, but I love that memory. It opened a new informal food frontier to me. Not just a fierce love of bacon, but how radical that my mother, a woman of grace and high culture, understood this animal-like need to gnaw. We consider the best part of a meat curry to be the fighting with the bones and in this way we often have very fibrous stalks and pods in vegetable dishes and chew the life out of them. The dessicated remnants are then placed delicately on the side of the plate, like a sophisticated Brahmin owl pellet. There, I've laid bare the green veg indignity that lurks in the kitchen holy of holies. We are not proud of it, but we should be. To extract every last shred of pulp from earthly gifts of greenery is surely a most appreciative end.

GREEN BEANS

These hold a very special place in the Indian kitchen and so deserve special mention. In India they grow in the winter and they grow with zeal. Like all green veg, they are bought daily at the market, as they shrivel and dry in the heat. Through the winter season, the bean baskets on the pavement display a breadth of colourful variety to brighten the shoppers' day – a white, green, red, maroon and speckled splendour. They come in every shape and size and are approached with the same joy. They are substantial, sweet and delicate all at the same time. Their strength of structure means that they are hard to overcook and destroy in your spice experimentation phase.

They also stand up to a good simmer in your finishing flavours. Interesting headnotes like panch poron draw complex and haunting flavours out of beans. Some have naturally extraordinary garlic hues, some are more nut-like in their taste. They are cooked with potatoes to add bulk and with peas to add sweetness. We eat them with roti flat breads or with rice. Generally, we fry beans separately prior to the spicing stage; then they can be simply tossed into the spiced oil, flashed with the finishing flavours and turned out quickly. What Indian diaspora love about green beans is that they can be grown simply in the smallest of foreign spaces – a doctor's plant pot or a high-rise window box can bring the bounty of a varanasi market. Topped, tailed, chopped, fried and then frozen, we can eat the results of our husbandry all the year around.

FORAGED GREENS

And now to Indians most generous love of foraged greens. To put matters in context, one must understand why these filched plant parts are so important. Marrow plants grow in the summer and grow with abundance. They can often be found swelling wild on various rubbish heaps around Indian villages. To use the leaves, shoots and fruit triples the culinary swag. The tops of beetroots, the seed pods of bolted radish plants, the stalks and leaves of runaway courgette plants, cut-and-come again veg patch spinaches and the pods and shoots of young pea plants (one might think it profligate to harvest sweet, delicate pea shoots, but peas grow in Indian winters with abandon and the shoots are fair game). The pea shoots are cooked like spinach with a delicate headnote and a touch of mustard and/or lemon to finish. There is a special place in our hearts for those vegetables we find between the cracks of the obvious. It was for these dishes that an orderly and greedy queue of guests formed outside my mother's home in the summer months.

OKRA

Okra is one of India's most beloved vegetables. They are prolific and hold their structure well and so do not shrink in the cooking. This is a great bonus in a vegetable. Tasty and generous, they are topped and tailed and fried before they are cooked as a main course. They are widely loathed for their slime, but frying them before cooking them into a sauce eliminates this. Also, finely sliced and fried to a nutty crisp is a very common way of enjoying them with rice.

CAPSICUM

Green peppers are commonly added into mixed vegetable dishes. They are cut into large chunks and add a fleshy bulk to pans of delicate and heavy ingredients.

Green beans with cumin, honey and pecans

A reliable dinner party recipe and the dish is always licked clean. The citrus tang of the cumin seed and powder works addictively well with the honey and lemon. The beans retain their garden-sweet integrity and the nuts take on a toffee smoke. This business about *al dente* vegetables is not one that is honoured in the Indian kitchen. I have tried to analyse this and it seems that hard veg are just not as yielding and absorbent of spicing. And we are all about the spicing. Thus, we are all about vegetables being cooked into permeable defeat. You can always cook the beans a little shy of soft, but I devised this dish because I love my beans soft and ribbon-like and like to let the honeyed, cumin pecans do the hard talking.

Prep Time: 5 mins
Cook Time: 10 mins
Serves: 4

Vegetable oil, 4 tbsp
Cumin seeds, 1 tbsp
Green beans, 250 g, topped and tailed, cut into thirds
Cumin powder, 1½ tsp
Ground turmeric, ¼ tsp
Chilli powder, ⅛ tsp
Pecan nuts, 100 g, roughly chopped into large pieces
Honey, 3 tbsp
Salt, ½ tsp
Juice of ½ lemon

Put the vegetable oil in a large wok over a medium-high heat and when hot, add the cumin seeds and fry until they turn dark brown and become fragrant, then turn the heat down to medium and add the green beans, cumin powder, ground turmeric and chilli powder. Fry for 8 minutes until the beans have completely softened and turned a nutty brown.

While the green beans are cooking, put a separate small non-stick frying pan over a medium heat and add the pecan nuts, honey and salt. Cook for 3–5 minutes until the nuts are fully coated and sticky, taking care not to burn.

When the nuts are done, put them into the wok with the green beans and toss until everything is fully combined. Finish with a squeeze of fresh lemon juice.

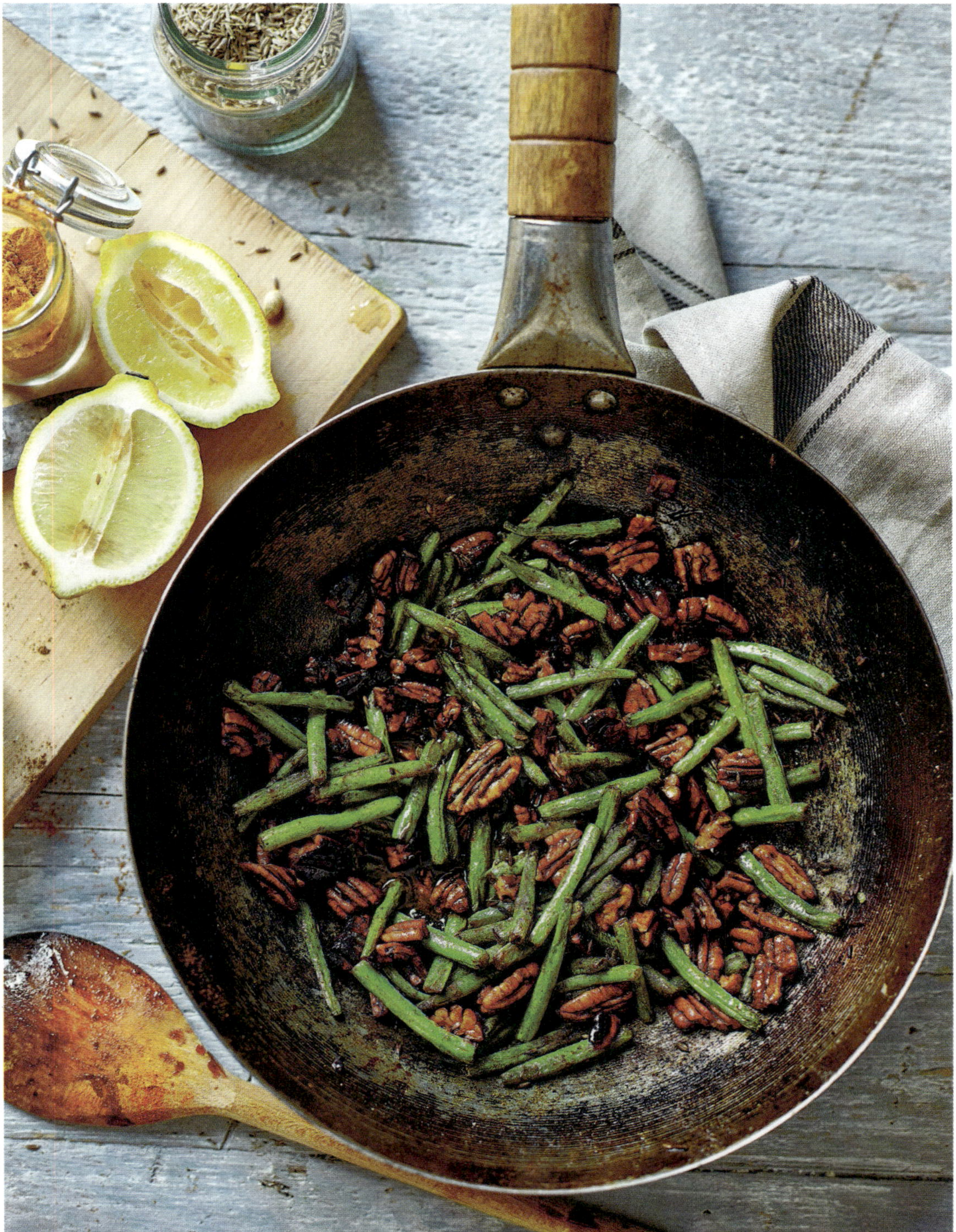

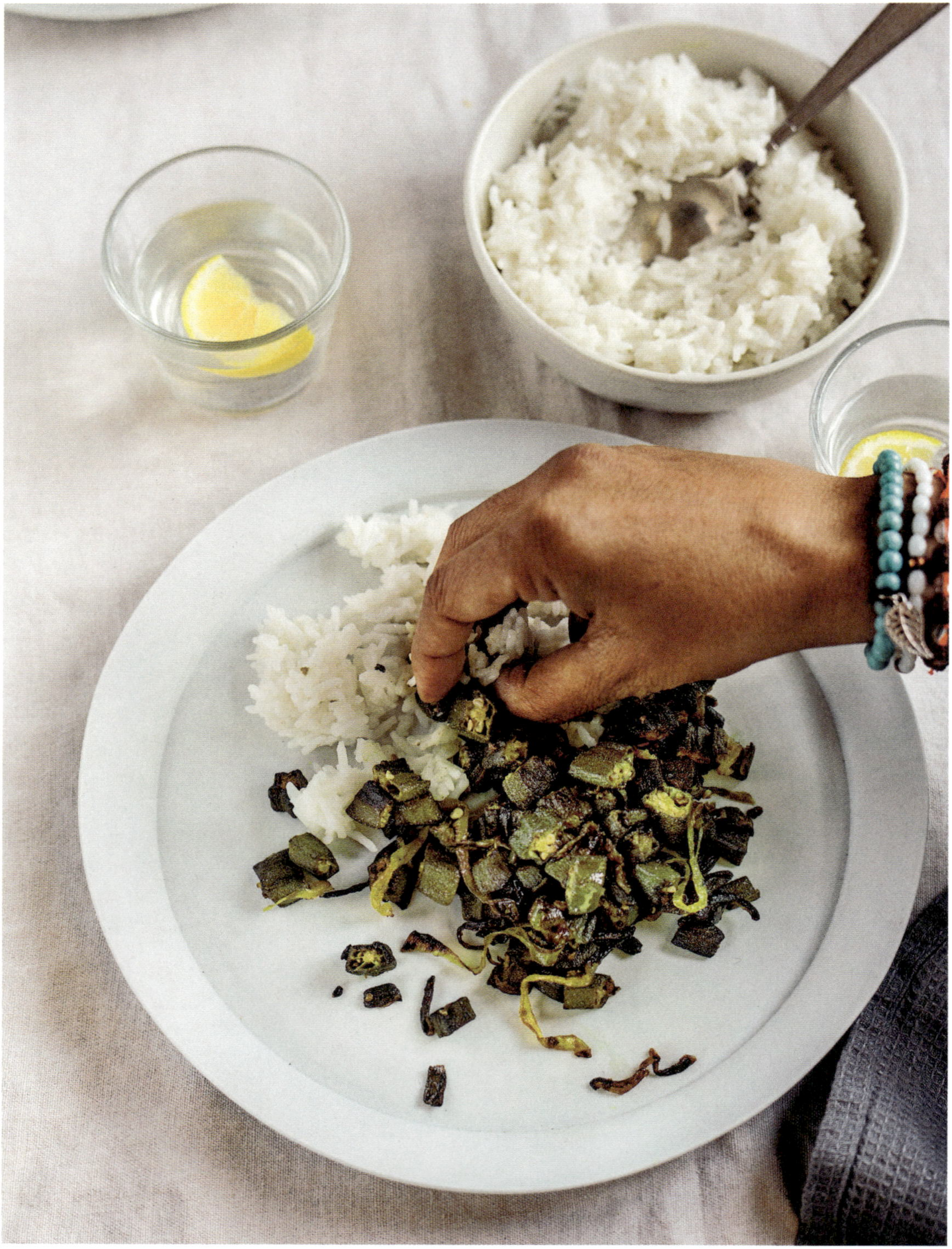

Crunchy okra with cumin

Okra is one of our most beloved vegetables. It saddens me how they are often loathed because of the slime they produce. All you need to do is chop them and then fry them to the point that the slime disappears. In this dish we fry them beyond that stage to a dark, caramelised crunch. We then eat those sweet, nutty discs, mashed into rice, with greedy fingers.

Prep Time: 10 mins
Cook Time: 30 mins
Serves: 4

Vegetable oil, 4 tbsp
1 large green chilli, deseeded and thinly sliced
1 large white onion, cut in half and thinly sliced
Okra, 500 g, topped and tailed, cut into 1 cm discs
Ground turmeric, ¼ tsp
Chilli powder, ⅛ tsp
Ground cumin, 1 tsp
Salt, 1 tsp
Juice of ½ lemon

Put the vegetable oil in a large non-stick frying pan set over a medium-high heat. When hot, turn the heat down to medium, add the green chilli and onion and fry for 10 minutes until the onion is golden and sweet. Now add the okra, ground turmeric and chilli powder and fry for another 20 minutes, tossing the okra, until it has turned crispy and brown.

Finish by tossing the okra with the ground cumin, salt and lemon juice just before serving.

Popped mustard radish pods

When radish plants bolt, they produce charming soft seed pods and increase their culinary use tenfold. The pods are a little bitter sweet and have a mesmeric popping texture. Choose the soft ones and don't be afraid to add small cubes of potato into the early stage of cooking to add some bulk. This is another degree-level curry dish, like the Cauliflower stalk yellow split dahl on page 149. It is very much one that is eaten in the privacy of the Indian kitchen, family gathered, curtains drawn. If you can't find radish pods, replace with mange tout or green beans.

Prep Time: 10 mins
Cook Time: 15 mins
Serves: 4–6

Vegetable oil, 2 tbsp
Mustard seeds, 1 tsp
Cumin seeds, ½ tsp
1 dried red chilli
1 large green chilli, pierced
Radish pods, 250 g
Ground turmeric, ¼ tsp
Chilli powder, ⅛ tsp
English mustard paste,
    1 tbsp, loosened with
    a little water
Salt, 1 tsp
Sugar, ½ tsp
Juice of ½ lemon

Put the vegetable oil in a large non-stick frying pan over a medium-high heat. When hot, add the mustard and cumin seeds and fry until the mustard seeds turn grey and the cumin seeds turn a deep brown.

Add the dried red chilli, green chilli, radish pods, ground turmeric, chilli powder, mustard paste, salt and sugar and cook gently, partially covered, for 10–15 minutes until the radish pods are tender and juicy.

Finish by stirring through the fresh lemon juice.

Okra curry

I know okra is considered an exotic and somewhat scary alien slime-emitting vegetable creature, but it is a great carte blanche for your Spice Tree experiments. Always top and tail each one, then halve and fry the okra until the slime has gone. In this tame and tasty form, it can even be frozen to add to your clever concoctions at your later convenience.

Prep Time: 10 mins
Cook Time: 40 mins
Serves: 4

Vegetable oil, 5½ tbsp
Okra, 500 g, topped and tailed, cut in half
Cumin seeds, 1 tsp
1 large green chilli, deseeded and thinly sliced
1 white onion, cut in half and thinly sliced
Ground turmeric, ¼ tsp
Chilli powder, ⅛ tsp
Tinned chopped tomatoes, 200 g
Water, 400 ml
English mustard paste, 1 tbsp, loosened with a little water
Salt, 1 tsp
Sugar, 1 tsp
Juice of ½ lemon
1 small bunch of fresh coriander, roughly chopped

Put half the vegetable oil in a large non-stick frying pan and set over a medium-high heat. When hot, add the sliced okra and fry until golden brown and all the sliminess has gone from the okra, then set aside.

In a separate large heavy-based pan set over a medium-high heat, add the remaining vegetable oil and when hot, add the cumin seeds and fry until they turn a deep brown, then add the green chilli and onion and fry for 6 minutes until the onion has softened.

Add the ground turmeric, chilli powder, chopped tomatoes, water and the fried okra and mix well. Turn the heat down to low, partially cover with a lid and simmer gently for 15 minutes.

Add the mustard paste, salt, sugar and lemon juice and continue to cook for a further 8 minutes until the sauce has become rich and thick. Finish by stirring through the fresh coriander just before serving.

Beetroot tops with mustard and lemon

The soft red stalks and purple-green leaves atop beetroot plants should be treated like spinach. They are great in dishes like this, as a stand-alone ingredient, or else simmer them into dahls or any meat curry for an added charm.

Prep Time: 10 mins
Cook Time: 35 mins
Serves: 4

Vegetable oil, 5 tbsp
Mustard seeds, 1 tsp
1 large dried red chilli
1 large potato, 200 g, cut into 5 cm chunks
Mooli, 200 g, peeled and cut into 5 cm chunks
Ground turmeric, ¼ tsp
Chilli powder, ⅛ tsp
English mustard paste, 1 tbsp, loosened with a little water
Salt, 1 tsp
Sugar, 1 tsp
1 bunch of beetroot tops/ greens, washed and roughly chopped
Juice of ½ lemon
Obligatory backup jug of water, to loosen the dish to your taste

Put the vegetable oil in a large heavy-based pan and set over a medium-high heat. When hot, add the mustard seeds and fry until they fizz, pop and turn grey, then add the dried red chilli, potato, mooli, ground turmeric, chilli powder, mustard paste, salt and sugar and mix everything together well. Reduce the heat to medium and cook, partially covered, for 20 minutes until the potato has softened.

Add the beetroot tops and continue to cook for a further 10 minutes until they have fully wilted down. Finish with the fresh lemon juice just before serving. Add a little water if necessary to loosen to your taste.

Capsicum curry

There is one ingredient I cannot stand and it is green capsicum. In this dish, however, it is a transformed creature with all bitterness turning to perfume. This is the simplest of dishes and it flows so perfectly and easily through the Spice Tree.

Prep Time: 10 mins
Cook Time: 40 mins
Serves: 4–6

Vegetable oil, 5 tbsp
Cumin seeds, 1 tsp
1 large white onion, roughly chopped
1 large potato, 200 g, peeled and cut into 3 cm chunks
3 large green capsicums, 500 g, deseeded and chunkily chopped
Ground turmeric, ¼ tsp
Chilli powder, ⅛ tsp
Tinned chopped tomatoes, 200 g
Water, 450 ml
English mustard paste, 1 tbsp, loosened with a little water
Coriander powder, ½ tsp
Obligatory backup jug of water, to loosen the dish to your taste

Put the vegetable oil in a large heavy-based pan and set over a medium-high heat. When hot, add the cumin seeds and fry until they turn dark brown, then add the onion and fry for 8 minutes until it is soft and golden.

Add the potato, green capsicums, ground turmeric, chilli powder and chopped tomatoes and fry for 4 minutes, until most of the water from the tomatoes has evaporated and the oil has started to split out of them.

Reduce the heat to low and add the water and mustard paste, stirring so everything is fully mixed. Partially cover and simmer gently for 25 minutes until the potato is cooked through and the sauce has become thick and rich.

Finish by stirring through the coriander powder just before serving. Add more water if necessary to loosen to your taste before serving.

Mustardy pea shoots and potatoes

Pea shoots are the sweetest and most delicious of ingredients. I love to buy a cheap pack of marrowfat peas and plant them in a pretty trough on my kitchen window. I reap and cook with the shoots when they get any growth and love their sweet cut-and-come-again generosity. When cooked, they are sweet and delicate but reduce dramatically and so the potatoes perform their usual bulkier, big brother role.

Prep Time: 10 mins
Cook Time: 30 mins
Serves: 4

Vegetable oil, 2 tbsp
Mustard seeds, 1 tsp
1 dried red chilli
3 medium potatoes, cut into 2 cm chunks
Ground turmeric, ¼ tsp
Chilli powder, ⅛ tsp
English mustard paste, 1 tbsp, loosened with a little water
Pea shoots, 75 g, chopped in half
Salt, 1 tsp
Sugar, ½ tsp

Put the vegetable oil in a large non-stick frying pan set over a medium-high heat. When hot, add the mustard seeds and fry until they crackle and turn grey, then add the dried red chilli, chopped potatoes, ground turmeric and chilli powder and toss everything together.

Reduce the heat to low and cook, partially covered, for 25 minutes, stirring occasionally, until the potatoes are soft and cooked through.

When the potatoes are cooked, add the mustard paste, chopped pea shoots, salt and sugar and stir everything together well.

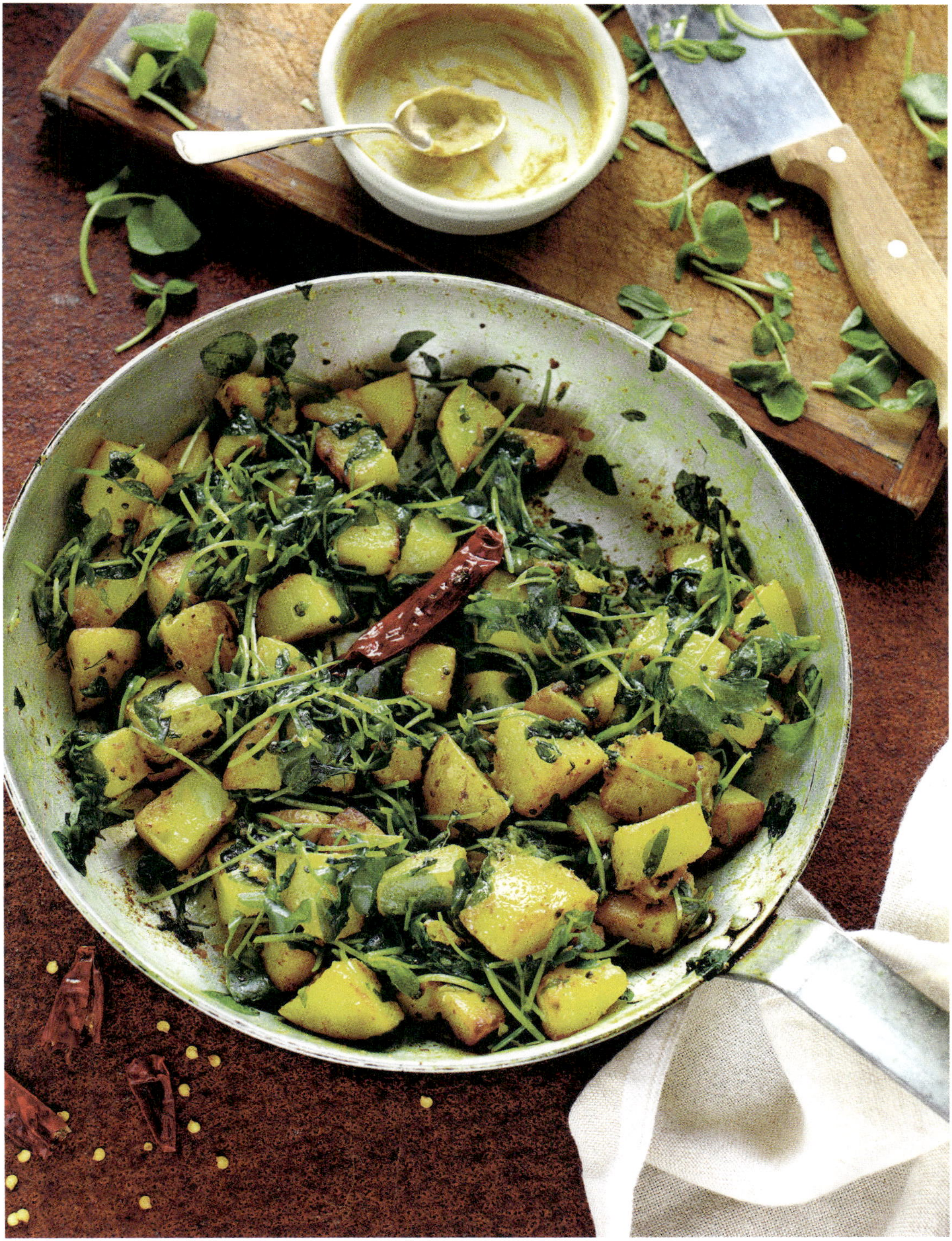

Mange tout and potato with panch poron

In India we believe in using every part of the vegetable, so even whole pea pods are thrown into curries. The sweet, snappy flesh is pulled from the husk between the teeth using your fingers. Mange tout makes a great, less antisocial alternative.

Prep Time: 10 mins
Cook Time: 40 mins
Serves: 4

Vegetable oil, 4 tbsp
1 large dried red chilli
Panch poron, 1 tsp
2 small white onions, cut in half then thinly sliced lengthways
2 medium potatoes, peeled and cut into 2 cm cubes
Ground turmeric, ¼ tsp
Chilli powder, ⅛ tsp
Mange tout, 300 g
Salt, 1 tsp
Sugar, 1 tsp
English mustard paste, 1 heaped tbsp, loosened with a little water
Coriander powder, 1 tsp

Put the vegetable oil in a large non-stick frying pan set over a medium-high heat. When hot, add the dried red chilli and panch poron and fry for 30 seconds until the nuggets of fenugreek turn a golden brown and the mustard seeds turn grey. Lower the heat to medium, add the sliced onions and fry for 8 minutes until they soften.

Turn the heat down to low, add the potatoes, ground turmeric and chilli powder and stir until everything is fully mixed with the onions. Partially cover and cook gently for 20 minutes, stirring occasionally, until the potatoes are soft and cooked through. Add the mange tout and continue to cook for a further 10 minutes until tender.

To finish, add the salt, sugar and mustard paste and mix well, stirring the coriander powder through just before serving.

Green beans with panch poron and coriander

This is a great simple signature dish, which allows you the freedom to play with the Spice Tree. You can interchange panch poron for the more citrus cumin or nuttier mustard seeds. And have some fun with the finishing flavour combinations. Frozen beans work brilliantly, but they won't need cooking, just add them with the spices and heat through. You can turn out a swisher dish by mixing in a handful of pine or cashew nuts.

Prep Time: 5 mins
Cook Time: 20 mins
Serves: 4

Vegetable oil, 4 tbsp
Panch poron, 1 tsp
1 large white onion, thinly sliced
Green beans, 300 g, topped and tailed
Ground turmeric, ¼ tsp
Chilli powder, ⅛ tsp
Tinned chopped tomatoes, 3 tbsp
English mustard paste, 1 tbsp, loosened with a little water
Coriander powder, 1½ tsp
Salt, 1 tsp
Sugar, 1 tsp

Put the vegetable oil in a large, heavy-based saucepan and set over a medium-high heat. When hot, add the panch poron and fry until the nuggets of fenugreek turn dark brown, then turn the heat down to medium and add the onion, frying for 8 minutes until soft and nutty.

Add the green beans, ground turmeric, chilli powder and chopped tomatoes and cook for 8–10 minutes until the green beans are completely tender.

Finish by stirring through the mustard paste, coriander powder, salt and sugar.

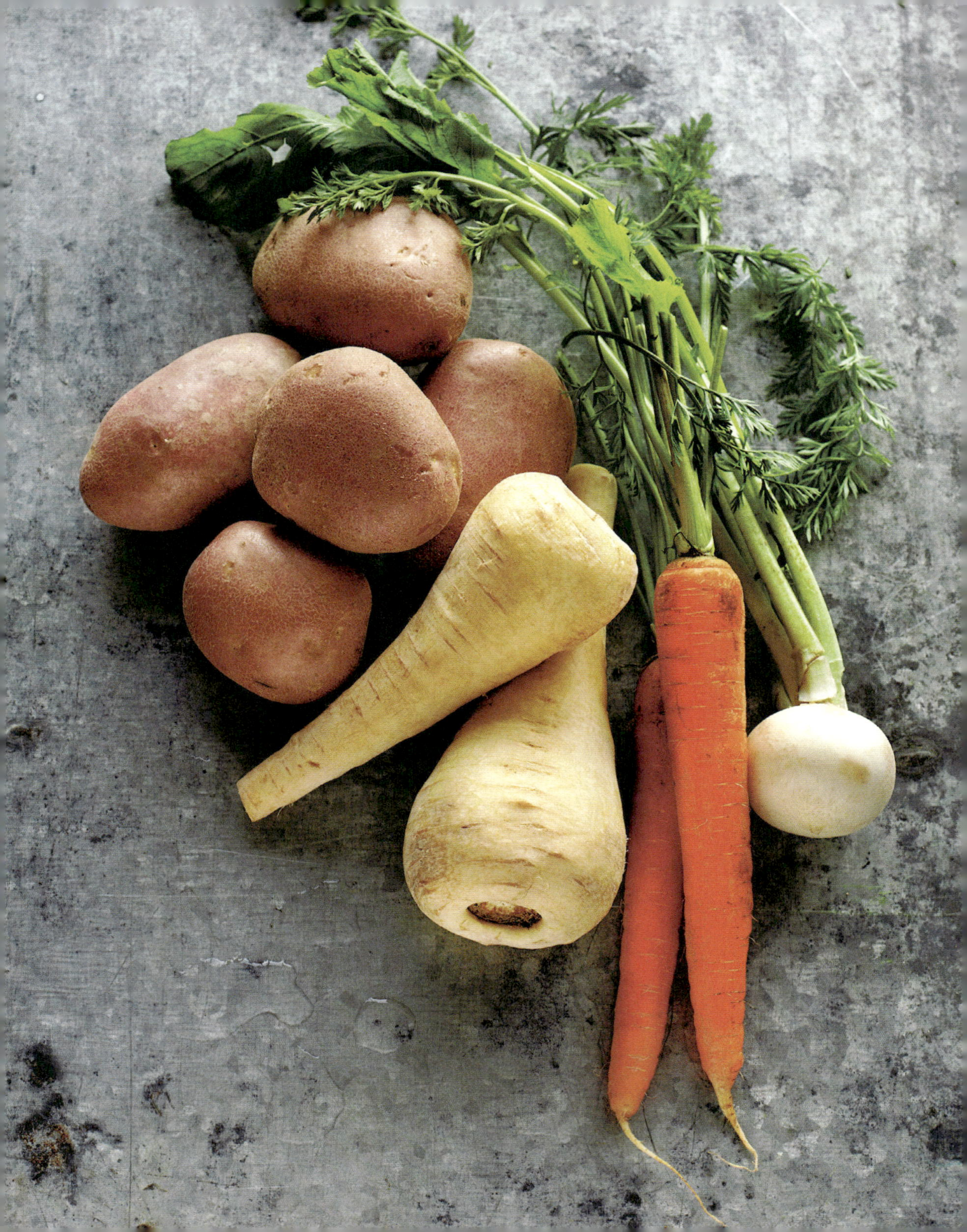

Root Vegetables

1
Pick ONE starter ball from the root system and fry the spice in a pan with a drizzle of oil.

2
Add your root veg to the pan.

3
Now travel up the trunk, adding turmeric and chilli powder. Add salt and sugar, to taste.

4
From the leaves, choose one or more of the ingredients to finish your dish. Play around and have fun – this is how you personalise your curry.

KEY

● = Mustard Seed, Dried Red Chilli and Curry Leaf
SOUTH INDIAN TRIO

● = Fenugreek Seed and Asafoetida
NUCLEAR TRIO

● = Mustard Seed, Dried Red Chilli, Cumin Seed and Asafoetida
GUJRATI QUARTET

The Root Veg Tree

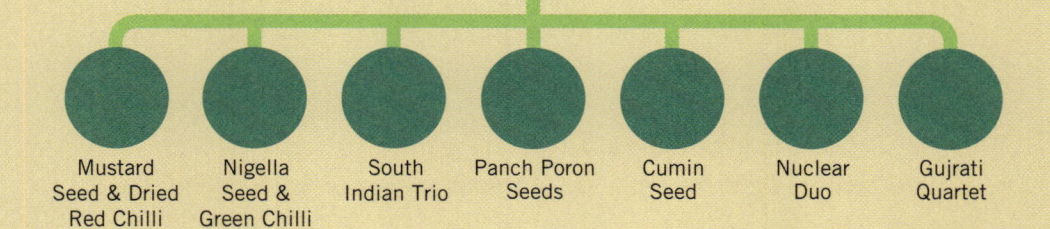

Coriander Leaf

Coriander Powder

Green Chilli

Tomato

Sugar

Salt

Turmeric

Chilli powder

English Mustard Paste

White Poppy Seed

Mustard Seed & Dried Red Chilli

Nigella Seed & Green Chilli

South Indian Trio

Panch Poron Seeds

Cumin Seed

Nuclear Duo

Gujrati Quartet

Root vegetables are treated like background noise in the Indian kitchen. They are always available, filling, generous and beloved ingredients, but we often take them for granted, chopping them up and adding them into other vegetable dishes without barely a mention.

They are such a gracious genre of ingredient. They naturally thicken the dishes in which they are cooked, while holding their flavour so well. They are almost always diced, and are often cooked with squashes to absorb excess liquids. Dense and heavy, they are often started with light, zingy, citrus cumin seeds as a headnote spice. Common finishing flavours are refreshing ginger and floral coriander powder, which also leaven the weight of these hefty veg.

To experiment with root vegetable curries, start with a cumin seed headnote spice and then add in your veg. This is when you need to cook on a low heat – partially covered – and introduce turmeric and chilli. The finishing flavours come once the vegetables are soft. Root veg work best with tomato and with mustard paste. The sharpness of lemon works with mooli, but not so well with potatoes and yams.

POTATOES
More tuber than root, these grow all year round in India. Goodness, this small sentence embodies a love sonnet between Indians and the humble spud. This small fact keeps the wolf from the door through the months of paucity and makes the potato a giant amongst all our most beloved ingredients. It is not an oblique side veg; it is central to the curries that feature it.

Potatoes in India are often red and the Indian diaspora tend to favour red Desiree potatoes. My mother will cook with nothing else.

We don't want our potatoes too waxy or they won't absorb the spiced oils with which we cook. Too floury, and they don't keep their structure in the cooking pot. We look for a balance. When cooking potato curry, we want some of them to break a little and some to keep general form. If your potatoes start to fragment during the cook, please embrace the mess. My mother makes a new potato curry with her crop called *aloo dom*. She starts by frying a cumin and bay leaf headnote spice, and adds tomato, coriander powder, water and fresh ginger for a long, loose poach. It is one of her favourite curries. I don't like it at all, and this is a constant bone of contention between us. We understand most things about each other, but this love and loathe of *aloo dom* makes us feel like strangers. I can't bring myself to write a formal recipe of it, but here it is in the subtext: fry cumin and bay leaf, add your new potatoes, ground turmeric, chilli powder, tomato, water, salt, sugar, coriander powder and freshly grated ginger and simmer away. Fresh coriander is stirred in as a finishing garnish. Then enjoy. Or not.

CARROTS

In India these are usually red and sweet. They are not the moist orange giants of the West, but are much drier and, hence, they hold their shape better when cooked with other vegetables. They often take a lead role in mixed vegetable dishes, adding sweetness, and going in with the cauliflower and potatoes, which cook at the same pace.

Because they are so sweet, gruff cumin seeds work so well as a headnote spice, but do also play with panch poron. It is so variously fragrant that every time I cook carrots with it, it seems to draw out different flavours from the vegetable.

Indian carrots also take pickling spices well as they carry much more crunch than their orange cousins. The dish in which they feature in isolation is a sweet dish called *gajar halwa*, which is grated carrots boiled up with sweet cardamom milk.

YAMS

The ugly cave trolls of the root vegetable genus. But they are little pet trolls from whom little is expected by way of flavour, but much by way of pot filler. They are very popular in south Indian cuisine and, remember, this means headnotes of mustard seed and curry leaf combined with asafoetida as a headnote. They are a pretty bland veg, and so they are generally cooked in the same way as meat and heavy pulses.

They are also starchy, carb-rich entities, lauded for their phosphorous, calcium and vitamin C content and hence are shoehorned into many dishes. They require the onion, ginger and garlic precursors to wrestle flavour into their flesh, much like meat and pulses do. But because they are vegetables, they also require the perfumed nod of a strong headnote seed spice, usually cumin.

They are variously called elephant yam, purple yam, greater yam or lesser yam, but they are all approached the same way – using ground aromatic meat spicings like garam masala and cumin powder.

Yams are pesky little vegetables in that they cause irritation to the skin and mucus membranes. My grandmother, in her best Joan Crawford voice, would tell my mother that this only affected children who lie. But they affect all our forked tongues so, to remove the irritants, they are frequently diced and par-boiled with salt and lemon or tamarind water. Before handling them, Indians will smear their hands with oil. The more I started to cook with yams, the more phrases like 'puffer fish' and 'why bother?' sprang to mind, but don't let me put you off.

SWEET POTATOES

Originating from America and shipped to Asia by the Chinese in the fifteenth century, these play the same role as carrots in Indian cooking

– successfully maintaining their form when cooked and providing a sweetness to dishes. They are usually white in India, approximating more to the Western pink ones, not the orange ones.

Use sweet potato as you would use its regular potato cousin. We very often add them into mixed vegetable curries, started with a panch poron headnote and a mustard paste finish. They are usually cooked with other vegetables rather than as a stand-alone curry ingredient.

BEETROOT
Cherished not only for their roots, but also their leaves and stalks. The tops are cut and cooked like chard or spinach. The roots are cooked exactly in the way that potatoes are used. This is a great accolade for a vegetable, to be as ubiquitous as our Lord's own tuber. Beetroot are often fried up with the strong meat spice, garam masala, potato and peas, then mashed and formed into patties that Indians call chops. They, in turn, are dipped in beaten egg and breadcrumbs and fried. However, the rule of thumb is you can turn the obedient beetroot into any kind of curry by applying whichever headnotes and finishing flavours work with potato.

Sweet-and-sour beetroot and carrot with panch poron

This dish is eaten as a curry but, in truth, when it is cold it can almost be served as a pickle. Fenugreek seeds in the aromatic panch poron makes a superb pickling spice. So play with this and take your pick. Warm banquet or cold buffet.

Prep Time: 20 mins
Cook Time: 35 mins
Serves: 4

Vegetable oil, 4 tbsp
1 large dried red chilli
Panch poron, 1 tsp
1 large white onion, cut in half then thinly sliced lengthways
Carrots, 350 g, peeled and cut into 3 cm pieces
Red beetroot, 350 g, peeled and cut into 3 cm pieces
Ground turmeric, ¼ tsp
Chilli powder, ⅛ tsp
Salt, 1 tsp
Sugar, 1 tsp
Juice of ½ lemon
Obligatory backup jug of water, to loosen the dish to your taste

Put the vegetable oil in a large non-stick frying pan and set over a medium-high heat. When hot, add the dried red chilli and panch poron and cook for a few seconds until the nuggets of fenugreek turn golden brown and the mustard seeds crackle and turn grey. Lower the heat to medium, add the sliced onion and fry for 8 minutes until the onion turns the colour of deep caramel.

Turn the heat down to low, add the carrots, beetroot, ground turmeric and chilli powder and toss until everything is fully mixed with the onion. Partially cover and cook gently for 25 minutes, stirring occasionally and adding a little water if necessary, until the carrots and beetroot are tender and juicy.

To finish, toss with the salt, sugar and fresh lemon juice.

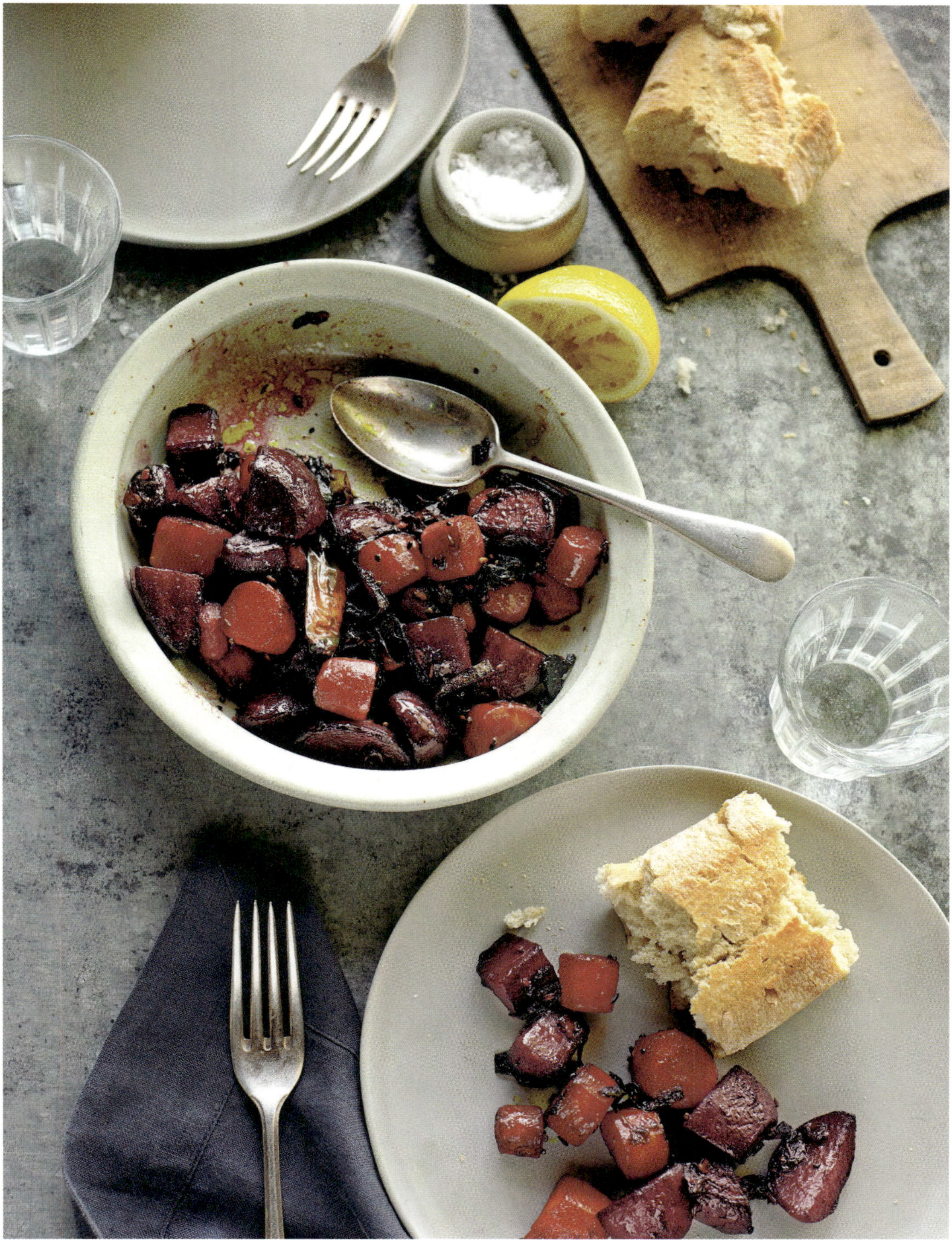

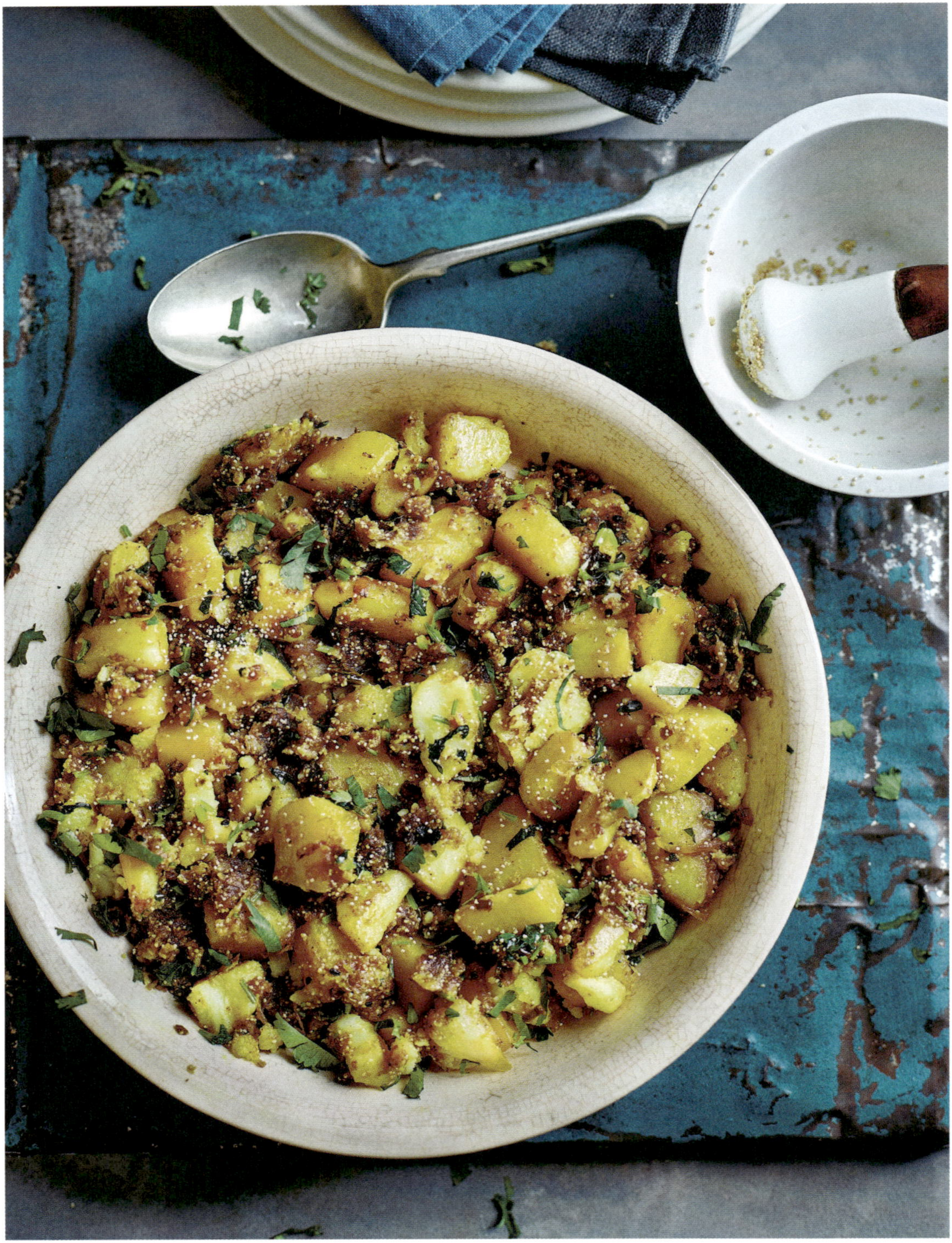

Potato with nigella, onion and poppy seed

Poppy seed, nigella seed and onion are quite a special trilogy in the Bengali kitchen. Remember too, that nigella seed goes hand in hand with the fresh waft of green chilli. Poppy seeds, when fried, have the nuttiest and most addictive quality. They are not opiates, I promise you, but their effect on soft, earthy potatoes, lifted by their heady poppy seed crunch, is the addiction of many an Indian glutton.

Prep Time: 10 mins
Cook Time: 45 mins
Serves: 4

Vegetable oil, 4½ tbsp
Nigella seeds, 1 tsp
2 large green chillies, deseeded and thinly sliced
1 small white onion, cut in half then thinly sliced
4 large Maris Piper potatoes, 800 g, peeled and cut into 2 cm cubes
Ground turmeric, ¼ tsp
Chilli powder, ⅛ tsp
Salt, 1½ tsp
White poppy seeds, 2 tbsp
1 small bunch of fresh coriander, stalks and leaves, roughly chopped

Put 3 tablespoons of the vegetable oil in a large non-stick frying pan over a medium-high heat. When hot, add the nigella seeds and fry until they start to crackle and become fragrant. Lower the heat to medium, add the green chillies and sliced onion and continue to fry for 8 minutes until the onion softens and turns golden brown.

Turn the heat down to low and add the potatoes, ground turmeric, chilli powder and 1 teaspoon of the salt and stir until mixed with the onion. Partially cover and cook gently for 25–30 minutes, stirring occasionally, until the potatoes are completely soft and cooked through. Remove the lid and continue to cook for a further 5 minutes until the potatoes have browned around the edges and crisped up a little.

Meanwhile, grind the white poppy seeds in a pestle and mortar until they turn into a paste, then in a separate medium-sized saucepan, heat the remaining 1½ tablespoons of vegetable oil over a high heat, add the white poppy seed paste and fry for 20 seconds, taking care not to burn, until it turns a light brown.

Once the potatoes are cooked through and tender, stir the browned poppy seed paste through the potatoes, then season with the remaining salt and finish with the fresh coriander just before serving.

Indian chips

No Indian would fry potatoes without first rubbing them with turmeric and salt. Turmeric, an earthy root, deepens the savoury nature of potatoes. These chips were a real childhood treat for me, only enjoyed on rare occasions. For her grandchildren, however, my mother knocks them out with gay abandon.

Prep Time: 10 mins
Cook Time: 40 mins
Serves: 4–6

5 large Maris Piper potatoes, 1 kg, peeled and sliced into chunky chips
Ground turmeric, 1 tbsp
Sea salt, 1 tbsp

Bring a large saucepan of salted water up to the boil, reduce the heat to low and then completely submerge your chips, simmering for 8–10 minutes until they start to soften around the edges but are still firm. Drain in a colander and sprinkle over the ground turmeric, giving them a good shake to make sure they are covered in the turmeric.

Heat the oil in a deep heavy-bottomed pan to 170°C on a cooking thermometer, or a piece of bread browns in 20 seconds. Using a large metal slotted spoon, carefully submerge the chips in the oil and cook for 8–10 minutes until golden and crispy. You will probably need to cook them in 2 batches. Once cooked, remove gently and place on kitchen paper to drain. Finish with a generous sprinkle of sea salt and serve.

Carrot and green chilli pickle

This is one of the most common Indian pickles. It is such a far cry from the mango or lime pickles served in a rotating carousel at the curry house. This is typical of home-style pickles in that it is light, fresh and crunchy and eaten alongside vegetable dishes and wholemeal roti breads. We don't serve pickles with meat curry; they are used, instead, to bring dry and quiet ingredients to life. Try this in your lacklustre work lunch sandwiches and you, too, will see the glory of the carrot pickle.

Prep Time: 10 mins
Cook Time: 10 mins
Serves: 4

Vegetable oil, 4 tbsp
Mustard seeds, 1 tsp
Fenugreek seeds, ½ tsp
Asafoetida, ½ tsp
3 dried red chillies
2 large green chillies, deseeded and thinly sliced
4 large carrots, peeled and cut into 1 cm batons
Salt, 1 tsp
Sugar, 1 tsp
Juice of 1 lemon

Put the vegetable oil in a large non-stick frying pan and set over a medium-high heat. When hot, add half the mustard seeds and the fenugreek seeds and fry until the mustard seeds turn grey and the fenugreek nuggets turn a deep golden brown, then add the asafoetida, dried red chillies and the green chillies.

Turn the heat down to low and add the carrots, salt, sugar and lemon juice and continue to cook for 6 minutes or until the carrots have just started to soften around the edges.

Crush the remaining mustard seeds in a pestle and mortar and add them to the carrot mix, stirring until everything is fully mixed.

Spoon the carrot pickle into a sterilised jar and seal; it will keep for a week in the fridge.

Pictured overleaf

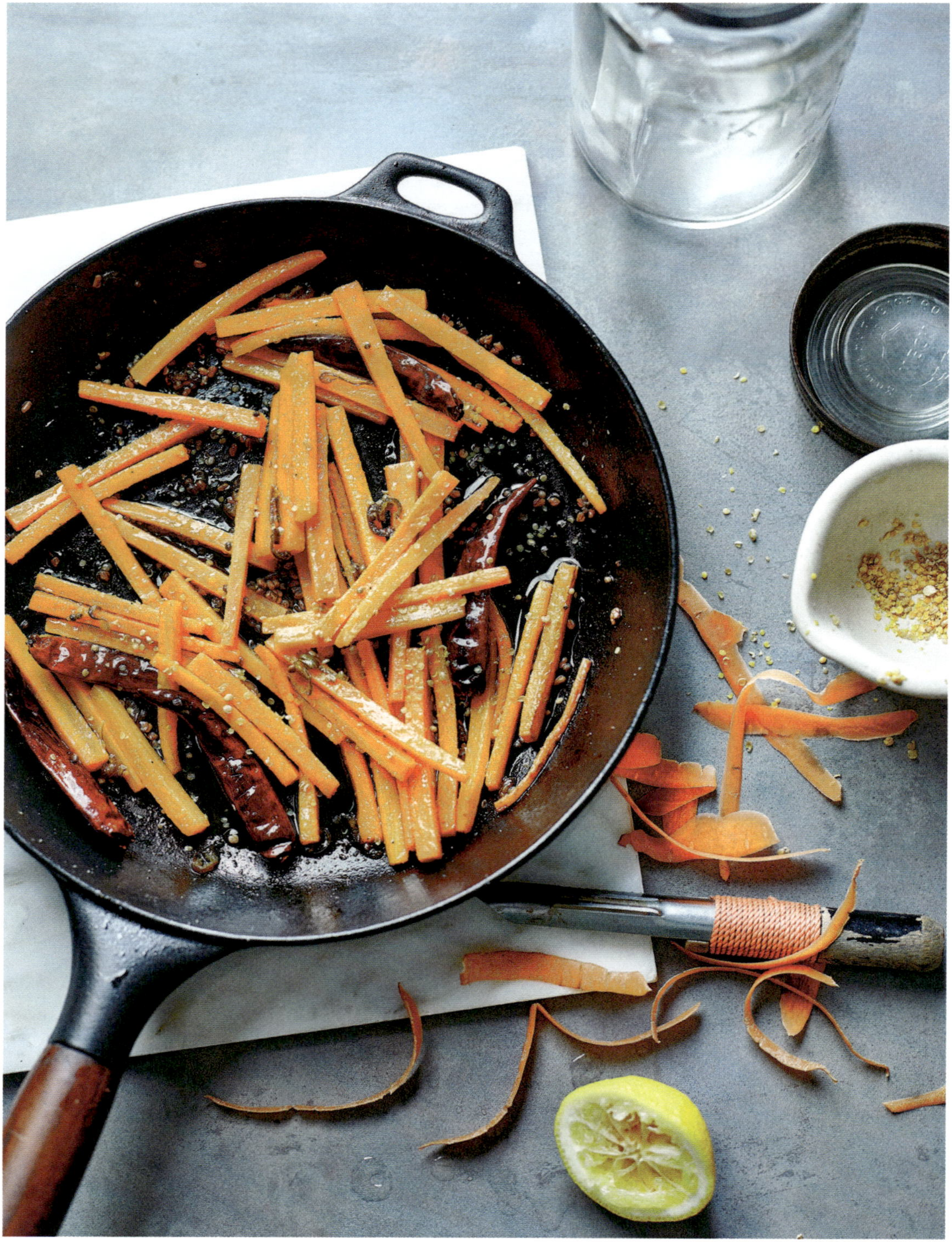

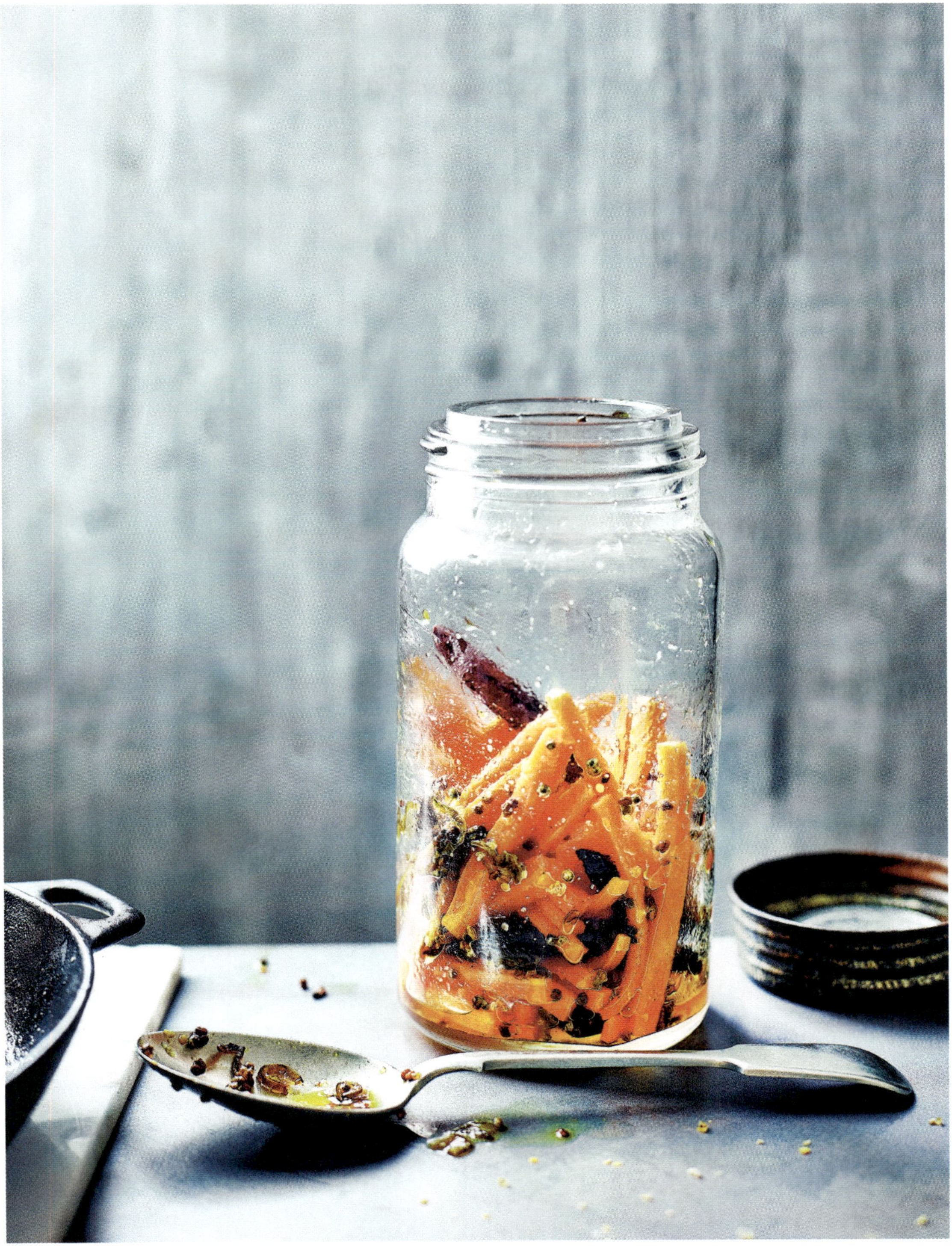

Village turnip

This is a simple dish that my uncle used to enjoy, cooked over the embers, in his Patna village. You need to get the turnips good and soft on a low heat so that they drink in the spices. If you have no amchoor, just use a squeeze of lemon.

Prep Time: 5 mins
Cook Time: 30 mins
Serves: 4

Vegetable oil, 3 tbsp
Cumin seeds, 1 tsp
1 large turnip, 500 g, peeled and cut into 5 cm chunks
Ground turmeric, ¼ tsp
Chilli powder, ⅛ tsp
Amchoor, 1 tsp
Obligatory backup jug of water, to loosen the dish to your taste

Put the vegetable oil in a large non-stick frying pan and set over a medium-high heat. When hot, add the cumin seeds and fry until they turn a dark brown and become fragrant.

Turn the heat down to low and add the turnip, ground turmeric and chilli powder and give everything a good toss together. Partially cover and cook gently for 20–25 minutes, adding a splash of water if necessary, until the turnip is tender and juicy.

Finish by tossing the cooked turnip with the amchoor.

Gujrati potato with parsnip

Although this dish opens with the simple Gujrati trio of asafoetida, cumin and mustard seed, there are myriad layers of other flavours going on. The tomato makes it a moist dish – although you don't want to create a full-on sauce as vegetable flavours can leach away like that. Just add enough for a tangy slick.

Prep Time: 15 mins
Cook Time: 45 mins
Serves: 4

Vegetable oil, 5 tbsp
Cumin seeds, 1 tsp
Mustard seeds, 1 tsp
Asafoetida, ¼ tsp
1 dried red chilli
5 cm piece of fresh ginger, 20 g, peeled and grated
Tinned chopped tomatoes, 200 g
Ground turmeric, ½ tsp
Chilli powder, ¼ tsp
3 large Maris Piper potatoes, 600 g, peeled and cut into 2 cm cubes
3 large parsnips, 350 g, peeled and cut into 5 cm batons
Salt, 1 tsp
Sugar, 1 tsp
Juice of ½ lemon
Coriander powder, 1 tbsp
1 small bunch of fresh coriander, stalks and leaves, roughly chopped

Put the vegetable oil in a large non-stick frying pan and set over a medium-high heat. When hot, add the cumin and mustard seeds and fry until the cumin seeds turn dark brown and fragrant, and the mustard seeds crackle and turn grey, then add the asafoetida and dried red chilli and fry for 10 seconds. Lower the heat to medium and add the grated ginger and chopped tomatoes. Continue to cook for 5 minutes until most of the water has evaporated and the oil starts to split out of the tomatoes.

Turn the heat down to low and add the ground turmeric, chilli powder, potatoes and parsnips and stir until everything is fully mixed. Cover and cook gently for 35 minutes, stirring occasionally, until the parsnips and potatoes are cooked through and soft.

Add the salt, sugar, lemon juice and coriander powder and finish with chopped fresh coriander just before serving.

Hot sweet potatoes with chilli and tomato

Green chilli and tomato give this dish its sweet heat. I've used spinach here, but this is a very simple staple recipe into which you can add any other or leftover cooked vegetables and make it your own.

Prep Time: 10 mins
Cook Time: 35 mins
Serves: 4

Vegetable oil, 4 tbsp
Nigella seeds, 1¼ tsp
3 green chillies, deseeded and thinly sliced
2 large sweet potatoes, 700 g, peeled and cut into 4 cm chunks
Ground turmeric, ¼ tsp
Chilli powder, ⅛ tsp
Sugar, 1 tsp
Salt, 1 tsp
Tinned chopped tomatoes, 200 g
Water, 150 ml
Spinach, 250 g, washed and drained
Juice of ½ lemon

Put the vegetable oil in a large non-stick frying pan set over a medium-high heat. When hot, add the nigella seeds and fry for around 30 seconds until they crackle, then add the green chillies, sweet potatoes, ground turmeric, chilli powder, sugar, salt and chopped tomatoes and fry for 6–8 minutes until the oil starts to split out of the tomatoes.

Turn the heat down to low, add the water and simmer gently, partially covered, for 15–20 minutes or until the sweet potatoes are soft and cooked through.

Add the spinach and give everything a good mix together. When it has wilted, finish by stirring through the fresh lemon juice.

Picnic potatoes with radish and panch poron

Typical Indian picnics will usually include a good tangy potato dish like this, as its flavour almost enhances when it cools. Other inevitable cool box culprits are soft puri breads, sliced red onion and green chillies. Try any potato curry, rolled in a roti bread, and chase it up with red onion and – if you dare – green chilli. That is how it tasted to be a 12-year-old Indian in the Chester Zoo car park, windows up lest the smell of foreign food scares the good Cheshire folk parked up in their driving gloves and Mondeos.

Prep Time: 10 mins
Cook Time: 45 mins
Serves: 4

Vegetable oil, 5 tbsp
1 large dried red chilli
Panch poron, 1 tsp
2 small white onions, cut in half then thinly sliced lengthways
2 large Maris Piper potatoes, 400 g, peeled and cut into 2 cm cubes
Ground turmeric, ¼ tsp
Chilli powder, ⅛ tsp
Red radishes, 200 g, halved or mooli, 200 g, peeled and cut into 3 cm cubes
Tinned chopped tomatoes, 200 g
Salt, 1 tsp
Sugar, 1 tsp
English mustard paste, 1 tbsp, loosened with a little water

Put the vegetable oil in a large non-stick frying pan set over a medium-high heat. When hot, add the dried red chilli and panch poron and cook for 30 seconds until the nuggets of fenugreek turn a golden brown and the mustard seeds turn grey. Lower the heat to medium, add the sliced onions and fry for 8 minutes until they turn a deep golden brown.

Turn the heat down to low, add the potatoes, ground turmeric, chilli powder, radishes and chopped tomatoes and stir until everything is fully mixed with the onions. Partially cover and cook gently for 30 minutes, stirring occasionally, until the potatoes are soft and cooked through. Remove the lid and continue to cook for a further 5 minutes until the oil has started to separate out from the tomatoes.

To finish, add the salt, sugar and mustard paste and mix well.

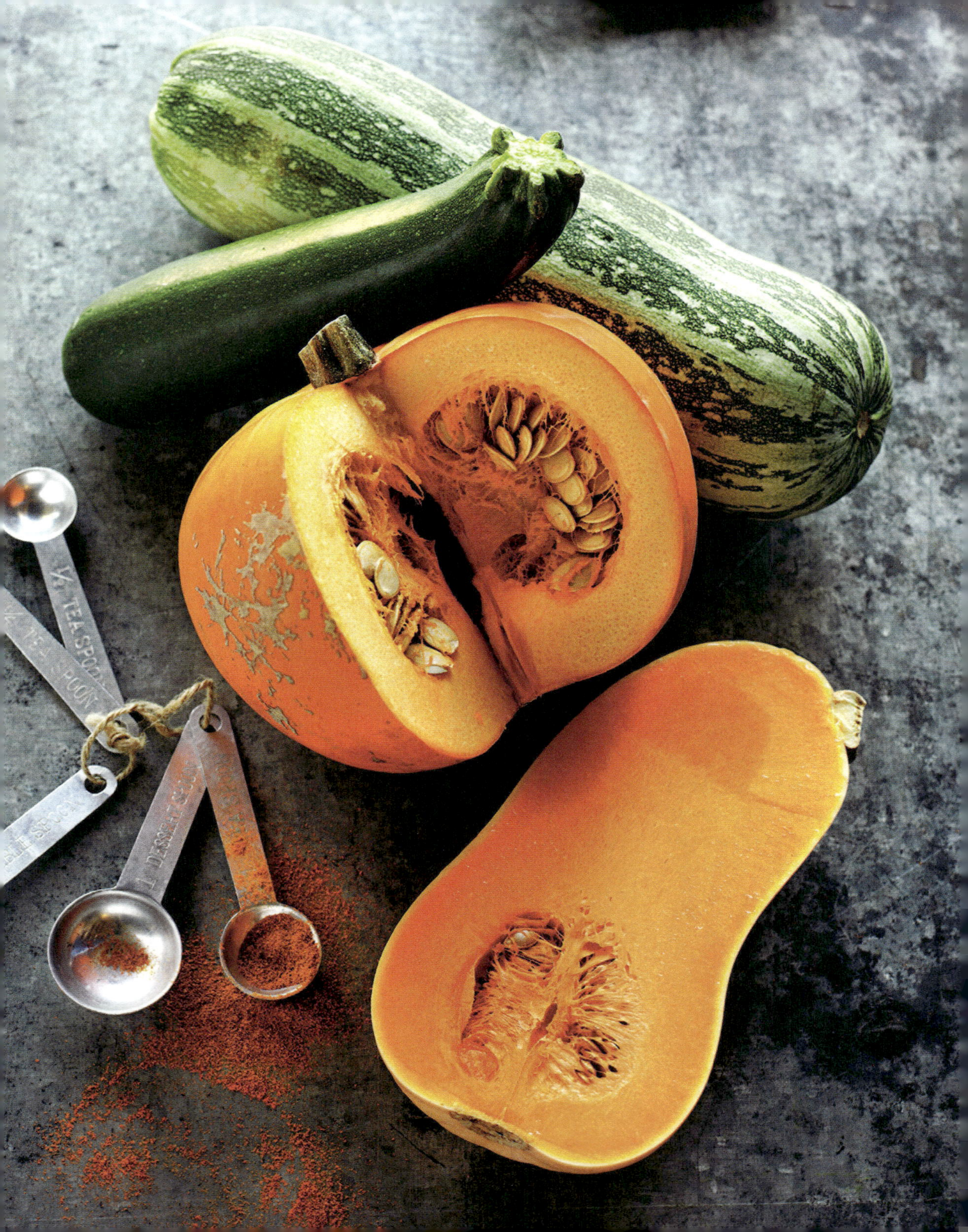
¼ TEA SPOON
1 DESSERT SPOON

Squashes

1

Pick ONE starter ball from the root system and fry the spice in a pan with a drizzle of oil.

2

Add your squash to the pan.

3

Now travel up the trunk, adding turmeric and chilli powder. Add salt and sugar, to taste.

4

From the leaves, choose one or more of the ingredients to finish your dish. Play around and have fun – this is how you personalise your curry.

KEY

● = Mustard Seed, Dried Red Chilli and Curry Leaf

SOUTH INDIAN TRIO

● = Fenugreek Seed and Asafoetida

NUCLEAR TRIO

● = Mustard Seed, Dried Red Chilli, Cumin Seed and Asafoetida

GUJRATI QUARTET

The Squash Tree

- Coriander Leaf
- Coriander Powder
- English Mustard Paste
- Lemon
- Amchoor
- Garlic
- White Poppy Seed
- Sugar
- Salt
- Turmeric
- Chilli powder

- South Indian Trio
- Nuclear Duo
- Mustard Seed & Dried Red Chilli
- Gujrati Quartet
- Panch Poron Seeds

Squashes and gourds come with the joy of summers in India. This family includes the familiar pumpkin, butternut squash, cucumber, marrow, courgette and aubergine, but it is the gourd clan that makes for the most interesting cooking.

Since much of Indian cooking is vegetarian or vegan for at least most of the week, squashes and gourds, therefore, are beloved for their firm flesh that provides a texture reminiscent of meat protein. They are substantial, and don't shrink during cooking. They are bland but absorbent, which makes them versatile in the kitchen and wonderful vehicles for clever spicings.

Any squash works brilliantly with the headnote combination of asafoetida and fenugreek seeds. They are utterly uncompromising. They will tear into the dull and flaccid, and rip flavour and sweetness from their recalcitrant fists.

PUMPKINS AND PUMPKIN-TYPE SQUASHES
By this I mean on the orange spectrum and with a sweet, compact flesh. They are available in so many shapes and sizes in Indian grocers, from the intriguing Turk's Turbans to the smaller greenish or pale red squat shelf fillers. They feel so impenetrable and labour intensive in your hand, but when their skins come off, their seeds are removed and they are cooked, this could not be further from the truth.

Pumpkins in the West feel a little removed from the genre of food and feature more often in the Halloween activity part of the brain. The poor blighters are piled high in October in supermarket lobby areas next to wheelbarrows and patio heaters. Greengrocers stack them outside as comedy cousins of the proper vegetable inside.

It does not help that the giant Atlantic pumpkins, the ultimate activity pumpkin, are also short on flavour. Those of us who do cook our Halloween excavations are often left reaching for a sweet potato or butternut squash to give them an extra boost.

The small, less beautiful pumpkins of the Asian grocers, however, are much more compact in their flesh, and much sweeter. They are not as sweet as the butternut squash, which is veg rack's golden boy, but that's no bad thing. These small pumpkins have tougher skins, but they cook quickly and don't need to be removed. Although the flesh is more compact, it, too, cooks quickly and so once the seeds have been scooped out and the squash diced, you are usually 15 minutes from dinnertime.

Pumpkins are great in dahls. They work especially well with pea-soupy asafoetida and gruff cumin, providing a sweet mouthful of respite. Pumpkin is often cooked with other vegetables in curries to add substance, rather like a potato, and we, in fact, often cook pumpkins with potatoes, as they absorb the spiced juices and thicken dishes beautifully.

COURGETTES AND MARROWS

Courgettes and their larger siblings marrows have a tendency to arrive en masse, but a glut of courgettes in the summer or early autumn is like a mudslide to a pig. We dip courgette flowers in gram flour bhaji batter and deep fry them. The flesh of the marrow is manna from heaven; we cannot get enough of it. Marrows and courgettes are often stuffed in the West; a noble end, but they are just vehicles at the end of the day. They do lose a lot of water when they cook, so my aunty Geeta's favourite trick is to dry-fry a few channa dahl lentils in a pan and throw them in during the cooking process. This absorbs the water and also gives a pleasant, nutty crunch to the finished dish.

There are a number of spice combinations that spring to mind that can transform the ignominious dull waters of these two squashes. The secret is a powerful and invasive headnote combination and then a fizzing, sharp finishing flavour.

GOURDS

These are the confusing, green, percussive, fat, glossy vegetables in damp misshapen boxes on Asian grocer floors. Alien, but obviously sophisticated in their heft and popularity, how can it be that most of us have no idea how to cook them? Please bear with me – the importance of many vegetables to the Indian's mind often comes from their perceived medicinal value.

As a child I grew up wondering why on earth any human would want to eat bitter gourds. They can be bitter in a 'stay the hell away from me I may be poisonous' way. Well, first, bitter gourds are widely thought to help with diabetes. Diabetes to Indians is like head lice to pre-schoolers – it's there or it's lurking. My parents ate gourds every night, chopped into thin rings, rubbed with salt and turmeric and fried to a dark crisp. They would then mash them into their rice and dahl, which I thought was like eating drawing pins, utterly masochistic. However, they are, in fact, an utterly addictive, albeit acquired taste and I urge you to try them not once, but three times. If you hate them after three attempts, then give up. But it is on the third push that they break through the 'red alert, ear wax on biro' area of the tongue to the 'I will pop one of those into my shopping basket' part of the brain.

They keep for ages in the fridge so go ahead, give them a go. I have included my parent's favourite recipe in this chapter so you can experience how 1970s evenings in Lancashire tasted for me (see page 128).

In the way that fishermen show their prowess by holding up large carp, Indians like to pose with their home-grown bottle gourds or *laukis*. These huge, pale green, long vine gourds grow like cucumbers. We cook the leaves and stalks as well as the fruit. Not only that, even the peelings of the fruit itself make the most divine dishes. Thickly peeled and shredded, they are cooked with a mustard seed headnote and seasoning, but no finishing flavours. The stalks and leaves are cooked with potatoes with a 5-spice headnote, mustard paste and poppy seeds to finish.

AUBERGINE

Oh, aubergine, it is with a heavy heart that I write about the aubergine for I know that my words can never do justice to where this vegetable sits in the hearts of Indians. (Actually it often sits along the arteries in the form of cholesterol because the blighters usually sail into the food chain on an ocean of oil.)

My mother and I were sitting in the kitchen but two nights ago, trying to unravel the reason we loved the vegetable so much. A popular recipe is very similar to the one for bitter gourd. Simply rub thick slices of aubergine with salt and turmeric and shallow fry. This is then mashed with rice and gives a vegan meal the 'flesh' component. There is no need to gild the aubergine with spices. As my mother and I sampled these fried aubergine slices, we detected flavours of mustard and garlic, pungent but sweet. The texture was that of a rare steak or a soft puffball fungus if you have ever been lucky enough to find one. It was all things to all mouths for us at that moment. There is also the flick of astringency to the tongue towards the end, and remember astringency is one of the six areas of the tongue that wants satisfying, but rarely gets a look in.

As an Indian child you are taught how to select good vegetables from the grocers. Each box is a beauty parade and there is no grabbing the cheapest top-of-the-box floozy and running. No. My matriarchs were very exacting when they inspected the vegetable purchases. For okra or ladies' fingers, the ends of each had to be snapped off with ease to show they were fresh and not bendy with age. With aubergines, however, you must take two in two hands and keep the lighter one. Repeat until you have chosen the lightest ones in the box. The heavy ones are full of seeds you see. Hmmm, I doubt the logic of this domestic tyranny, but I pass it on to you because just maybe the ancients were right.

There is something heady about the flavour of aubergine. It may come from what taste like mustard and garlic undertones and their interaction of the copious oils soaked up by the sponge-like aubergines. This heady intoxicating tone is paired brilliantly and appropriately with ground white poppy seeds. This gift from the opium plant works together to provide pure intrigue and intoxication in a pan. Not literally, as there is nothing opiate about the poppy seed itself, but it is a dish that leaves you wanting ever more.

The headnote spices that work with squashes in their many forms are mustard seed, fenugreek seed and asafoetida. Play around, but do try to use the fenugreek-asafoetida nuclear pairing to really send your squashes off to an optimum start.

Remember, whenever you start a dish with mustard seed, you must also add a dried red chilli, and if you want a south Indian curry, add in curry leaf to complete the south Indian trio.

Experiment with your finishing flavours, but it is with the sharp edge of lemon or amchoor that these sweet, dense vegetables tend to work best.

Courgette and potato with panch poron and amchoor

The fenugreek seeds in the panch poron work with virtuosity on the likes of courgette and potato. The water released from the courgette should be absorbed by the potato over a low heat. These kinds of squash dishes need to be quite dry, so simmer low, lid off, until the flavour intensifies and the waters evaporate.

Prep Time: 10 mins
Cook Time: 40 mins
Serves: 4

Vegetable oil, 4 tbsp
Panch poron, 1 tsp
1 large white onion, cut in half and thinly sliced
2 medium potatoes, peeled and cut into 2 cm chunks
Ground turmeric, ¼ tsp
Chilli powder, ⅛ tsp
Tinned chopped tomatoes, 200 g
1 courgette, 200 g, cut into 2 cm cubes
Salt, 1 tsp
Juice of ½ lemon
Sugar, 1 tsp
Amchoor, 2 tsp

Put the vegetable oil in a large non-stick frying pan set over a medium-high heat. When hot, add the panch poron and fry until the nigella seeds start to crackle and the fenugreek nuggets turn a dark brown. Turn the heat down to low, add the onion and fry for 6 minutes or until the onion turns the colour of caramel.

Add the cubed potatoes, ground turmeric and chilli powder and fry gently, partially covered, for 20–25 minutes or until the potatoes are soft and cooked through.

Turn the heat down to low and add the chopped tomatoes, fry until the oil starts to split out of them and then add the cubes of courgette. Give everything a good stir together and continue to cook for 5 more minutes until the courgette is tender.

Finish with the salt, lemon juice and sugar and finally stir the amchoor through just before serving.

Pumpkin and ginger curry

Pumpkins are available widely in India in every shape and size and we love them because they retain their bulk. Their sweet, copious flesh works so well with the big spices in this recipe and also with the sharp fragrance of ginger.

Prep Time: 10 mins
Cook Time: 35 mins
Serves: 4–6

Vegetable oil, 4 tbsp
Fenugreek seeds, ½ tsp
Asafoetida, ¼ tsp
1 small pumpkin, 800 g, skin left on (if soft), deseeded and cut into 5 cm chunks
Water, 250 ml
Ground turmeric, ¼ tsp
Chilli powder, ⅛ tsp
Salt, 1 tsp
Sugar, 1 tsp
Garam masala, 1 tbsp
5 cm piece of fresh ginger, 20 g, peeled and grated
Juice of ½ lemon
Obligatory backup jug of water, to loosen the dish to your taste

Put the vegetable oil in a large non-stick frying pan set over a medium-high heat. When hot, add the fenugreek seeds and, being careful not to burn, fry until they turn fragrant and dark brown, then quickly add the asafoetida and fry for a further 10 seconds until it releases its pungent aroma.

Add the chopped pumpkin, water, ground turmeric, chilli powder, salt and sugar and stir until everything is mixed, then partially cover and gently cook on a low heat for 25 minutes or until the pumpkin is tender.

When the pumpkin is cooked through, add the garam masala and grated ginger, then continue to cook for a further 5 minutes. Finish with the fresh lemon juice. Add more water if necessary to loosen to your taste.

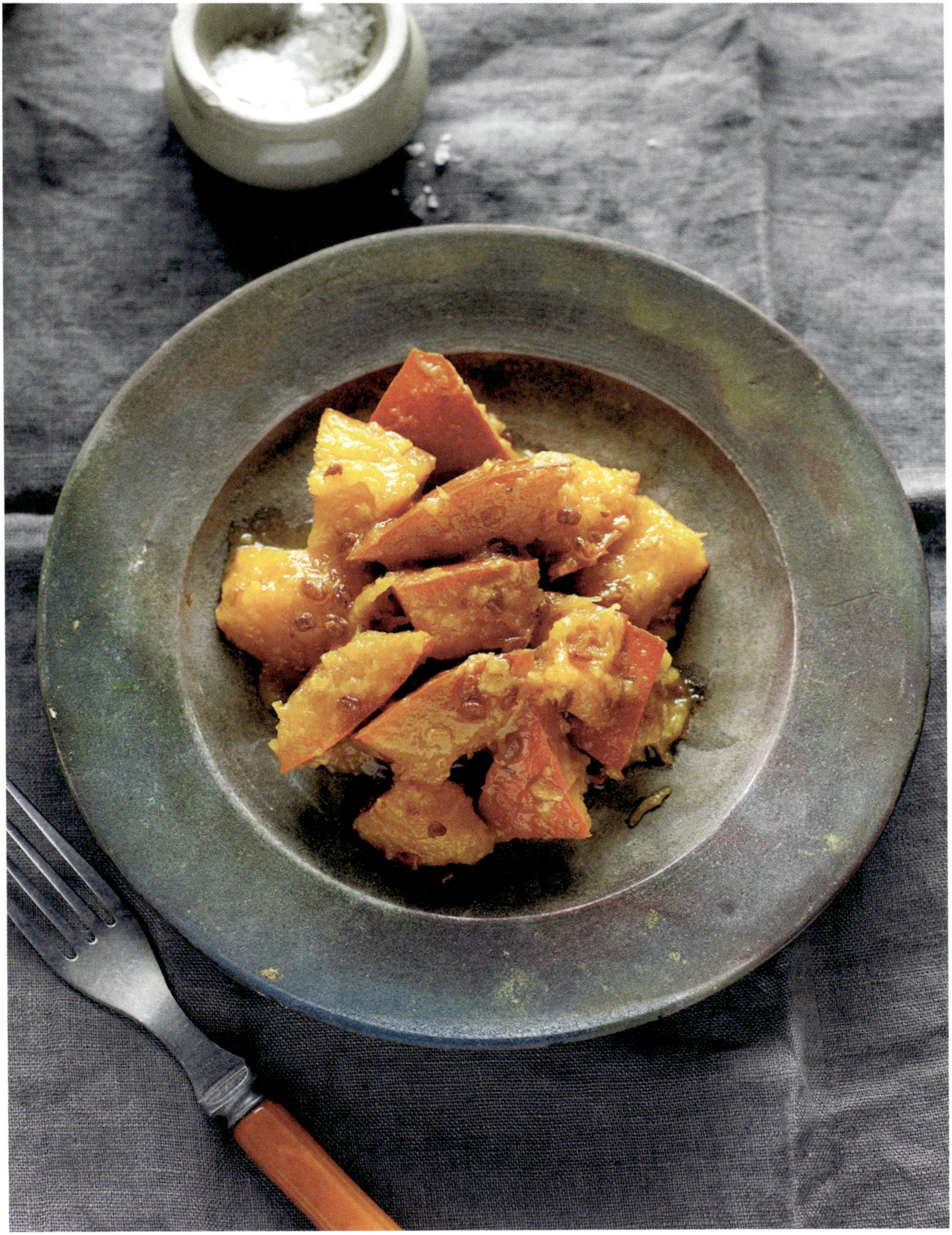

Mona's nutty marrow

It is dishes like this that turned me into a curry evangelist. Never again will a glut of marrows have a negative connotation. The nuclear duo of asafoetida and fenugreek take muted marrow and sets it alight with autumn flavour. Aunty Mona taught me the trick with this dish of adding dry-roasted channa lentils to give a wonderful nutty crunch and also to soak up some of the marrow water. It's a good tip with any vegetable dish. Give it a go – channa lentils are simply chickpea lentils. Dry roast a jar load and you have curry crunch forever at your fingertips.

Prep Time: 5 mins
Cook Time: 25 mins
Serves: 4

Vegetable oil, 4 tbsp
Dried fenugreek leaves, ½ tsp
Asafoetida, ½ tsp
1 dried red chilli
Marrow, 800 g, cut into large chunks
Ground turmeric, ¼ tsp
Chilli powder, ⅛ tsp
Salt, 1 tsp
Sugar, 1 tsp
Channa dahl, 100 g
Amchoor, 1 tsp
Obligatory backup jug of water, to loosen the dish to your taste

Put the vegetable oil in a large non-stick frying pan set over a medium-high heat. When hot, add the fenugreek leaves, asafoetida and dried red chilli, fry for 10 seconds until the asafoetida turns a deep golden brown, then quickly add the chopped marrow, ground turmeric, chilli powder, salt and sugar and toss everything together. Turn the heat down to low and gently cook for 10 minutes.

As the marrow is cooking, put a separate non-stick frying pan on a medium-high heat and dry roast the channa dahl for 8–10 minutes until it turns light brown, then pour it into the pan with the marrow and mix everything together.

Continue to cook for a further 5 minutes, adding a little water if necessary. Finish by stirring through the amchoor just before serving.

Milk lau

Keep an eye open for these large tympanic bottle gourds. They are a great greenhouse vegetable and you can make a fabulous curry from the soft stalks and leaves. They are sweet and firm and this is a quirky, but very Indian home-kitchen way of treating them.

Prep Time: 10 mins
Cook Time: 35 mins
Serves: 4

Vegetable oil, 4 tbsp
Mustard seeds, 1 tsp
1 large dried red chilli
1 large lau, 500 g, peeled, deseeded and cut into 5 cm chunks
Ground turmeric, ¼ tsp
Chilli powder, ⅛ tsp
Salt, 1 tsp
Sugar, 1 tsp
Whole milk, 200 ml
Mustard paste, 1 tbsp

Put the vegetable oil in a large non-stick frying pan and set over a medium-high heat. When hot, add the mustard seeds and fry until the nuggets turn golden. Add the dried red chilli and fry for 8 minutes.

Add the chunks of lau, the ground turmeric, chilli powder, salt and sugar, partially cover and simmer gently for 20 minutes or until the lau is tender and cooked through.

When the lau is soft, turn the heat up to high and pour in the milk and add the mustard paste. Cook vigorously for a further 5 minutes, stirring occasionally, until the sauce has reduced slightly.

Pictured overleaf

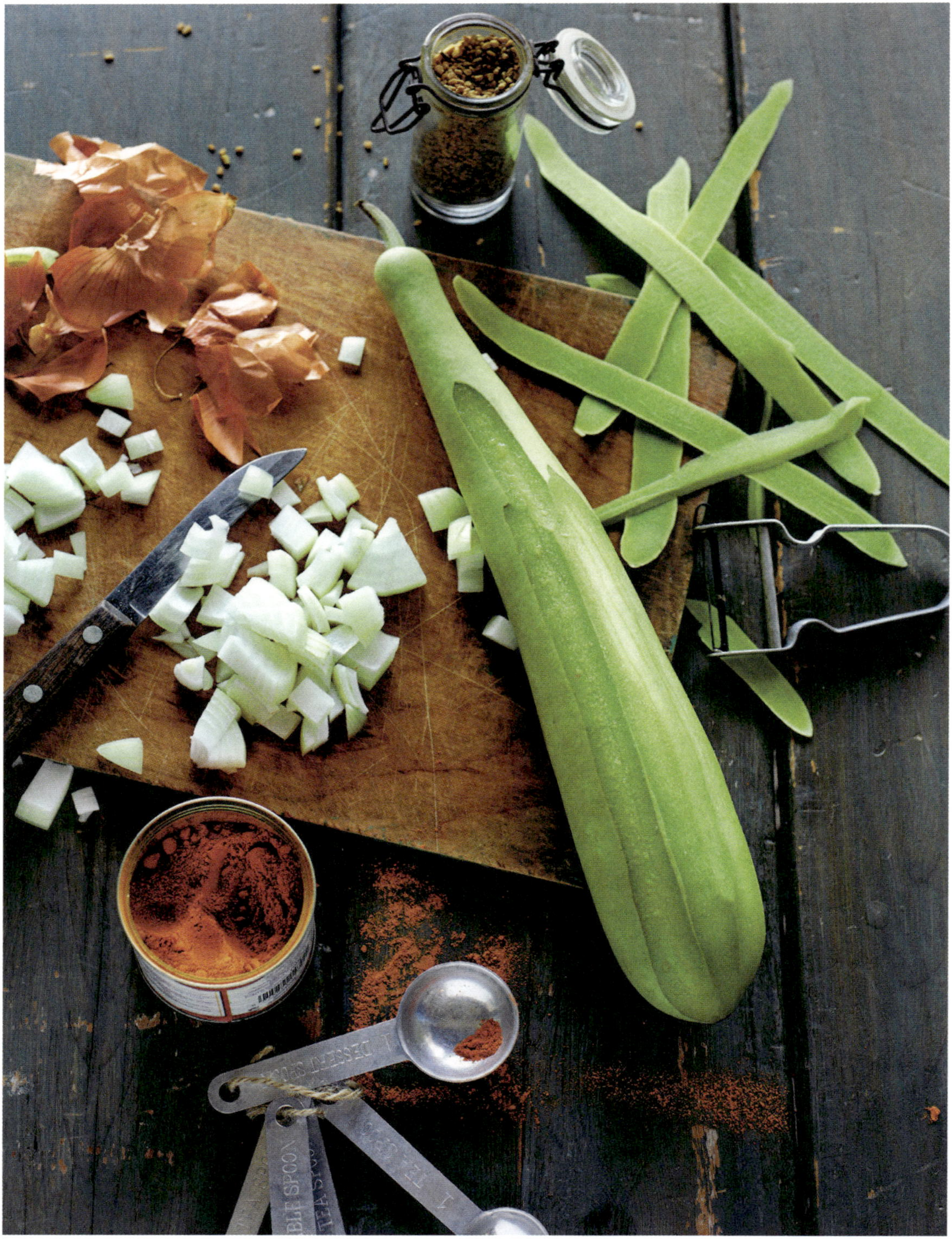

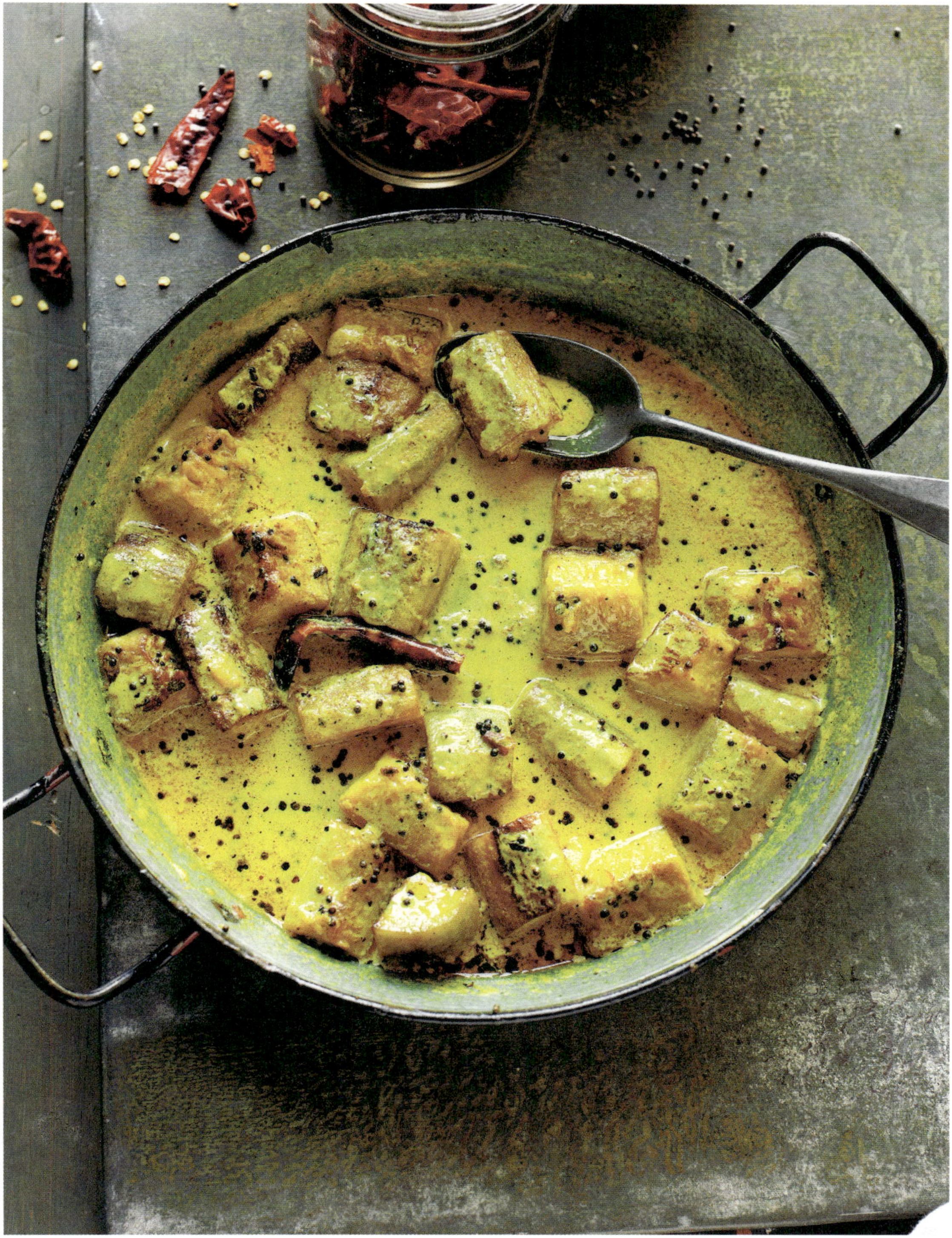

Hot bitter gourds

I felt so clever once these crocodile-shaped cucumbers stretched into my understanding. As a child, I would taste them from my father's plate; they were so blindingly bitter and to justify such a gall, he, like many Indians, would declare them to be 'good for diabetics'. It's something often levelled at inexplicable vegetables. My mother, too, loves them and her theory is that one must eat them at the start of the meal and, thereafter, everything you eat tastes sweet.

Prep Time: 10 mins
Cook Time: 25 mins
Serves: 4

Vegetable oil, 6 tbsp
1 large gourd, sliced lengthways, deseeded and sliced into 2 cm chunks
Nigella seeds, 1 tsp
1 large white onion, cut in half and thinly sliced
2 large green chillies, deseeded and thinly sliced
Ground turmeric, ¼ tsp
Chilli powder, ⅛ tsp
Salt, 1 tsp
Sugar, 1 tsp
Juice of ½ lemon

Put 3 tablespoons of the vegetable oil in a large non-stick frying pan and set over a medium-high heat. When hot, add the sliced gourd and fry for 10 minutes or until browned and soft, then set aside.

In a separate non-stick frying pan set over a medium-high heat, add the remaining 3 tablespoons of vegetable oil and when hot, add the nigella seeds and fry until they start to crackle. Add the onion and sliced green chillies and fry for 8 minutes until the onion is soft and golden brown.

Add the fried gourd into the onion pan, then add the ground turmeric, chilli powder, salt and sugar and toss, making sure the gourd is fully covered in the spices. Finish with the fresh lemon juice just before serving.

Funeral aubergine and potato

This is one of my mother's dishes, with its cacophony of easy-hit flavours. Its charm lies in the slow cooking of the quartered onions and big chunks of lobbed-in veg. These big rustic cubes of onion, potato and aubergine so affronted my father that his pet name for this dish was 'The Aubergine's Funeral'. He loved it mind. Well, with fenugreek, garlic and coriander... that's a hell of a way to go.

Prep Time: 10 mins
Cook Time: 40 mins
Serves: 4

Vegetable oil, 3 tbsp
Fenugreek seeds, 1 tsp
1 garlic clove, peeled and minced
2 small white onions, quartered
2 large potatoes, 400 g, peeled and cut into large chunks
Ground turmeric, ¼ tsp
Chilli powder, ⅛ tsp
Salt, 1 tsp
Sugar, 1 tsp
1 large aubergine, cut into 6–8 pieces
Coriander powder, 1 tsp

Put the vegetable oil in a large non-stick frying pan over a medium-high heat. When hot, add the fenugreek seeds and fry until the nuggets turn golden brown. Quickly add the garlic and fry for 10 seconds, taking care not to colour. Add the onions and fry for 8 minutes until they become soft and turn golden brown.

Add the potatoes, ground turmeric, chilli powder, salt and sugar, turn the heat down to low, stir everything together and partially cover. Cook gently for 20 minutes or until the potatoes have softened.

Add the aubergine chunks and continue to cook for a further 8 minutes, until the aubergine is tender and juicy. Finish by stirring through the coriander powder just before serving.

Aubergine with nigella and poppy seed

This is a Rolls-Royce of a dish. Poppy seed and mustard seem to dive straight into the endorphins. I implore you to please master ground white poppy seeds, as they are one of those Indian kitchen secrets that will change your world. Grind them and they will keep in a jar for weeks. Do make play of the spice formula in this recipe – try it with green beans, courgettes and potato and let the scales fall from your eyes.

Prep Time: 10 mins
Cook Time: 20 mins
Serves: 4

Vegetable oil, 3½ tbsp
Nigella seeds, 1 tsp
1 large green chilli, pierced
2 large aubergines, 800 g, sliced into quarters then 2.5 cm slices
Ground turmeric, ¼ tsp
Chilli powder, ⅛ tsp
Salt, 1 tsp
Sugar, 1 tsp
White poppy seeds, 5 tbsp, crushed in a pestle and mortar or blender
Tinned chopped tomatoes, 250 g
English mustard paste, 1 tsp, loosened with a little water

Put the vegetable oil in a large non-stick frying pan set over a medium-high heat. When hot, add the nigella seeds and fry until they start to crackle, then add the green chilli and aubergine slices and, turning the heat down to low, partially cover and cook for 15–20 minutes or until the aubergine is golden brown and tender. Toss to make sure the aubergine are evenly fried.

Stir in the ground turmeric, chilli powder, salt, sugar, white poppy seeds and the chopped tomatoes and fry for a further 8–10 minutes until the oil has started to split out of the tomatoes. Finish by stirring through the mustard paste.

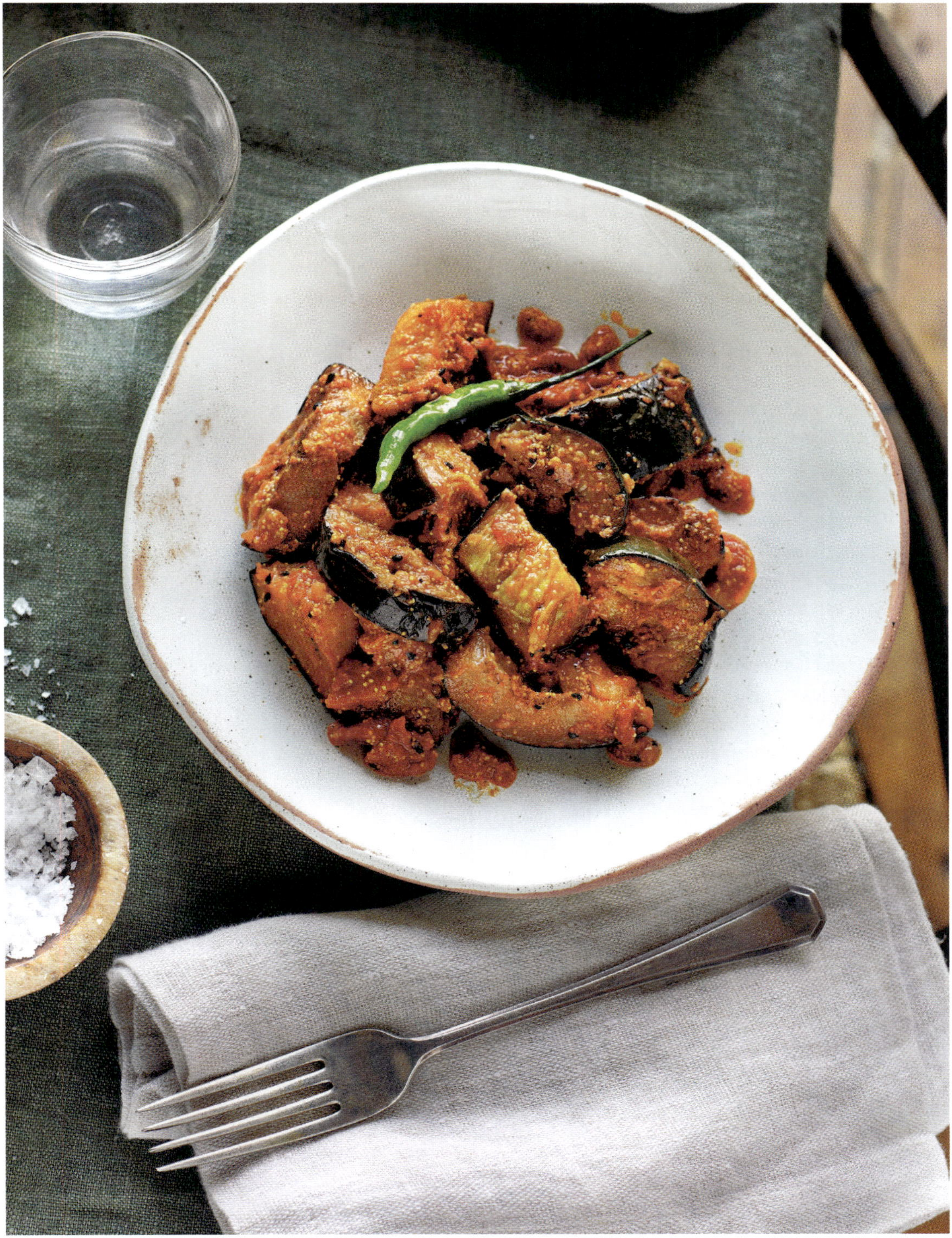

Butternut squash curry

It's strange to see garam masala used in a vegetable dish, isn't it? The punchy powder is, of course, the meat headnote spice (see page 31). However, it is sometimes used towards the end of a vegetable dish, as a finishing flavour. We tend not to do this with delicate vegetables, but butternut squash is a good solid weight bearer. In India, pumpkins are used. Sweet and red with compact flesh, pumpkins come in all shapes and sizes and are a most popular vegetable as they thicken and sweeten and create a most deliciously filling dish.

Prep Time: 10 mins
Cook Time: 50 mins
Serves: 4

Vegetable oil, 4 tbsp
Cumin seeds, 1 tsp
2 large white onions, cut in half and thinly sliced
2 green chillies, deseeded and thinly sliced
2 bay leaves
1 large butternut squash, peeled, deseeded and cut into 4 cm cubes
Ground turmeric, ½ tsp
Chilli powder, ⅛ tsp
Salt, 1¼ tsp
Water, 400 ml
Amchoor, 1 tsp
Garam masala, 1½ tsp
Obligatory backup jug of water, to loosen the dish to your taste

Put the vegetable oil in a large heavy-based pan and set over a medium-high heat. When hot, add the cumin seeds and fry until they turn dark brown, then add the onions and fry for 8 minutes until they are soft and golden.

Next add the green chillies and bay leaves and fry for 30 seconds, then add the butternut squash, ground turmeric, chilli powder and salt and stir well until everything is fully mixed.

Pour over the water, reduce the heat to low and simmer gently, partially covered, for 35–40 minutes or until the butternut squash is cooked through and tender.

Finish by stirring through the amchoor and garam masala just before serving, adding a little more water if necessary to loosen to your taste.

Courgette stalks and leaves

This dish comes from the holy of holies of the Bengali home kitchen. Courgette leaves and tender stems are as prized and loved as the fruit. There is a culture in India of chewing terse, fibrous vegetables and politely leaving the chaff on the side of the plate – there is a uniquely lush sweetness trapped in those hard-working stems and leaves. Dishes like this make for such interesting eating. Make sure you choose the softest stalks, and don't fear the owl pellet of authenticity.

Prep Time: 10 mins
Cook Time: 35 mins
Serves: 4

Vegetable oil, 5 tbsp
Mustard seeds, ¾ tsp
Fenugreek seeds, 1 tsp
1 dried red chilli
1 mooli, 200 g, peeled and cut into 3 chunks
1 medium potato, peeled and cut into 3 cm chunks
200 g tender stalks and tender leaves from 3 courgettes, stalks cut into 2–3 cm pieces (if not available, use spinach tops)
1 large aubergine, cut into 2–3 cm chunks
1 tsp ground turmeric
¼ tsp chilli powder
Salt, 1 tsp
Sugar, 1 tsp
English mustard paste, 1 heaped tbsp, loosened with a little water

Put the vegetable oil in a large, deep pan and set over a medium-high heat. When hot, add the mustard and fenugreek seeds and fry until the mustard seeds turn grey and the nuggets of fenugreek become caramel brown.

Add the dried red chilli, mooli and potato and toss everything together. Fry for 6–8 minutes or until the potato starts to colour and soften around the edges, then turn the heat down to medium and add the courgette stalks, aubergine, ground turmeric and chilli powder and fry for around 6 minutes, mixing well.

Add the salt, sugar, mustard paste and courgette leaves, turn the heat down to low and cover with a lid. Cook gently, stirring occasionally, for 15–20 minutes until the potato is cooked through and tender.

Fried courgette flowers

Courgette flowers tend to appear in one form in India and it is this. They are not stuffed, they are simply dipped and fried and we don't mind a thick batter. Often it seems the gram flour batter is the main feature and the flower, just a vehicle. This recipe is here because these flower bhajis fill trays on many an Indian street corner. I think though, that to many, the spicing of these flowers may feel like the gilding of the lily.

Prep Time: 10 mins
Cook Time: 15 mins
Serves: 4

Rice flour, 2 tbsp
Gram flour, 200 g
Coriander powder, ½ tsp
Cumin powder, ½ tsp
Chopped fresh coriander, 2 tbsp
2 garlic cloves, peeled and crushed
2 green chillies, deseeded and finely chopped
Salt, 1½ tsp
Freshly ground black pepper, 1 tsp
Ground turmeric, ½ tsp
Chilli powder, ¼ tsp
Bicarbonate of soda, ¼ tsp
Warm water, 300 ml
Sunflower oil, for deep frying
8 courgette flowers

Combine the flours, spices, fresh coriander, garlic, green chillies, salt, pepper, ground turmeric, chilli powder and bicarbonate of soda in a large mixing bowl and mix thoroughly. Add the warm water and mix together to form a smooth, loose batter.

Heat the sunflower oil to a depth of 8 cm in a large wok over a high heat. Check the temperature has reached frying heat by dropping a touch of batter into the hot oil. It should bubble and float to the surface in a few seconds, golden brown, if the oil is at the right temperature.

Gently drop the courgette flowers, two at a time, into the batter, making sure they are fully coated.

Transfer the battered courgette flowers to the hot oil and fry for 2 minutes. Turn and fry for a further 2 minutes until they are evenly golden brown. Remove from the oil and drain on kitchen paper. Repeat in batches of two.

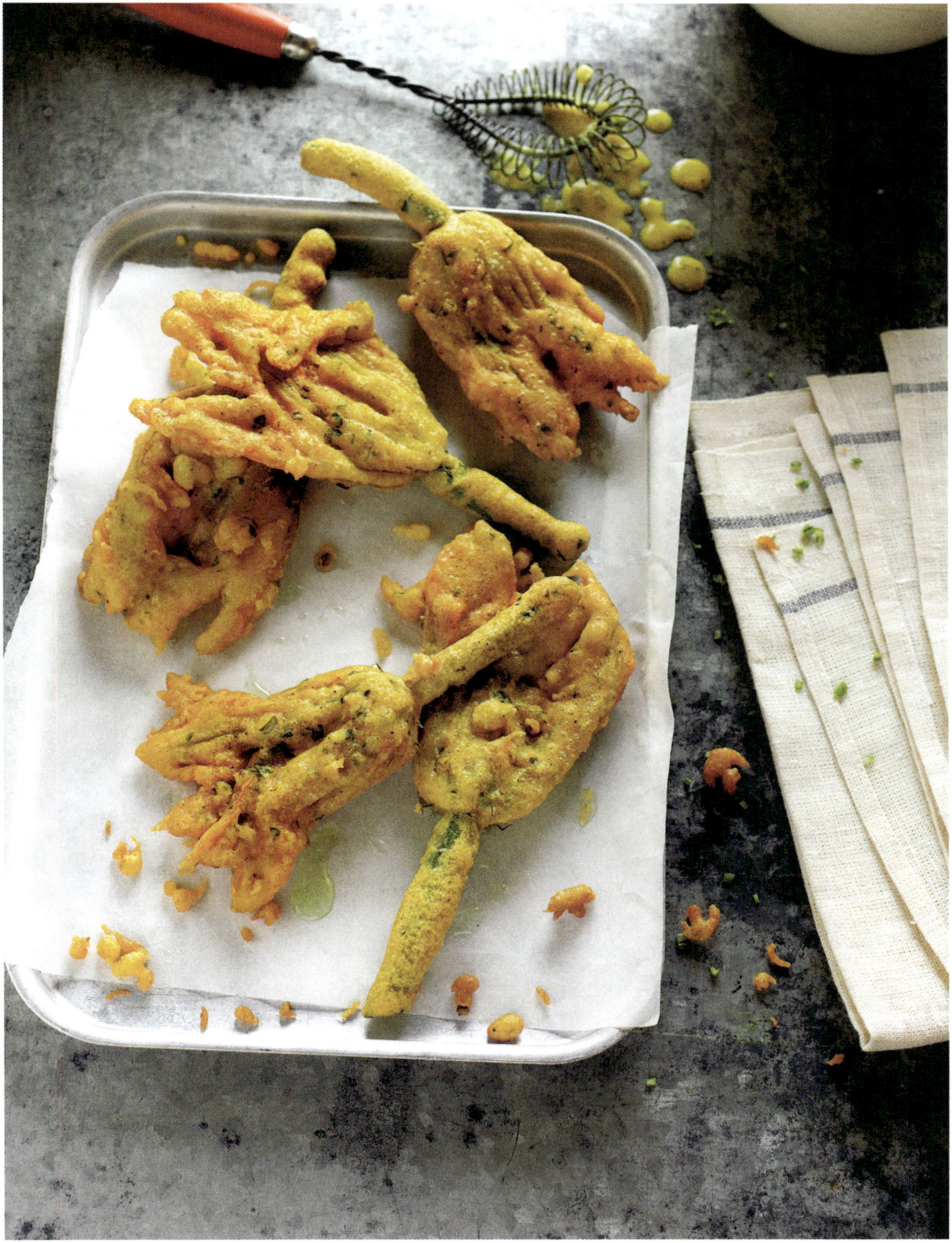

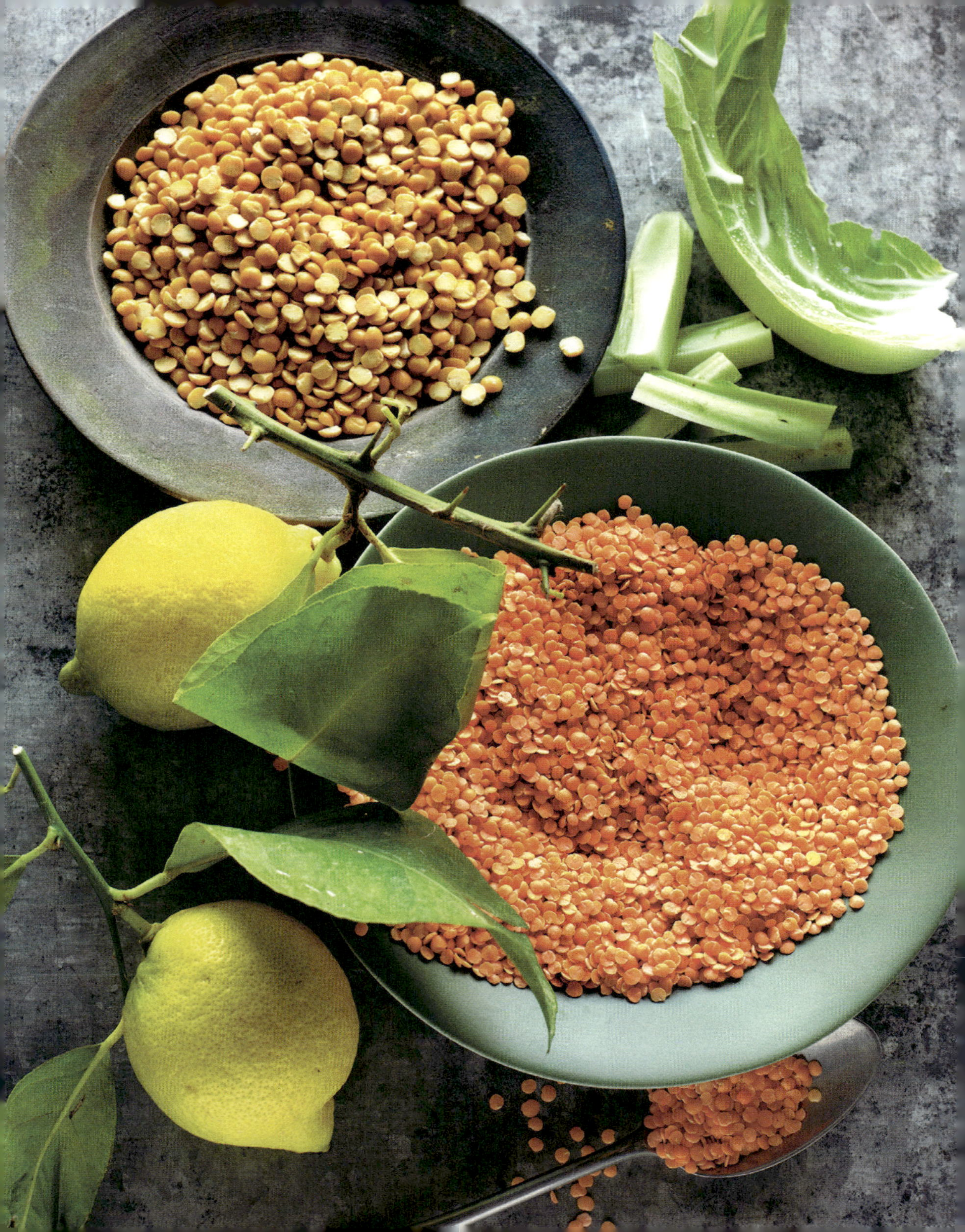

Light Lentils and Dahls

1

Pick ONE starter ball from the root system and fry the spice in a pan with a drizzle of oil.

2

Add your lentils to the pan.

3

Now travel up the trunk, adding turmeric and chilli powder. Add salt and sugar, to taste.

4

From the leaves, choose one or more of the ingredients to finish your dish. Play around and have fun – this is how you personalise your curry.

KEY

● = Mustard Seed, Dried Red Chilli and Curry Leaf

SOUTH INDIAN TRIO

● = Mustard Seed, Dried Red Chilli, Cumin Seed and Asafoetida

GUJRATI QUARTET

The Lentil and Dahl Tree

Coriander Leaf

Tomato

Lemon

Fruit & Veg

Green Chilli

Tamarind

Sugar

Salt

Turmeric

Chilli powder

South Indian Trio | Nigella Seed & Green Chilli | Mustard Seed & Dried Red Chilli | Gujrati Quartet | Cumin Seed | Panch Poron Seeds

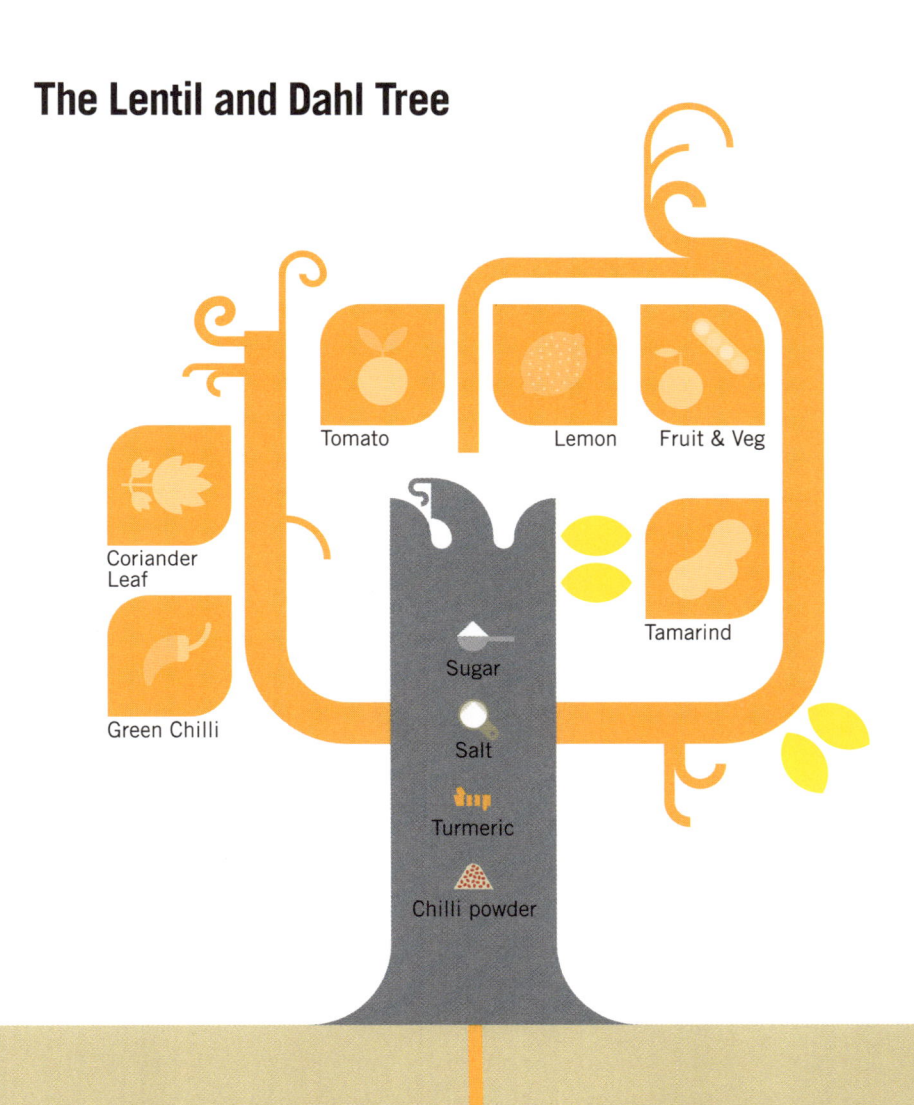

Just to be clear: lentils mean dahls. Dahls are highly savoury, soup-like dishes that Indians use to lubricate food. The truth is, most vegetable curries are quite dry. The idea of a sloppy, saucy curry is a Western one, borne from a culture that loves gravy. Indians don't have gravy; they have dahl.

The bags and bags of multi-coloured, variously textured lentils on the shelves of Asian supermarkets can be confounding. Do they all taste the same? What is the point of the skin being left on? Indeed, why would one buy skinless lentils?

I think, perhaps, the array of lentils is similar to the array of different types of potatoes to the Western consumer. Lentils are such a familiar staple to Indians that even the most subtle difference in flavour is as prominent as the difference between a baby new potato and an ancient floury one.

This chapter deals with lentils that are yellow or red in colour. Those NOT yellow or red have their skins on and require a very different cooking method. The rough rule of thumb is that the orange and yellow lentils are the de-husked ones. They are the quickest to cook and the easiest to digest. Not only does this make them ideal for the toothless and the frail – babies and the elderly alike – it also makes them great recuperation fodder. Any kind of gastric upset was treated by my grandmother with lightly spiced boiled lentils and rice. Notice the words 'lightly spiced'. The hand of an Indian cook is incapable of doing 'no spice'.

Remember the ancient Hindu view of ying and yang ingredients, *rajasic* and *satvic*? *Rajasic* ingredients – the yang – like meat, onions and garlic – are seen as heavy, hard to digest and tainting and are, therefore, 'heating' ingredients. *Satvic* foods, in contrast, are more ying, such as green veg and pulses. They are easier to digest, needing less intestinal legwork and are, therefore, cooling.

Light lentils are very much the cooling, pure, permissible ingredients. The heavier lentils, like the green, black or brown, I will cover in the next chapter, Heavy Pulses and Grains (see page 157). They have their skin on, they are harder to digest, they take longer to cook and need more by way of tenderising ingredients.

Because the red and yellow light lentils are so gentle in their flavour, they are great vehicles for other ingredients. And, of course, they are the basis of one of Indian cooking's most treasured dishes: dahl.

My mother makes a stunning dahl where she adds lightly fried batons of cauliflower stalks. Green beans, even frozen and smashed over the pan, provide a beautiful, sweet green bite. My favourite additions are chunks of semi-ripe mango and lemon juice. Basic dahl is a dish where you, as a cook, can reveal your greatest flair. The lentils provide just enough flavour to prevent you producing anything tasteless and have enough depth to buffer any wilder ingredients you may choose.

My grandmother loved to make a sour dahl. When she would visit England, the ingredients she added to achieve this were gooseberries or rhubarb. Those ingredients loved their exotic holiday home in the turmeric sunshine of dahl. So wondrous was her rhubarb dahl that I put it on my restaurant menu, and it has become a best seller.

Weeds, like nettle and fat hen, as well as beetroot tops and radish pods all make the most stupendous dahls and are ingredients that Indians often reach for when others are thin on the ground. Dahl is also a great place for health by stealth for any chlorophyll-averse children you may have.

One pan of dahl can absorb a bucketload of baby leaf spinach, which wilts down to nothing. All that Wizard of Oz goodness barely snags on their repulsion radar.

Asafoetida, or devil's dung, is a spice that works brilliantly with dahls. Boiling lentils in water will reveal their pungent, boiled-egg odour. Just as we do with brassicas (see pages 55–71), with dahl we capitalise on the depth of this pungency by using onion and asafoetida with gay abandon. In the way that stock and bacon are seen to bring out the best in lentils to the Western palate, so we in the Indian kitchen feel that asafoetida, fried lightly and added to dahl, gives the equivalent boost.

For a simpler spice pairing, let us turn once more to aunty Geeta: 'All dahls need green chilli to start and coriander leaf to finish, but if you don't have any, use lemon zest'. Wise words. And don't reach for the garlic – it will only muffle and overpower your spices.

Always bear in mind that lentils will continue to cook once left, so the next day your dahl will be much thicker, but also much more flavourful, as the spices continue to permeate and absorb into the lentils. To reheat it, simply ladle a desired amount into a pan and add enough water to loosen it to the consistency that you want. It is quite expected that you have a bowl of ageing dahl in the fridge for those munchies-at-midnight moments. But boy, what a wholesome and very righteous midnight snack it makes.

Alas, we can't discuss dahls without discussing the effect they have on the bowels. They are roughage, they are 'motivating' and they will not let your gut lining sleep. ALL good but, if they are not fully cooked through, they can continue to cook in your system and, in doing so, produce gas in the process. This can make for a little workout in the intestines and make long car journeys interesting. The secret is, if you don't want to be the embarrassing Labrador under the table, cook them until as soft as possible.

It is a shame to do this though as, very often, particularly with red and channa dahls, they are delicious with a little bite. Try them a little undercooked when you don't have visitors, and see what your body will allow of you.

In this chapter I have given you recipes for channa dahl, red dahl, yellow split peas and toor dahl, but know this: the formula works for any of the skinless 'yellow' pulses. Feel free to interchange and experiment to your heart's content. Yellow moong dahl is a great alternative to red lentils. It is seen as a very light dahl and good for your health. Red lentils and moong lentils are the go-to dahl for patients and invalids.

Channa dahl, yellow split peas and toor dahl are seen as heavier lentils and a little harder to digest, which means a little longer in the cooking. Let the pressure cooker do the work of your guts.

I have been teaching Indian cooking for many years and there are two lessons that I have tried and tried to impress: One, meat should always be cooked on the bone. Ha! Two, pressure cookers are a gift of the gods.

In India everyone has a pressure cooker. They are so beloved and so revered that they are part of the damned dowry system. I remember seeing the dowry gifts for my uncle arranged on a bed in our ancestral home: opulent bejewelled saris, bangles for the ladies, silk ties for the silverback males and a gleaming, rubber-sealed Prestige pressure cooker. I kid you not. The pressure cooker is THAT important AND the dowry monster still gnashes its ugly teeth even in the most enlightened homes.

In the West, pressure cookers are one of the bits of serious economical, energy-saving technology that we have not yet grasped with both hands. This might come from the fact that we never really have to worry about how much fuel we are using to cook with. This may also have something to do with the fact that in the West, vegetables are expected to be al dente and cooking time is not such a deal breaker. In the Indian kitchen we like our vegetables cooked with spices and to eat meat rare is to dance with the tapeworm. While leisurely cooking, for many years in the East, was a fuel-guzzling luxury few could entertain. However, light lentils only take 15 minutes in a normal pan, so don't be disheartened by all this pressure cooker talk.

Dahl is to Indians what buttered toast is to the West. No home fridge is complete without a gleaming bowl of day-old dahl. It is the comfort at the end of a 2 a.m. stagger home, it is what we feed our beloved babies, our elderly and our infirm and for most Indians, it is the very taste of a mother's love.

Gooseberry dahl

My grandmother used to love a sour dahl. In India she would achieve this with tart green mangoes, but when she came to visit us one hot autumn, she discovered the tricky prickle of the Lancashire gooseberry and combined it beautifully with the creamy luxury of yellow split peas.

Prep time: 10 mins
Cook Time: 40 mins
Serves: 4–6

Yellow split peas, 250 g
Ground turmeric, ¼ tsp
Water, 900 ml
Vegetable oil, 3 tbsp
Ghee, 1 tbsp (optional)
Cumin seeds, 1 tsp
Mustard seeds, ½ tsp
2 green chillies, pierced
Fresh gooseberries, 250 g
Chilli powder, ⅛ tsp
Sugar, 1 tsp
Salt, 2 tsp
Juice of ½ lemon
1 small bunch of fresh coriander, stalks and leaves, finely chopped
Obligatory backup jug of water, to loosen the dish to your taste

In a medium-sized saucepan, add the yellow split peas and turmeric, then cover with the water and stir together. Bring up to the boil, reduce the heat to low, cover and simmer gently for 25–30 minutes, stirring occasionally and adding more water if necessary, until the lentils are tender, then remove from the heat and set aside.

Put the vegetable oil (and ghee, if using) in a large non-stick frying pan set over a medium-high heat. When hot, add the cumin seeds, mustard seeds and green chillies and fry until the cumin seeds turn dark brown and the mustard seeds fizz, pop and and turn grey. Turn the heat down to low, then take the lentils and carefully ladle them into the pan, stirring until everything's mixed together.

Add the gooseberries, then bring up to the boil and add the chilli powder, sugar, salt and lemon juice.

Add a splash more water to loosen if necessary – the dahl should have the consistency of thick porridge. Finish by stirring through the chopped coriander just before serving.

White onion and nigella seed red dahl

This is an absolute classic home dahl. Dusty nigella seed is always accompanied by the open freshness of a single pierced green chilli in the hot oil, and the sweet thrill of the onion further cuts the earthy nigella notes. This majestic trinity – nigella, onion, green chilli – is one you need to really grasp and have fun with. Use it in a tomato base and play merry hell with your veg rack.

Prep Time: 10 mins
Cook Time: 30 mins
Serves: 4–6

Red lentils, 250 g
Tinned chopped tomatoes, 200 g
Ground turmeric, ¼ tsp
Water, 900 ml
Vegetable oil, 3 tbsp
Ghee, 1 tbsp (optional)
Nigella seeds, 1½ tsp
1 small green chilli, pierced
2 white onions, cut in half then thinly sliced
Chilli powder, ¼ tsp
Sugar, 1 tsp
Salt, 1 tsp
Juice of ½ lemon
1 small bunch of fresh coriander, stalks and leaves, finely chopped
Obligatory backup jug of water, to loosen the dish to your taste

In a medium-sized saucepan, add the red lentils, chopped tomatoes and ground turmeric, then cover with the water and stir together. Bring up to the boil, then reduce the heat to low, cover with a lid, and simmer gently for 18–20 minutes, stirring occasionally and adding more water if necessary, until the lentils are tender, then remove from the heat and set aside.

Put the vegetable oil (and ghee, if using) in a large non-stick frying pan set over a medium-high heat. When hot, add the nigella seeds and green chilli and fry for 30 seconds.

Turn the heat down to medium and add the onions and chilli powder and fry for 8 minutes until the onions are soft and golden brown. Take the lentils and carefully ladle them into the pan, stirring until everything is fully mixed. Bring up to the boil and add the sugar, salt and lemon juice, then remove from the heat.

Add a splash more water to loosen if necessary – the dahl should have the consistency of thick porridge. Finish by stirring through the chopped coriander just before serving.

Prep Time: 10 mins
Cook Time: 45 mins
Serves: 4–6

Red lentils, 250 g
Tinned chopped tomatoes, 200 g
Ground turmeric, ¼ tsp
Water, 900 ml
Vegetable oil, 3 tbsp
Ghee, 1 tbsp (optional)
Mustard seeds, 1 tsp
Cumin seeds, 1 tsp
Asafoetida, ½ tsp
Fresh curry leaves, 1 tbsp
2 small green chillies, pierced
Chilli powder, ⅛ tsp
1 large dried red chilli
Okra, 150 g, topped and tailed, cut into 1 cm slices
Red radishes, 150 g, quartered, or mooli, 150 g, peeled and cut into 2 cm cubes
Tamarind paste, 2 tsp
Sugar, 1 tsp
Salt, 2 tsp
Juice of ½ lemon
1 small bunch of fresh coriander, stalks and leaves, finely chopped
Obligatory backup jug of water, to loosen the dish to your taste

Tamarind, okra and radish red dahl

Tamarind concentrate or pulp makes your basic dahl round, fruity and sour. Into that you can add any vegetables you think are robust enough to peek their head above the clamour of flavour. Radish, to me, is all about pungency and bite. Both strong words. This dahl is full of strong flavours.

In a medium-sized saucepan, add the lentils, chopped tomatoes and ground turmeric, then cover with the water and stir together. Bring up to the boil, then reduce the heat to low, cover with a lid and simmer gently for 25–30 minutes, stirring occasionally and adding more water if necessary, until the lentils are tender, then remove from the heat and set aside.

Put the vegetable oil (and ghee, if using) in a large non-stick frying pan set over a medium-high heat. When hot, add the mustard and cumin seeds and cook for around 30 seconds until the cumin seeds turn dark brown and the mustard seeds fizz, pop and turn grey. Turn the heat down to medium and add the asafoetida, curry leaves, green chillies, chilli powder and the dried red chilli and continue to fry for a further 30 seconds.

Add the okra and radishes into the pan with the spices and fry for 6 minutes or until the okra is crispy and the radishes are tender.

Take the lentils and carefully ladle them into the pan, stirring until everything is fully mixed. Bring up to the boil and add the tamarind paste, sugar, salt and lemon juice, then remove from the heat.

Add a splash more water to loosen if necessary – the dahl should have the consistency of thick porridge. Finish by stirring through the chopped coriander just before serving.

Cauliflower stalk yellow split dahl

This dahl is like the A-level of dahl in its challenge to the Western mind and tongue. It is borne from husbandry, using every part of the vegetable: the stalks of brassicas are as precious to us as the florets. Remember how pungency is something that is celebrated and harnessed in Indian food? It is that secret sixth area of your tongue that is often overlooked and pussyfooted around. Not in this dish. Be brave, and please, please try it – it's so simple and is, honestly, one of the most comforting things you can eat. A pal of mine loves it cold, spread on hot buttered toast. The dahl that just keeps giving.

Prep Time: 10 mins
Cook Time: 50 mins
Serves: 4–6

Yellow split lentils, 250 g
Ground turmeric, ¼ tsp
Water, 900 ml
Vegetable oil, 3 tbsp
Ghee, 1 tbsp (optional)
Cumin seeds, 1 tsp
1 small green chilli, pierced
Chilli powder, ¼ tsp
Asafoetida, ½ tsp
Cauliflower stalks (select only the tender stalks), 200 g, cut into 5 cm batons
Sugar, 1 tsp
Salt, 2 tsp
Juice of ½ lemon
1 small bunch of fresh coriander, stalks and leaves, finely chopped
Obligatory backup jug of water, to loosen the dish to your taste

In a medium-sized saucepan, add the lentils and ground turmeric, then cover with the water and stir together. Bring up to the boil, then reduce the heat to low, cover and simmer gently for 35 minutes, stirring occasionally and adding more water if necessary, until the lentils are tender. Remove from the heat and set aside.

Put the vegetable oil (and ghee, if using) in a large non-stick frying pan set over a medium-high heat. When hot, add the cumin seeds and fry until they turn dark brown and become fragrant. Turn the heat down to medium and add the green chilli, chilli powder and asafoetida and fry for a further 30 seconds.

Add the cauliflower stalks and cook for 8 minutes until they are tender and nutty brown, then take the lentils and carefully ladle them into the pan, stirring until everything is fully mixed. Bring up to the boil and add the sugar, salt and lemon juice, then remove from the heat.

Add a splash more water to loosen if necessary – the dahl should have the consistency of thick porridge. Finish by stirring through the chopped coriander just before serving.

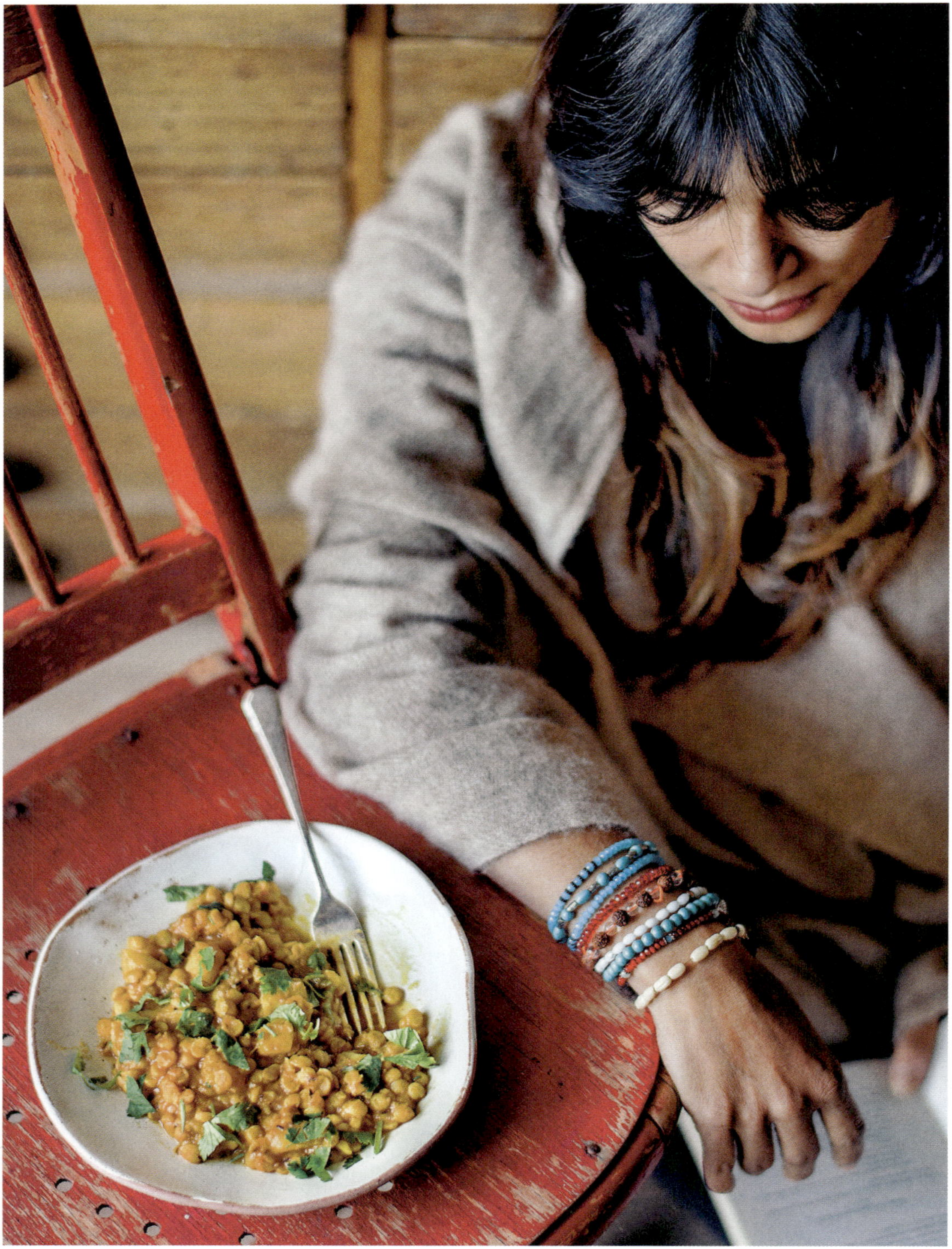

Green chilli and mango channa dahl

This sweet-sour and incredibly refreshing dahl works best with the flesh of big, happy South American mangoes that are available everywhere. Do not use the nasty, sour little green blighters from Asian stores. They are used to give edge, not joy. And this dish is all about sweet sunshine joy.

Prep Time: 10 mins
Cook Time: 45 mins
Serves: 4–6

Channa lentils 250 g
Tinned chopped tomatoes, 200 g
Ground turmeric, ¼ tsp
Water, 1 litre
Vegetable oil, 3 tbsp
Ghee, 1 tbsp (optional)
Cumin seeds, 1 tsp
4 medium green chillies, deseeded and chopped into 5 mm slices
Chilli powder, ¼ tsp
1 large unripe green mango, 300 g, peeled and cut into 1 cm chunks
Sugar, 1 tsp
Salt, 2 tsp
Juice of ½ lemon
1 small bunch of fresh coriander, stalks and leaves, finely chopped
Obligatory backup jug of water, to loosen the dish to your taste

In a medium-sized saucepan, add the lentils, chopped tomatoes and ground turmeric, then cover with the water and stir together. Bring up to the boil, then reduce the heat to low, cover and simmer gently for 30 minutes, stirring occasionally and adding more water if necessary, until the lentils are tender, then remove from the heat and set aside.

Put the vegetable oil (and ghee, if using) in a large non-stick frying pan set over a medium-high heat. When hot, add the cumin seeds and fry for 30 seconds until they turn dark brown and fragrant. Turn the heat down to medium and add the green chillies, chilli powder and the chunks of mango. Continue to fry for 3 minutes until the mango just starts to soften around the edges.

Take the lentils and carefully ladle them into the pan, stirring until everything is fully mixed, then bring up to the boil and add the sugar, salt and lemon juice, then remove from the heat.

Add a splash more water to loosen if necessary – the dahl should have the consistency of thick porridge. Finish by stirring through the chopped coriander just before serving.

Spinach and asafoetida yellow split dahl

When you see the combination of asafoetida and toor, you know a dahl is all about comfort. Asafoetida and cumin combined tend to give a very reassuring, almost pea and ham soup feel to dahl. And of course, where spinach works, so will kale, chard, beetroot tops or any delicate greens with which you would like to play.

Prep Time: 10 mins
Cook Time: 40 mins
Serves: 4–6

Yellow split lentils, 250 g
Ground turmeric, ¼ tsp
Water, 900 ml
Vegetable oil, 3 tbsp
Ghee, 1 tbsp (optional)
Cumin seeds, 1 tsp
2 medium green chillies, pierced
Asafoetida, ½ tsp
Chilli powder, ⅛ tsp
Spinach, 200 g, washed and drained
Sugar, 1 tsp
Salt, 2 tsp
Juice of ½ lemon
1 small bunch of fresh coriander, stalks and leaves, finely chopped
Obligatory backup jug of water, to loosen the dish to your taste

In a medium-sized saucepan, add the lentils and ground turmeric, then cover with the water and stir together. Bring up to the boil, then reduce the heat to low, cover with a lid and simmer gently for 30 minutes, stirring occasionally and adding more water if necessary, or until the lentils are tender, then remove from the heat and set aside.

Put the vegetable oil (and ghee, if using) in a large non-stick frying pan set over a medium-high heat. When hot, add the cumin seeds and green chillies and fry until the seeds turn brown and fragrant. Add the asafoetida and chilli powder and cook for a further 10 seconds. Turn the heat down to low, then take the lentils and carefully ladle them into the pan, stirring until everything's mixed together.

Add the spinach, then bring up to the boil and add the sugar, salt and lemon juice. When the spinach has wilted into the dahl, remove from the heat.

Add a splash more water to loosen if necessary – the dahl should have the consistency of thick porridge. Finish by stirring through the chopped coriander just before serving.

Green bean and cumin red dahl

I love dishes into which one can introduce a huge amount of health by a little stealth. This is such a simple dish. Red dahl cooks quicker than you can say 'good for the bowels', and this is a great resting place for your glut of garden greens. Most remarkably, this dish works brilliantly with frozen green beans, which can just be smashed over the pan, into the simmer.

Prep Time: 10 mins
Cook Time: 40 mins
Serves: 4–6

Red lentils, 250 g
Tinned chopped tomatoes, 200 g
Ground turmeric, ¼ tsp
Water, 900 ml
Vegetable oil, 3 tbsp
Ghee, 1 tbsp (optional)
Cumin seeds, 1 tsp
1 medium green chilli, pierced
Green beans, 250 g, topped and tailed, cut into 3 cm pieces
Chilli powder, ¼ tsp
Sugar, 1 tsp
Salt, 2 tsp
Juice of ½ lemon
1 small bunch of fresh coriander, stalks and leaves, finely chopped
Obligatory backup jug of water, to loosen the dish to your taste

In a medium-sized saucepan, add the lentils, chopped tomatoes and ground turmeric, then cover with the water and stir together. Bring up to the boil, then reduce the heat to low, cover and simmer gently for 25 minutes, stirring occasionally and adding more water if necessary, or until the lentils are tender, then remove from the heat and set aside.

Put the vegetable oil (and ghee, if using) in a large non-stick frying pan set over a medium-high heat. When hot, add the cumin seeds and green chilli and fry for 30 seconds until the seeds become brown and fragrant. Turn the heat down to low and add the green beans. Fry for 8 minutes until they become nutty brown and are completely soft.

Turn the heat up to medium, then take the lentils and carefully ladle them into the pan, stirring until everything is fully mixed. Bring up to the boil and add the chilli powder, sugar, salt and lemon juice, then remove from the heat.

Add a splash more water to loosen if necessary – the dahl should have the consistency of thick porridge. Finish by stirring through the chopped coriander just before serving.

Coconut and raisin channa dahl

This dahl is the benchmark of a good Bengali Hindu temple knees-up. It's absolutely vegan, of course, but by Jove, this is as hedonistic as one can get with lentils. The exotic weight of coconut is cut with the cheek of the sweet raisin. This is a dahl you can just eat with a spoon. No carbs required. It carries the very flavour of festival.

Prep Time: 10 mins
Cook Time: 40 mins
Serves: 4–6

Channa lentils 250 g
Tinned chopped tomatoes, 200 g
Ground turmeric, ¼ tsp
Water, 1 litre
Vegetable oil, 3 tbsp
Ghee, 1 tbsp (optional)
Cumin seeds, 1 tsp
1 small green chilli, pierced
Chilli powder, ⅛ tsp
1 large bay leaf
Raisins, 80 g
Coconut flakes, fresh or dried, 40 g
Sugar, 2 tsp
Salt, 1 tsp
Juice of ½ lemon
Obligatory backup jug of water, to loosen the dish to your taste

In a medium-sized saucepan, add the lentils, chopped tomatoes and ground turmeric, then cover with the water and stir together. Bring up to the boil, then reduce the heat to low, cover with a lid and simmer gently for 40 minutes, stirring occasionally and adding more water if necessary, until the lentils are tender, then remove from the heat and set aside.

Put the vegetable oil (and ghee, if using) in a large non-stick frying pan set over a medium-high heat. When hot, add the cumin seeds and fry until they turn dark brown and become fragrant. Turn the heat down to low and add the green chilli, chilli powder, bay leaves, raisins and most of the coconut flakes and continue to fry for a further 2 minutes until the raisins have started to plump and the coconut flakes turn brown.

Take the lentils and carefully ladle them into the pan, stirring until everything is fully mixed. Bring up to the boil and add the sugar, salt and lemon juice, then remove from the heat.

Add a splash more water to loosen if necessary, the dahl should have the consistency of thick porridge. Finish with the remaining coconut shavings over the top.

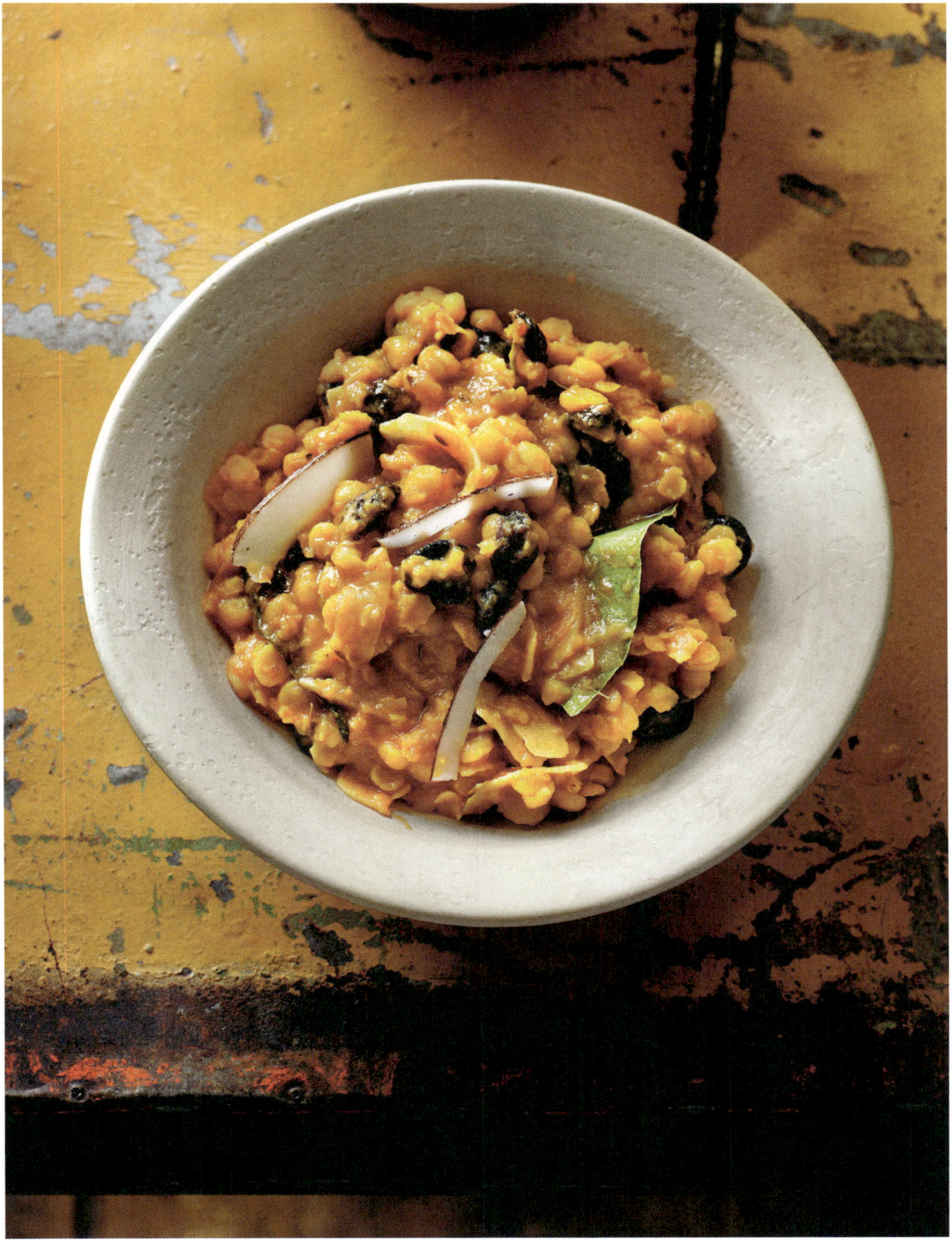

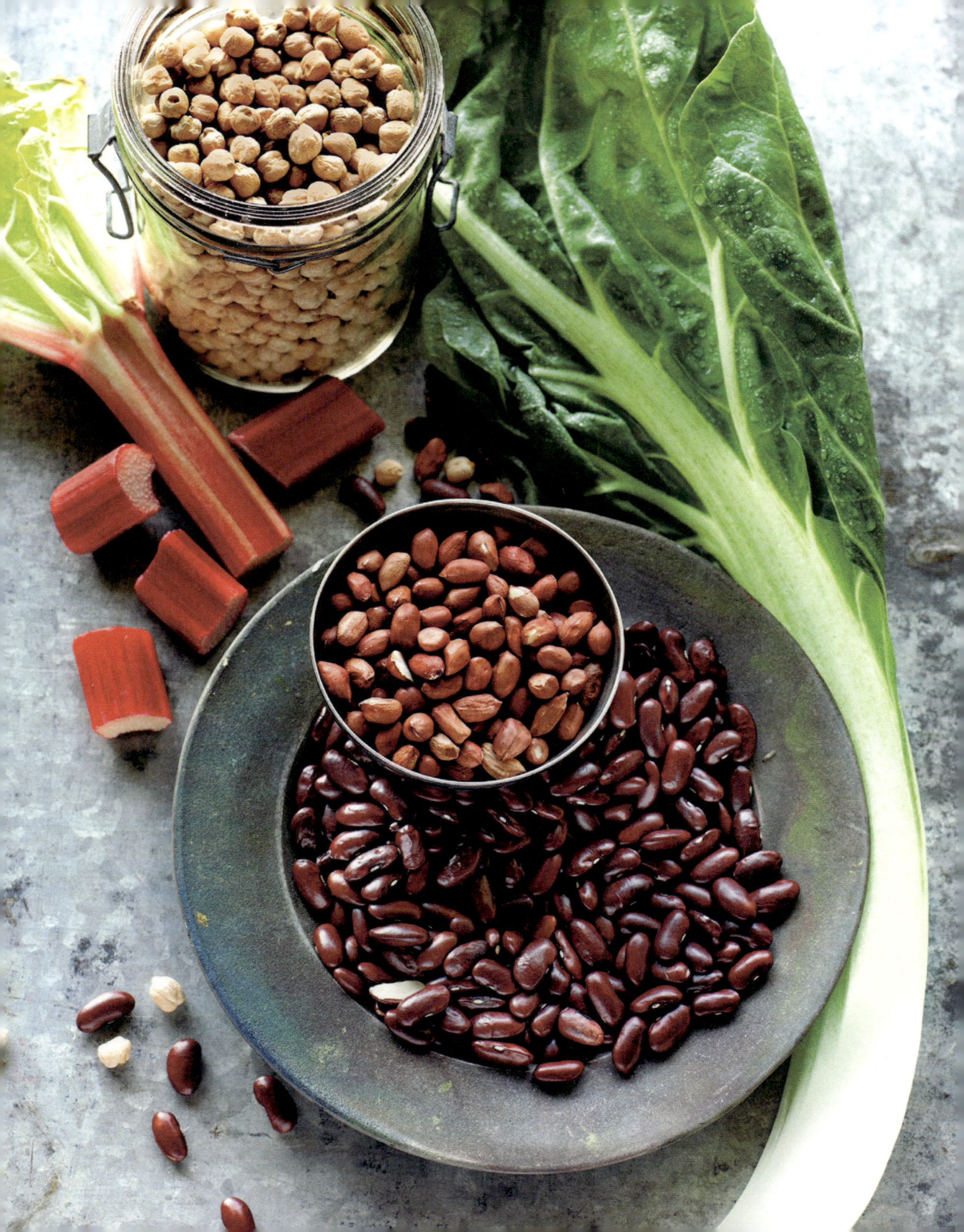

Heavy Pulses and Grains

1

Pick ONE starter ball from the root system and fry the spice in a pan with a drizzle of oil.

2

If you want a richer dish, add onion, ginger and garlic (the Meat Mantra that makes up the Meat-Veg Marriage) to the fried spices.

3

Add your pulses to the pan

4

Now travel up the trunk, adding turmeric and chilli powder. Add salt and sugar, to taste

5

From the leaves, choose one or more of the ingredients to finish your dish. Play around and have fun – this is how you personalise your curry.

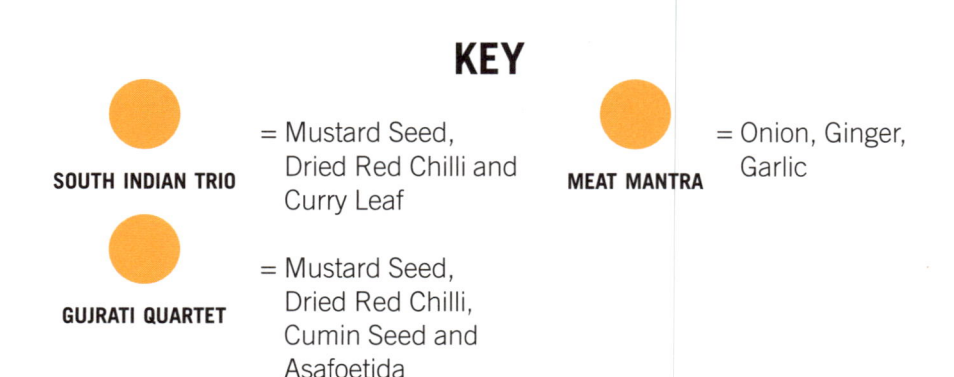

KEY

SOUTH INDIAN TRIO = Mustard Seed, Dried Red Chilli and Curry Leaf

MEAT MANTRA = Onion, Ginger, Garlic

GUJRATI QUARTET = Mustard Seed, Dried Red Chilli, Cumin Seed and Asafoetida

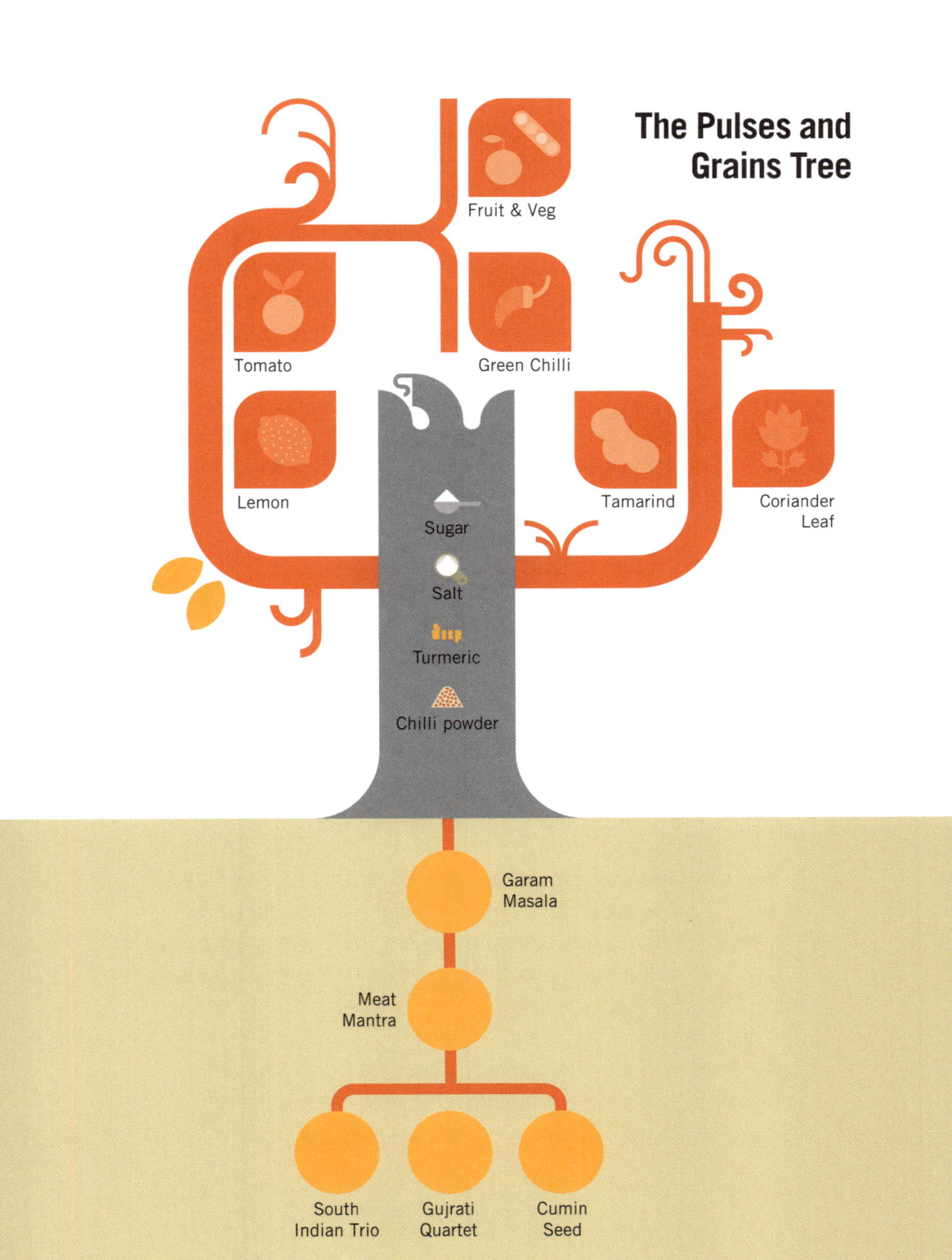

The Pulses and Grains Tree

Fruit & Veg

Tomato

Green Chilli

Lemon

Tamarind

Coriander Leaf

Sugar

Salt

Turmeric

Chilli powder

Garam Masala

Meat Mantra

South Indian Trio

Gujrati Quartet

Cumin Seed

In the previous chapter we discussed how when red and yellow lentils are unceremoniously stripped of their outer coverings, it is then that they become 'light'. 'Heavy' pulses make up the rest of this large family. Big, dry, impenetrable compact bolts, they often have their skins on. They include chickpeas, green moong lentils, white and black urad lentils, brown Puy lentils, kidney beans, butter beans, sweetcorn… if it keeps you regular, it's in this chapter.

I love how the spice tree philosophy applies so well to these heavy pulses. They sit as a hybrid between meats and vegetables but, as with all vegetable matter, a seed spice is selected and fried to start the dish. This is like the techniques used in fish cooking, another hybrid meat/non-meat ingredient.

However, because they are so meaty in their texture and structure, the heavy fragrance of the onion-ginger-garlic meat mantra (see page 31) is applied to penetrate these pulses' dense flesh. The finishing sauce is usually based on rich, tangy tomato in the way that many meat curries are finished. Powdered spices like cumin powder, coriander powder and garam masala work well with these heavy lentils and pulses, as the powders better infuse into the shells and hard flesh.

Grains in India are generally ground and used to make unleavened flat breads. We are not a nation to take grains and add them to salads or celebrate them for what they are. They need to go a long way. To grind them and bulk them with water in the form of bread made most sense historically.

The spice route for heavy pules and grains is a double whammy: Take your chosen seed headnote spice, then follow with the addition of garam masala and other ground spices added in along the way. Finishing flavours based on tomato work best because the acids help tenderise and also bring a much-needed sharpness.

CHICKPEAS

These spring first to mind above all. They tend to sit in the Western mind alongside notions of patchouli and tie-dye or else are pulverised into hummus. To Indians, though, they are a year-round lifeline. Because they can be dried, they provide a never-rotting source of filling, protein-rich nutrition during times when the land is parched and cruel. Chickpeas, if I may continue to wax lyrical, are not just 'curried' for kicks. Roasted and salted, they are to Indian village children what crisps are to kids in the West – only fat-free, protein-rich and as healthy as prescription medication.

My uncle AK was raised in a Patna village. He used to charm us with tales of how he travelled to school on his pet elephant Rani after a breakfast of boiled chickpeas with chopped onion, salt and tomato. School lunch would often be chickpea curry and rice. His home time treat would be… you guessed it… chickpeas, but this time roasted to a Monster Munch crunch. One would have thought he would have tired of chickpeas. One would think that once wealth and the middle class allowed it, he would never return to the chickpea, but, oh no, he has aunty Geeta running ragged, replenishing old coffee jars with roasted chickpeas of every flavour.

Sorry, I'm still on chickpeas. I tried to move on, but I can't without singing the praises of the panacea that is gram flour. This is flour made from ground dried chickpeas. Mixed with water, it is the batter that makes bhajis. I use it as a flour replacement in any batter: pancakes, fish batter, fried chicken coating. In India it is used to make *karhi*, which is a kind of dahl made on a natural yoghurt base (see page 175). Into it, one can simmer vegetables or indeed gram flour dumplings. It's like a sweet and sour dahl and extremely popular.

KIDNEY BEANS AND BLACK LENTILS

The staples for many Indians. Kidney beans are known as *rajma* and the black lentils become a dish called *mahdi dahl*. Both are strangely creamy when they have been cooked through. They do need a good long cook and so are perfect if you are a slow-cooker fan or able to use a pressure cooker. They are started with a cumin headnote, but with garam masala spices and onion, ginger and garlic – those classic meat combinations. They are always finished with tomato and sometimes you can add a slick of cream or natural yoghurt at the very end to give a velvet finish.

The Panjabis are especially deft with their meat seasonings, and so they cook up these both in a way that feel like the richest, most luxurious meat stews.

Black dahl has a special place in my heart. I remember cooking it for my little nephew Nayan who was convinced it was a gorgeous mincemeat creation. I showed him the jar of black shiny bullets, into which he dug his hands with confused and mesmerised respect. It was wonderful to see the humble, muscular lentil become a thing of magic in the eyes of a 10-year-old boy.

GRAINS, RICE AND MILLET

These form a very simple subsection. Rice is basmati rice. Always. And it accompanies everything. It has minor deity status. It is best boiled and served white as snow with a heady hint of musk. Rice grains can also be puffed (bought in bags like pillows of airy white puffs) and served as a cold street snack, tossed with chopped onion, tomato, mustard oil and roasted chickpeas. This is known as *bhel* and is dished into small newspaper cones outside every office and every railway station.

Rice is also rolled flat and cooked in the form of *powa*. It is first soaked to attain softness and then tossed into the formulaic spiced oil, with onions and potatoes (see recipe on page 166). Fried rice is simply rice that has been fried in spiced oil BEFORE boiling. It is a great vehicle for any added meats or vegetables – chuck what you like in during the frying stage, then boil up with the rice and chalk it up as a biryani. Indian dining customs generally dictate that rice is eaten with meat, fish and pulses, and that vegetables are eaten with flat roti breads. General rule, wet curries with rice, dry curries with breads. Easy. Er yes, but also the vegetables and breads are eaten before the rice and meat are unleashed. Gentle, untainting flavours first, then come the tongue boggling meat headnotes of onion, ginger, garlic and garam masala.

Millet is an ancient grain that always reminds me of BBC2 archaeology documentaries. As it happens, millet grains are not just found with fossilised fish bones in coffins of old. No, millet is alive and kicking in many areas of India where it is ground and its flour used to make flat breads. These flat breads are a little like the mediaeval horsebread of the West: unleavened, heavy, but gluten-free and terribly good for the gut. I include millet under the intro for grains because it is significant in the East. It is not something to which I attach a spice formula recipe, however. I leave you to add water, knead, roast on a flat pan and lubricate with rustic ale to your heart's content.

Boiled rice

Cooking rice is all about what you DON'T do. Step away from the pan and let the grain do the work. The proportion of water to rice is critical but simple: one cup of rice to two of water. Once you master that, master your nerves. When you start to wonder whether the rice is done or not, put the lid on, turn the heat off and leave it alone on the naughty step for 10 minutes. Nothing could be simpler.

Prep Time: 5 mins
Cook Time: 25 mins
Serves: 4

Basmati rice, 190 g
Water, 450 ml

Rinse the rice under cold running water until the water runs clear, then leave to drain.

Put the rice in a saucepan and add the water. Bring up to the boil, then simmer for about 10 minutes, uncovered, until almost dry and with a dimpled surface.

Cover the pan tightly, remove from the heat and leave to stand for 10 minutes.

Fluff up the grains with a fork before serving.

Prep Time: 10 mins
Cook Time: 35 mins
Serves: 4

Vegetable oil, 2 tbsp
Cumin seeds, 1½ tsp
3 cardamom pods
2 bay leaves
2 large white onions, medium diced
5 cm piece of fresh ginger, 20 g, peeled and grated
4 garlic cloves, peeled and minced
Dried fenugreek leaves, 1 tsp
Garam masala, 2 tbsp
   Plus 1 tsp more cumin powder and 1 tsp more cinnamon powder
Ground turmeric, ½ tsp
Chilli powder, ¼ tsp
Tomato purée, 3 tbsp
Tinned chopped tomatoes, 400 g
Water, 350 ml
2 x 400 g tins kidney beans, rinsed and drained
Salt, 1 tsp
Sugar, 1 tsp
Coconut milk, 200 ml
1 small bunch of fresh coriander, stalks and leaves, roughly chopped

Rajma curry

Known as *rajma*, kidney beans are incredibly popular in everyday dishes. They carry the weight of meat, but none of the moral and health implications! The dense, somewhat safe nature of the beans tames the heat in this dish, which can often be quite chilli heavy.

Put the vegetable oil in a large non-stick frying pan set over a medium-high heat. When hot, add the cumin seeds and fry until they turn dark brown and become fragrant. Quickly add the cardamom pods and bay leaves and fry for a couple more seconds, then add the onions, ginger and garlic, turn the heat down to low and fry for 6–8 minutes or until the onions become soft and dark brown.

Add the dried fenugreek leaves, garam masala, cumin powder, cinnamon powder, ground turmeric, chilli powder and tomato purée and fry for 2 minutes, then add the chopped tomatoes, water, kidney beans, salt and sugar and simmer gently for 15 minutes.

When the kidney beans are tender and cooked through, gently mash with a fork, add the coconut milk and cook uncovered for a further 5 minutes. Finish by stirring through half of the fresh coriander with the remaining half sprinkled on top.

Peanut and potato *powa*

This is a very common breakfast dish in Maharashtra. Flattened rice is known as *powa*, *pauwa* or *poha* and is such a widespread Indian ingredient – you can get it in any Indian grocer. I really wanted to give you this recipe as it opens a door onto a whole new world of carb-on-carb action. Curry leaves and mustard seeds take you immediately to the south of India. Play around with your headnote spices to travel elsewhere.

Prep Time: 10 mins
Cook Time: 20 mins
Serves: 4

Rice flakes, 150 g
Vegetable oil, 5 tbsp
Cumin seeds, 1 tsp
Mustard seeds, ½ tsp
1 dried red chilli
15 fresh curry leaves
1 large waxy potato, 200 g, cut into 1 cm chunks
Ground turmeric, 1 tsp
Salt, 1½ tsp
White sesame seeds, 4 tsp
Roasted unsalted peanuts, skin on, 100 g
Sugar, 2 tsp
Fresh coriander, stalks and leaves, 50 g, chopped
½ lemon, juiced

FOR THE MASALA SPICE PASTE
2 green chillies, deseeded
2 garlic cloves, peeled
5 cm piece of fresh ginger, 20 g, peeled
Pinch of salt

First create the masala spice paste by blitzing the ingredients in a blender or pounding in a pestle and mortar. You want a smooth paste.

Soak the rice flakes in enough warm water to cover them for 1 minute, then drain immediately.

In a large non-stick frying pan or wok, heat the vegetable oil over a medium heat. Drop in the cumin seeds and let them sizzle and turn brown. Add the mustard seeds and wait for them to fizz, pop and turn grey, then add the dried red chilli. Turn the heat to medium-low and add the curry leaves. They will begin to sizzle, but be careful not to let them turn brown. Turn the heat down to low.

Add the potato, ground turmeric and salt, increase the heat to medium and cook for 5 minutes, partially covered, stirring occasionally until the potato starts to soften.

Stir in the masala paste, sesame seeds, peanuts, sugar and half of the chopped coriander. Turn the heat down to low, cover and cook for a further 5 minutes, stirring occasionally, until the potato has cooked through.

Now add the drained rice flakes and 2 tablespoons of warm water. Stir very carefully to avoid breaking the grains too much, but make sure the ingredients have combined well. Cover and cook for 2 minutes, stirring occasionally to prevent anything sticking to the pan.

Stir in the lemon juice and continue to cook, covered, over a low heat until the rice flakes have absorbed all the liquid. The final dish should have a dry, loose finish. Serve sprinkled with the remaining coriander.

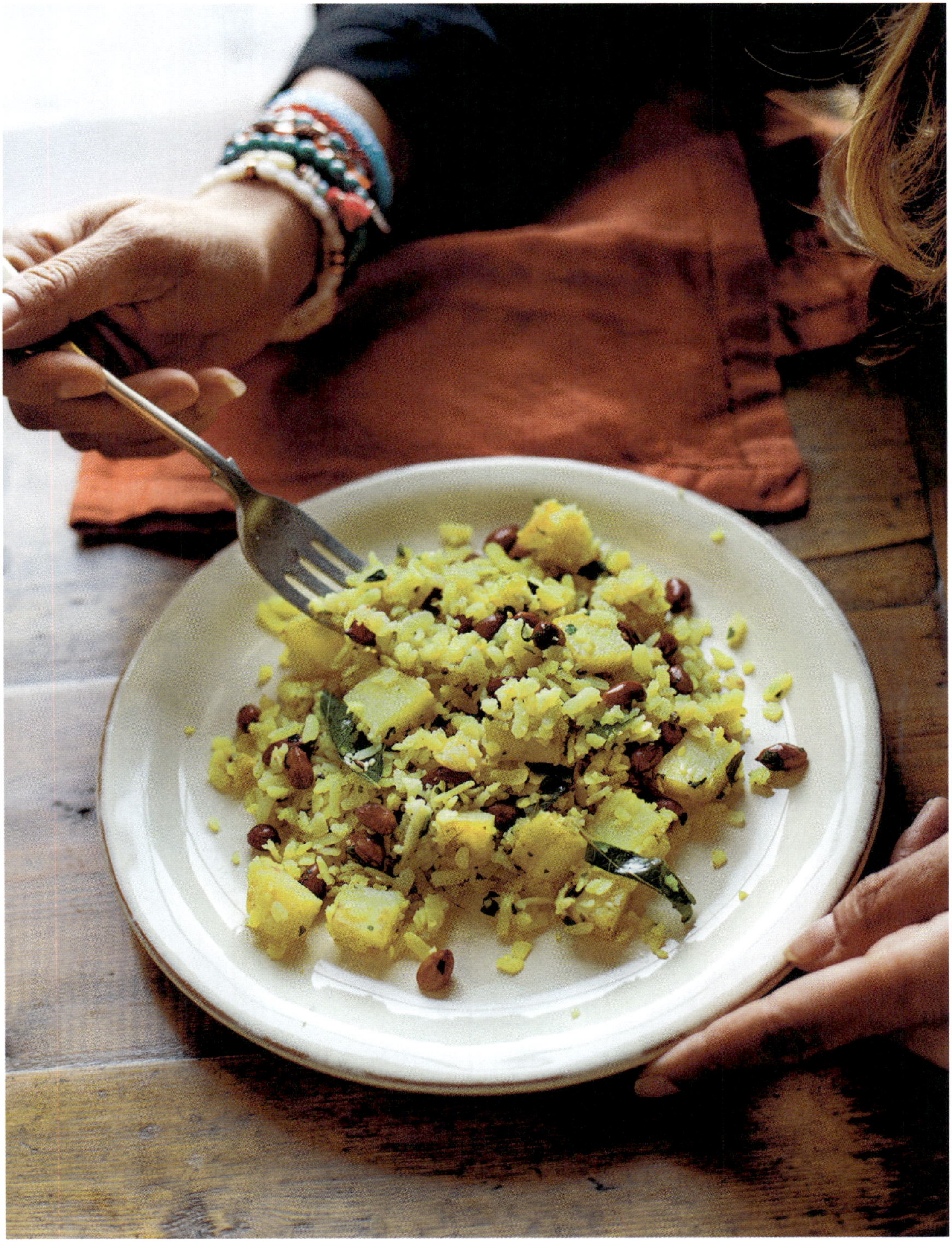

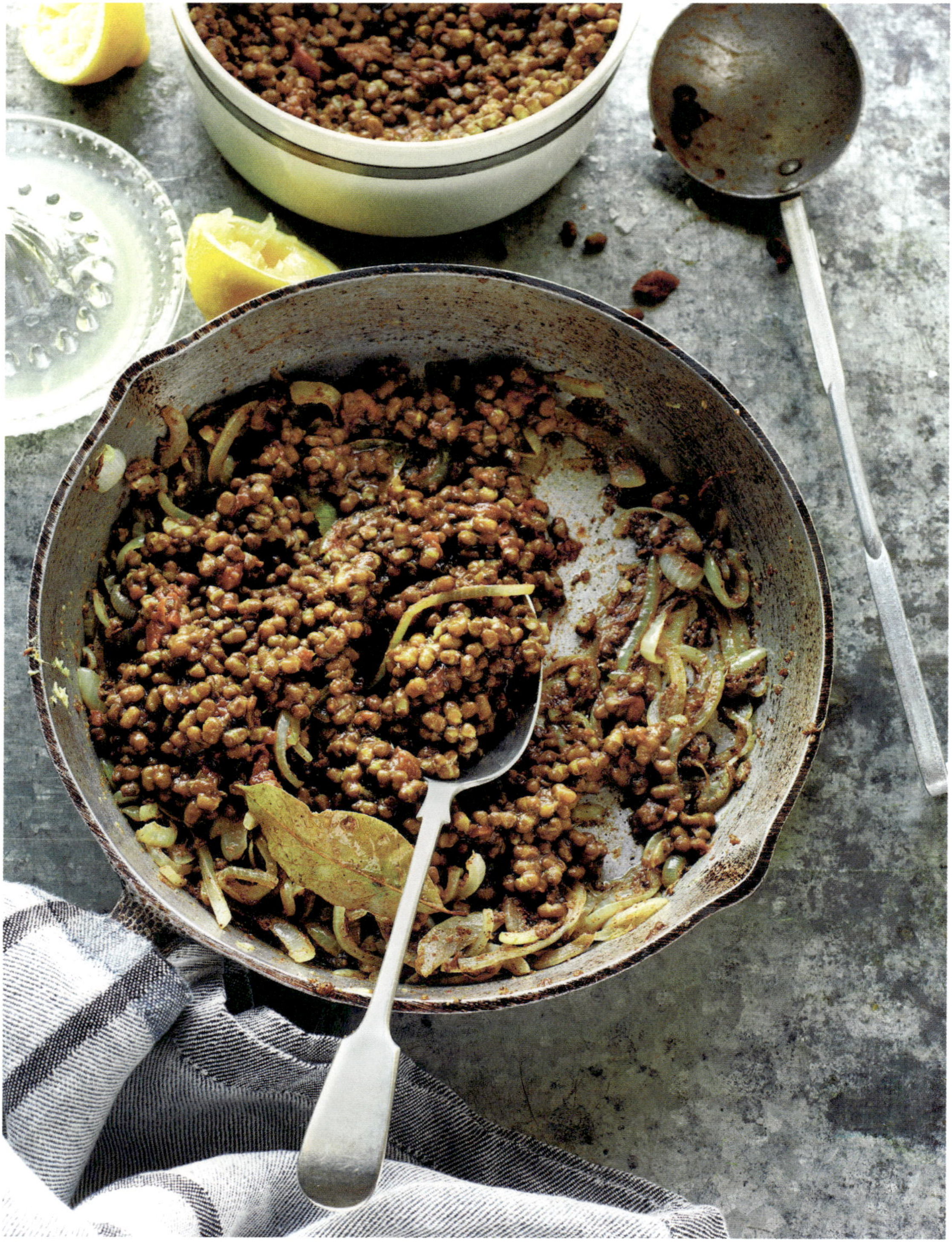

Garam masala black dahl

Prep Time: 10 mins
Cook Time: 2 hours
Serves: 4–6

Black urid or black gram lentils, 250 g
Tinned chopped tomatoes, 400 g
Ground turmeric, ¼ tsp
Water, 1.5 litres
Vegetable oil, 2 tbsp
Cumin seeds, 1 tsp
2 large green chillies, deseeded and thinly sliced
2 bay leaves
3 small white onions, thinly sliced
5 cm piece of fresh ginger, 20 g, peeled and grated
5 garlic cloves, peeled and minced
Garam masala, 1½ tbsp
Plus ¼ tsp more cardamom powder, 1 tsp more cinnamon powder and ¼ tsp more nutmeg powder
Chilli powder, ⅛ tsp
Juice of ½ lemon
Salt, 1 tsp
Sugar, 1 tsp
Fresh coriander, stalks and leaves, 50 g, finely chopped

Black, velvety and rich, this is one of the Punjab's most popular dahls. It is uncompromising in how much flavour and spices it contains – and they are the flavours and spices of the richest meat curry. I made this for my nephew recently and he could not believe that it wasn't made with minced lamb. For me, that was such a compliment. Be warned that these dense black lentils will take almost 2 hours to cook through, unless you use a pressure cooker. Despite the jeopardy of either, it is worth it.

In a medium saucepan, add the urid lentils, chopped tomatoes and ground turmeric, then cover with the water and stir together. Bring up to the boil, then reduce the heat to low, cover and simmer gently for 1½–1¾ hours until the lentils are tender, then set aside.

Put the vegetable oil in a large non-stick frying pan set over a medium-high heat. When hot, add the cumin seeds and fry until they turn dark brown. Add the green chillies and bay leaves and fry for a further 20 seconds. Add the onions, ginger and garlic and fry for 8 minutes until they soften and turn golden brown.

Add the garam masala, cardamom, cinnamon, nutmeg and chilli powders and fry for 30 seconds. Carefully ladle the cooked lentils into the pan and stir until everything is fully mixed.

Bring the lentils up to the boil, adding more water if necessary, then stir through the lemon juice, salt and sugar – the dahl should have the consistency of thick porridge. Finish by stirring through the fresh chopped coriander.

Roasted chickpeas

Chickpeas are to Indians what potatoes are to the West. In Indian villages they are depended on in their every form. These roasted chickpeas are found in most homes, in an old coffee jar where they keep for weeks. They are eaten instead of potato crisps. Cup of tea in one hand, jar of mouthwatering crunch in the other.

Prep Time: 5 mins
Cook Time: 40 mins
Serves: 4–6 as a snack

Tinned chickpeas, 400 g, drained and dried
Coconut oil, 3 tbsp
Cumin powder, 1 tsp
Coriander powder, 1 tsp
Mild chilli powder, ⅛ tsp
Salt, ½ tsp
Ground turmeric, ½ tsp
Amchoor, ½ tsp

Preheat the oven to fan 210°C/230°C/450°F. In a bowl, mix the drained chickpeas with all the other ingredients except the amchoor. Make sure the chickpeas are evenly coated and then spread in an even layer on a baking sheet.

Roast the chickpeas in the oven for 30–40 minutes, making sure to give them a good shake every 10 minutes so that they don't catch. Remove when they are crispy and golden.

To finish, toss the chickpeas while still hot with the amchoor powder.

Prep Time: 15 mins
Cook Time: 35 mins
Serves: 4

Vegetable oil, 3 tbsp
Cumin seeds, 1 tsp
2 bay leaves
2 white onions, finely chopped
5 cm piece of fresh ginger, 20 g, peeled and grated
3 garlic cloves, peeled and minced
Garam masala, 1½ tbsp
 Plus 1 tsp cumin powder and 1 tsp more coriander powder
Chilli powder, ⅛ tsp
Ground turmeric, ¼ tsp
Tinned chopped tomatoes, 400 g
2 x 400 g tins chickpeas, rinsed and drained
Strong Darjeeling tea, 350 ml
Salt, 1 tsp
Sugar, 1 tsp
Spinach, 200 g, washed and drained and roughly shredded
1 small bunch of fresh coriander, stalks and leaves, roughly chopped

Tea-steeped chickpeas

Back in the 1970s, my dad and Mr Jagota – brave owner of one of the only Asian shops in Liverpool – used to share tales of back home, over fried breads and these chickpeas, which were simmered in a huge muslin full of Darjeeling tea. The gentlemen and chickpeas were rich and full of nostalgia. Good tea adds a pleasant and bitter quickening.

Put the vegetable oil in a large heavy-based pan set over a medium-high heat. When hot, add the cumin seeds and fry until they turn brown and fragrant, then add the bay leaves, onions, ginger and garlic and fry for 8 minutes until the onions are soft and dark brown.

Add the garam masala, cumin powder and coriander powder and cook for 2 minutes, then add the chilli powder, ground turmeric, chopped tomatoes, chickpeas, Darjeeling tea, salt and sugar and simmer gently for 20–25 minutes until thick and tangy.

Finish by stirring through the shredded spinach leaves and chopped coriander.

Family fried rice

I make this fried rice for every dinner party. It is the one that my mother, grandmother and great-grandmother before me relied on to woo the masses. Black cardamom has a unique ability to turn rice into something elegant and majestic.

Prep Time: 10 mins
Cook Time: 40 mins
Serves: 4–6

Vegetable oil, 3 tbsp
Cumin seeds, 1 tsp
3 black cardamom pods
6 whole cloves
Basmati rice, 225 g, soaked in cold water for 2 hours, rinsed and drained
Water, 350 ml
Any leftover cooked veg

Heat the vegetable oil in a saucepan over a medium-high heat. When hot, add the cumin seeds, black cardamom pods and cloves and allow them to sizzle for 1 minute.

Add the washed rice grains and toss them in the oil with the whole spices for 1 minute, then pour in the water. Bring up to the boil, then turn the heat down, cover and cook very gently for 20 minutes. Add the cooked veg and continue to cook for a further 5 minutes until the rice is tender and all the water has been absorbed.

Cover with a tightly fitting lid and turn off the heat. Leave the pan undisturbed for 10 minutes, then serve hot.

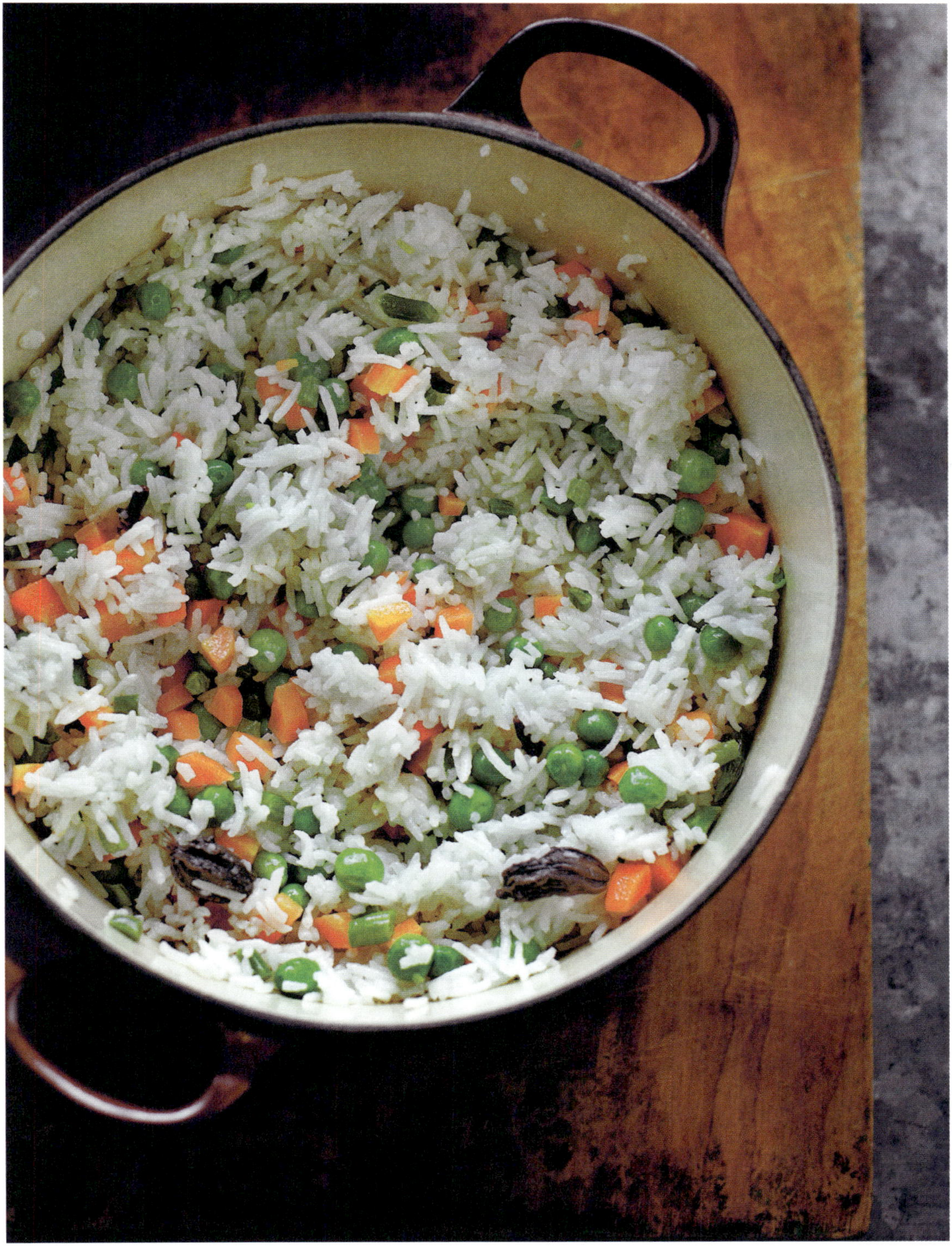

Green dahl with rhubarb and ginger

Rhubarb and ginger dahl is one of the best sellers at my restaurant, Mowgli. The flavours are zingy and clean. This is so unlike anything one would expect from the jaded stereotypes of Indian food and it's a great ambassador for the way we really eat at home.

Prep Time: 10 mins
Cook Time: 1¼ hours
Serves: 4–6

Green mung beans, 250 g
Water, 1 litre
Tinned chopped tomatoes, 200 g
Ground turmeric, ¼ tsp
Chilli powder, ⅛ tsp
Vegetable oil, 5 tbsp
Cumin seeds, 1 tsp
1 large green chilli, pierced
2 bay leaves
3 small white onions, thinly sliced
5 cm piece of fresh ginger, 20 g, peeled and grated
2 garlic cloves, peeled and grated
Fresh rhubarb, 200 g, cut into 5 cm pieces
Juice of ½ lemon
Salt, 1 tsp
Sugar, 1 tsp
1 small bunch of fresh coriander, stalks and leaves, roughly chopped
Obligatory backup jug of water, to loosen the dish to your taste

In a medium saucepan, add the mung beans, water, chopped tomatoes, ground turmeric and chilli powder, then bring up to the boil, reduce the heat to low and simmer gently for 50–60 minutes or until the lentils are tender, then set aside.

In a large non-stick frying pan set over a medium-high heat, add the vegetable oil. When hot, add the cumin seeds and fry until they turn dark brown, then add the green chilli, bay leaves, onions, ginger and garlic and fry for 8 minutes until the onions are soft and golden.

Turn the heat down to medium, then take the lentils and carefully ladle them into the pan. Add the chopped rhubarb, lemon juice, salt and sugar and bring up to the boil. Reduce the heat to low and simmer gently for 6 minutes or until the rhubarb is cooked through and tender.

Finish by stirring through the fresh coriander. Add a splash more water to loosen if necessary – the dahl should have the consistency of thick porridge.

Karhi (Pronounced 'Car-heee')

Indians don't have the word 'curry', although it is thought that *karhi* – a popular dahl-type sauce – might be the root of this Western term. Authentic Indian dishes are actually often quite dry, and dahl and *karhi* act as the lubricant. Eat *karhi* with rice or use a roti bread to spoon it straight into the mouth. Note the Gujrati roots to this dish: that flow of curry leaf, asafoetida and mustard seed. This recipe is one of my aunty Geeta's favourites, using mixed vegetables. Often *karhi* is served as a soup with fried discs of Crunchy okra with cumin (see page 83) sprinkled on top. You can really experiment here. Garnish with what you love.

Prep Time: 15 mins
Cook Time: 20 mins
Serves: 4

Vegetable oil, 6 tbsp
1 stick celery, cut into 2–3 cm batons
1 small swede, cut into 2–3 cm batons
2 large carrots, cut into 2–3 cm batons
3 tomatoes, roughly chopped
Ground turmeric, ¼ tsp
Natural yoghurt, 200 g
Water, 350 ml
Gram flour, 4 tbsp
Mustard seeds, 1 tsp
Asafoetida, ¼ tsp
3 fresh curry leaves
Chilli powder, ¼ tsp
2 dried red chillies, chopped
Salt, 1 tsp
Sugar, 1 tsp
1 small bunch of fresh coriander, stalks and leaves, roughly chopped

Put 4 tablespoons of the vegetable oil in a large heavy-based pan set over a medium-high heat. When hot, add the celery, swede and carrots and fry for 6 minutes until the vegetables start to soften. Then add the chopped tomatoes and ground turmeric and continue to fry for a further 4 minutes.

Add the yoghurt and water and bring up to the boil, then reduce the heat to low and add the gram flour, stirring well. When everything is fully mixed, set aside.

In a separate non-stick frying pan, add the remaining 2 tablespoons of vegetable oil. When hot, add the mustard seeds and fry until they fizz, pop and turn grey. Add the asafoetida and fry for 10 seconds until it turns a deep brown, then add the curry leaves, chilli powder and dried red chillies.

Quickly pour this into the *karhi* and add the salt and sugar, stirring well. Put back over a medium heat, simmer for 5 minutes and then finish by stirring through the fresh coriander just before serving.

Prep Time: 10 mins
Cook Time: 35 mins
Serves: 4–6

Puy lentils, 250 g
Ground turmeric, ¼ tsp
Water, 900 ml
Vegetable oil, 2 tbsp
3 cardamom pods*
2 bay leaves*
1 green chilli, pierced
2 large white onions, thinly sliced
5 cm piece of fresh ginger, peeled and grated
3 garlic cloves, peeled and grated
Garam masala, 1½ tbsp
    Plus 1 tsp more coriander powder and ¼ tsp more cumin powder
Chilli powder, ⅛ tsp
Juice of ½ lemon
Salt, 1 tsp
Sugar, 1 tsp
Swiss chard, 250 g (or any other leafy green vegetable), leaves and stalks finely chopped
Obligatory backup jug of water, to loosen the dish to your taste

Puy lentils and chard with cardamom and garam masala

Puy lentils, cooked using this rich, warming base, are such a far cry from the cold hippy salads of yesteryear's vegetarian bistros.

In a medium saucepan, add the Puy lentils and ground turmeric, then cover with the water and stir together. Bring up to the boil, then reduce the heat to low, cover and simmer gently for 20–25 minutes until the lentils are tender, then set aside.

Put the vegetable oil in a large non-stick frying pan set over a medium-high heat. When hot, add the cardamom pods and bay leaves and fry for 10 seconds. Add the green chilli and fry for a further 20 seconds. Add the onions, ginger and garlic and fry for 8 minutes or until they soften and turn golden brown.

Add the garam masala and coriander, cumin and chilli powders and fry for 30 seconds. Carefully ladle the cooked lentils into the pan and stir until everything is fully mixed.

Bring the lentils up to the boil, adding more water if necessary, then stir through the lemon juice, salt, sugar and Swiss chard. Simmer gently for 5 minutes until the chard has wilted down. The dahl should have the consistency of thick porridge.

*Note: Bay and cardamom, as with cumin and coriander powders, are already found in garam masala. In this recipe you are simply adding more to elevate these 'voices'.

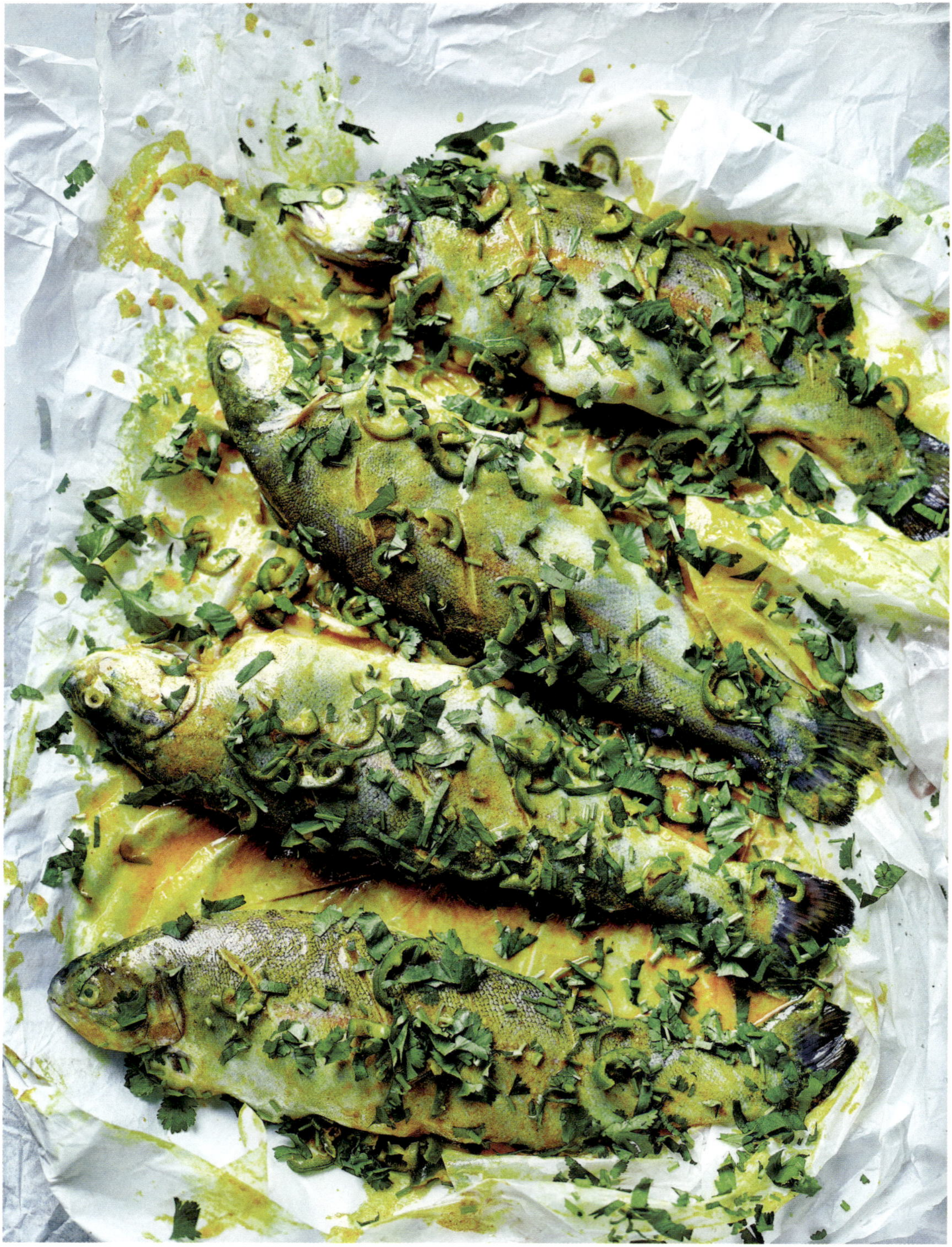

Fish and Shellfish

1
Pick **ONE** starter ball from the root system and fry the spice in a pan with a drizzle of oil. Rub your fish in turmeric and flash-fry it in a separate pan to seal it.

2
If you want a richer dish, add onion, ginger and garlic (the Meat Mantra that makes up the Meat-Veg Marriage) to the pan with the fried spices.

3
Now travel up the trunk, adding turmeric and chilli powder. Add salt and sugar, to taste.

4
From the leaves, choose one or more of the ingredients to finish your dish. Play around and have fun – this is how you personalise your curry.

5
Add your flash-fried fish now and cook through.

TIP: Add a little water to loosen the sauce so that you can submerge the delicate fish fillets without having to prod and break them.

KEY

● = Mustard Seed, Dried Red Chilli and Curry Leaf
SOUTH INDIAN TRIO

● = Onion, Ginger, Garlic and one Seed Spice
MEAT-VEG MARRIAGE

The Fish and Seafood Tree

Yoghurt
Coriander Leaf
Tomato
Coconut Milk
Green Chilli
Lemon
Tamarind
Sugar
Salt
Turmeric
Chilli powder

South Indian Trio | Nigella Seed & Green Chilli | Mustard Seed & Dried Red Chilli | Panch Poron Seeds | Cumin Seed | Meat-Veg Marriage

In ancient times, Hindu Brahmin priests came to the controlling conclusion that meat was aggression-inspiring and should be banned. These pot-bellied pontiffs, however, could not bring themselves to remove the lush flesh of fish from their diets. They therefore considered fish to be essentially 'fruit of the sea'. This meant that fish was cooked according to vegetarian principles, the beginning of which involves the frying of a headnote seed spice in a little oil.

Fish, like heavy pulses and eggs, thus sit in that strange hybrid world between meat and vegetables. Although a headnote seed starts the dish, it is often the case that onions, ginger and garlic – the meat mantra – can then be added, along with any of the powdered meat spices.

To understand how fish is eaten in India, one must first imagine the historical context of kitchen organisation. The early morning fishermen would bring their catch to a very early market. I recall heading to these slithering, dazzling, undercover fish markets first thing, and choosing live fish from buckets for lunch. The more they wriggled, the more attractive they were to the consumer.

The head, the egg sack and the tail end were all precious. The guts and gills were removed with a foot-held scythe and the scales removed and fish cut in a particular way for curry – in horizontal sections with a cylinder disc of spine running through each piece. The smell of the flesh was overwhelmingly sweet and my infant memories of fish are of this sweet smell and the beauty of the scales.

Even in the 1970s when I was growing up, fridges were not common in many Indian homes. Hence, it was customary for fish to be eaten at lunchtime when it was still fresh, as opposed to the late evening meal, which always occurs after the sun has gone down and so can often be as late as 10 p.m. or 11 p.m. This late dining is a hangover from when it was important that the houses in India were cool enough to tolerate the firing of the ovens.

Turmeric and fish have a special alliance. Turmeric is the earthiest of the spices and it is usually the case that fish is rubbed with turmeric and often salt, and then fried, before being simmered in a light curry sauce. This makes eminent sense for a number of reasons. Turmeric, with its taste of the very earth of India, almost gives fish a pair of 'land legs'. It takes away all scent of fishiness and replaces it with a grounded scent – it makes mammal of sea life. Turmeric is also known for its preservative and antiseptic qualities, and hence it seems rubbing fish with this powdered root goes some way to extending its freshness and life in the heat of the midday sun.

It is this charming steer that nature imposed on Indian chefs that gave birth to the great British breakfast, kedgeree. There is no such thing as kedgeree in India. Instead, what has always existed, especially as a comfort food for the elderly and the infirm, is a dish known as *kitchuri*. It is a simple dish of light lentils cooked with rice, with very light spicings. It challenges neither teeth nor gut. The chefs serving the breakfast tables of the British during the days of the Raj, thought to kill two birds with one stone. *Kitchuri* was a very simple, almost porridge-like breakfast that found favour with the delicate constitutions of the memsahibs – the Indian elite. But further, resourceful chefs would use the early morning catch in the breakfasts of the British who could not countenance a meal without flesh of some kind. Eggs were added in to give even more 'meat to the breakfast bones'.

The headnote spices that work best with fish are the gentle tones of nigella seed and mustard seed. Cumin seed can be too overpowering but is used.

The gentle structure and sweetness of fish flesh requires little propping. Nigella seed, with her ever accompanying pierced green chilli, has the same 'earth' notes as turmeric and works in the same way: it replaces the wet scent of sea with that of grass and ground.

Mustard seed is one of the gentlest of headnotes. Once fried, it has a playful popcorn nuttiness that sits on top of the flavour of fish without drowning its natural charm. In the south of India, mustard seed goes hand in hand with fragrant curry leaves and green chilli. This chlorophyll-rich, verdant duo again remove any overly fishy edge your fish may have.

Goa, on the west coast of India, is known for its hot-and-sour, tamarind-based fish curries. Remember that the hybrid of the meat and vegetable spice formulas apply to this special middle ingredient, fish. Hence, Goans often start their fish dishes with mustard seed and curry leaf in the way they might make a vegetarian dish. But then onions, ginger and garlic are added with tamarind paste and chilli, which are more often seen alongside meaty dishes elsewhere. The resulting flavours are huge, sweet, hot and powerful. The fish that are common to the Goan and south Indian areas can take this assault of flavours, however, as they are often sea fish whose flesh is more robust than the gentler river fish of the north.

FISH

It is vitally important to understand the difference between river fish and sea fish as they often require different cooking methods. In northern India, particularly in the Bengal, the area from which my ancestors hail, the land is punctuated by rivers. River fish, skilfully negotiating these twisting, flowing streams, have complicated and fine bone structures that allow them to move constantly and in tight turns. This makes them fiendishly hard to eat, as the bones are as fine as hairs and numerous, too. One of the tests of a good Hindu wife is her ability to negotiate the bones of the Hilsa river fish. One might wonder why one bothers? I thought the same for many years, but there is something uniquely delicate and delicious in the flesh of river fish that has been cleaved to bone and fed by sweet water all its life.

Koi is a fish that is prized for its flesh in India. I struggle with the notion of eating Koi. I have always had pet Koi who I love to hand feed and stroke like aquatic kittens. Hence I see a sweet pescetarian victory in the fact that their bones are the most treacherous. They are glass-like tiny hooks and they compound the horror of eating these mockingbirds of the oceans. Good on you, kindly Koi.

Sea fish on the other hand seem to have an easier life. Lurking in the stillness of the deep, their bones are bigger, and their structure less complex. The resulting flesh is denser and meatier in its flavour. Think of monkfish and how its scowling in sedentary deep seas has made its flesh almost steak-like. Amongst the sea fish most loved by the Indians are pomfret, mackerel and king fish.

PRAWNS, LOBSTERS AND CRABS

These are very much loved in coastal areas. My grandmother used to catch big crabs in the River Ganges when she went for her early morning holy dip. She cooked them with a typical meat and veg hybrid spice formula, separating the white and dark meat and treating each one slightly differently.

MOLLUSCS

An interesting genre, I have never seen cockles, mussels, scallops, whelks and the like in India, let alone eaten them. My family and their Bengali friends never came across dishes made with molluscs or squid. But it seems that coastal regions, particularly in the south, make a good clam or mussel curry, and squid is something of which they are not afraid. Northern Indians, however, appear to look more askance at this kind of shellfish. My grandmother and her generation of north Indians believed that clams or cockles in a watery curry were good for stomach illness and that this was their main value. That was the only time such ingredients were mentioned in my ancestral home, as a kind of mysterious healing potion.

So you see the attitude towards the mollusc is so very different across India. If you want to try them, simply use the fish formula and poach them in towards the end of the simmer of the sauce.

The curry formula of the south would, of course, be a mustard seed and curry leaf headnote spice to which you can add a rich slick of coconut milk. For a north Indian dish, look at the crab recipe on page 198 and simply loosen it with water, then steam in your mollusc of choice for the last few minutes. Of course, discard the ones that remain shut after cooking.

South Indian monkfish

Prep Time: 10 mins
Cook Time: 30 mins
Serves: 4

- Vegetable oil, 4½ tbsp
- Mustard seeds, 1 tsp
- 3 large fresh curry leaves
- 1 large green chilli, deseeded and thinly sliced
- 2 white onions, cut in half then thinly sliced lengthways
- 5 cm piece of fresh ginger, 20 g, peeled and grated
- 4 garlic cloves, peeled and grated
- Monkfish fillet, 750 g, cut into large cubes
- Ground turmeric, ½ tsp
- Chilli powder, ⅛ tsp
- Coconut milk, 200 ml
- Natural yoghurt, 200 g
- Water, 200 ml
- 1 small bunch of fresh coriander, stalks and leaves, roughly chopped
- Obligatory backup jug of water, to loosen the dish to your taste

This is a great generic south Indian fish recipe. I use monkfish here because it is an easy fish to eat and an easy recipe for you to have in your armoury. Try this recipe with any fish; shellfish and clams work well in it, too. If you feel you want more oomph, add more green chilli and perhaps add in some coriander powder and more leaf. This makes for a fresh, herby, gentle strength.

Put 3 tablespoons of the vegetable oil in a large pan set over a medium-high heat. When hot, add the mustard seeds and fry until they fizz, pop and turn grey, then turn the heat down to medium and add the curry leaves, green chilli, onions, ginger and garlic and fry for 8 minutes until the onions are soft and brown.

Rub the chunks of monkfish lightly with the ground turmeric, then in a separate large non-stick frying pan set over a medium-high heat, add the remaining 1½ tablespoons of vegetable oil and when hot, flash fry the fish for 1 minute until coloured, then set aside.

Add the chilli powder, coconut milk, yoghurt and water to the onion mixture and bring up to the boil, then reduce the heat to low, gently add the fish to the sauce and simmer for 8–10 minutes or until the fish is tender and cooked through.

Finish by stirring through the fresh coriander just before serving. Add more water if necessary to loosen to your taste.

Goan fish curry with tamarind

In the heat and colour of Goa, stronger flavours in curry are celebrated. Unlike elsewhere, they do not frown upon the meat triumvirate of onions, ginger and garlic joining forces with strong, firm sea fish. Tamarind is a very common Goan addition. Hot-and-sour dishes are seen as sweat-inducing, which, in the tropical heat of the Goan coast, is considered cooling.

Prep Time: 10 mins
Cook Time: 30 mins
Serves: 4

Vegetable oil, 4½ tbsp
Panch poron, 2 tsp
2 white onions, cut in half then thinly sliced lengthways
5 cm piece of fresh ginger, 20 g, peeled and grated
4 garlic cloves, peeled and grated
Skinless cod fillets, 650 g, cut into large chunks
Ground turmeric, 2½ tsp
Tinned chopped tomatoes, 200 g
Chilli powder, ⅛ tsp
Tamarind paste, 1 tbsp
Soft brown sugar, 1 tbsp
1 small bunch of fresh coriander, stalks and leaves, roughly chopped
Obligatory backup jug of water, to loosen the dish to your taste

Put 3 tablespoons of the vegetable oil in a large heavy-based pan set over a medium-high heat. When hot, add the panch poron and fry until the nuggets of fenugreek turn deep golden brown, then turn the heat down to medium and add the onions, ginger and garlic and fry for 8 minutes until the onions are soft and brown.

Rub the chunks of cod lightly with 2 teaspoons of the ground turmeric, then, in a separate large non-stick frying pan set over a medium-high heat, add the remaining 1½ tablespoons of vegetable oil and when hot, flash fry the fish for 1 minute, then set aside.

Add the chopped tomatoes to the onion mixture and cook gently for 6 minutes or until most of the liquid has evaporated, then add the remaining ½ teaspoon of ground turmeric, the chilli powder, tamarind paste and brown sugar and give everything a good mix together.

Gently add the fish to the sauce and simmer for 8–10 minutes or until the fish is tender and cooked through. Finish by stirring through the fresh coriander just before serving. Add a little water if necessary to loosen to your taste.

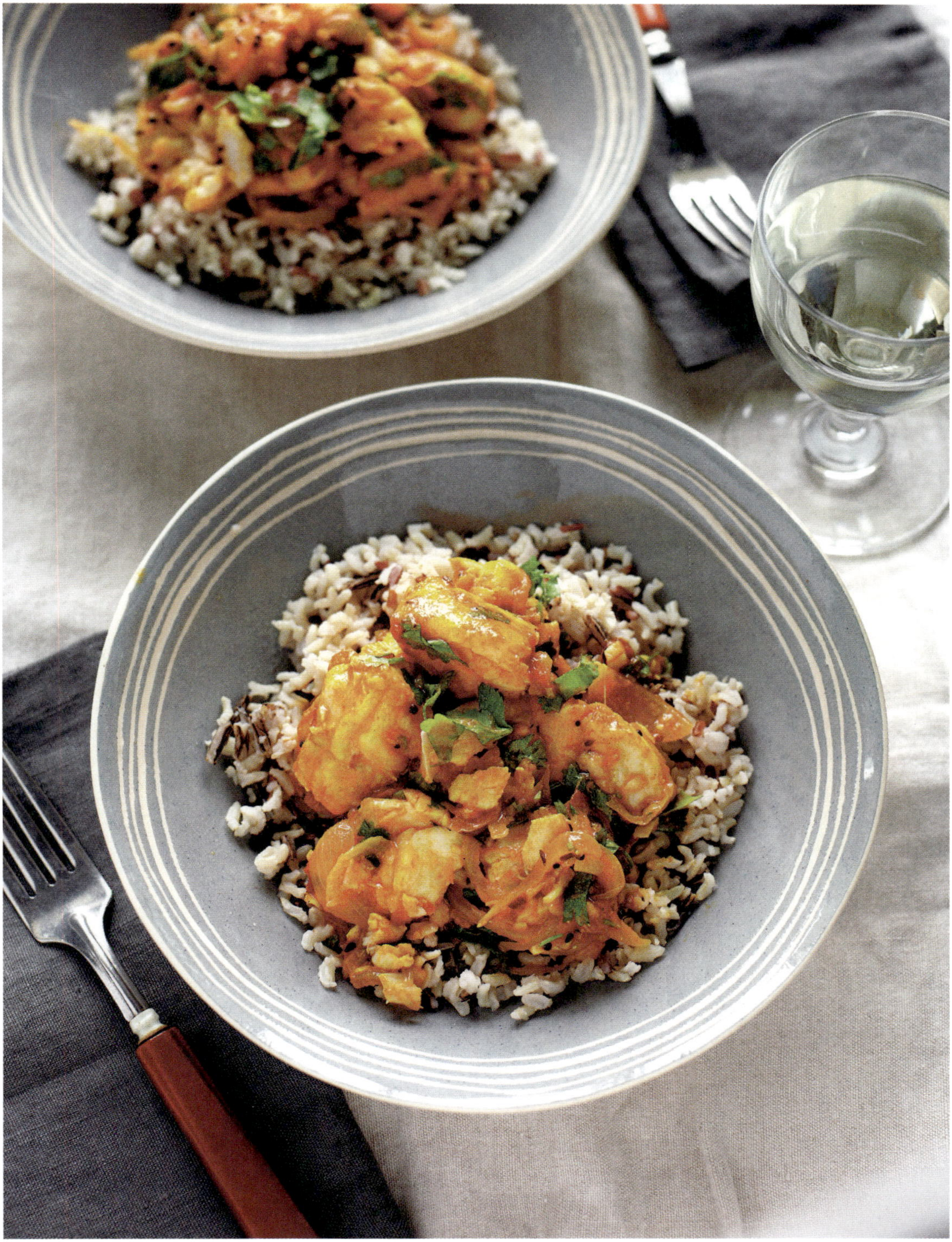

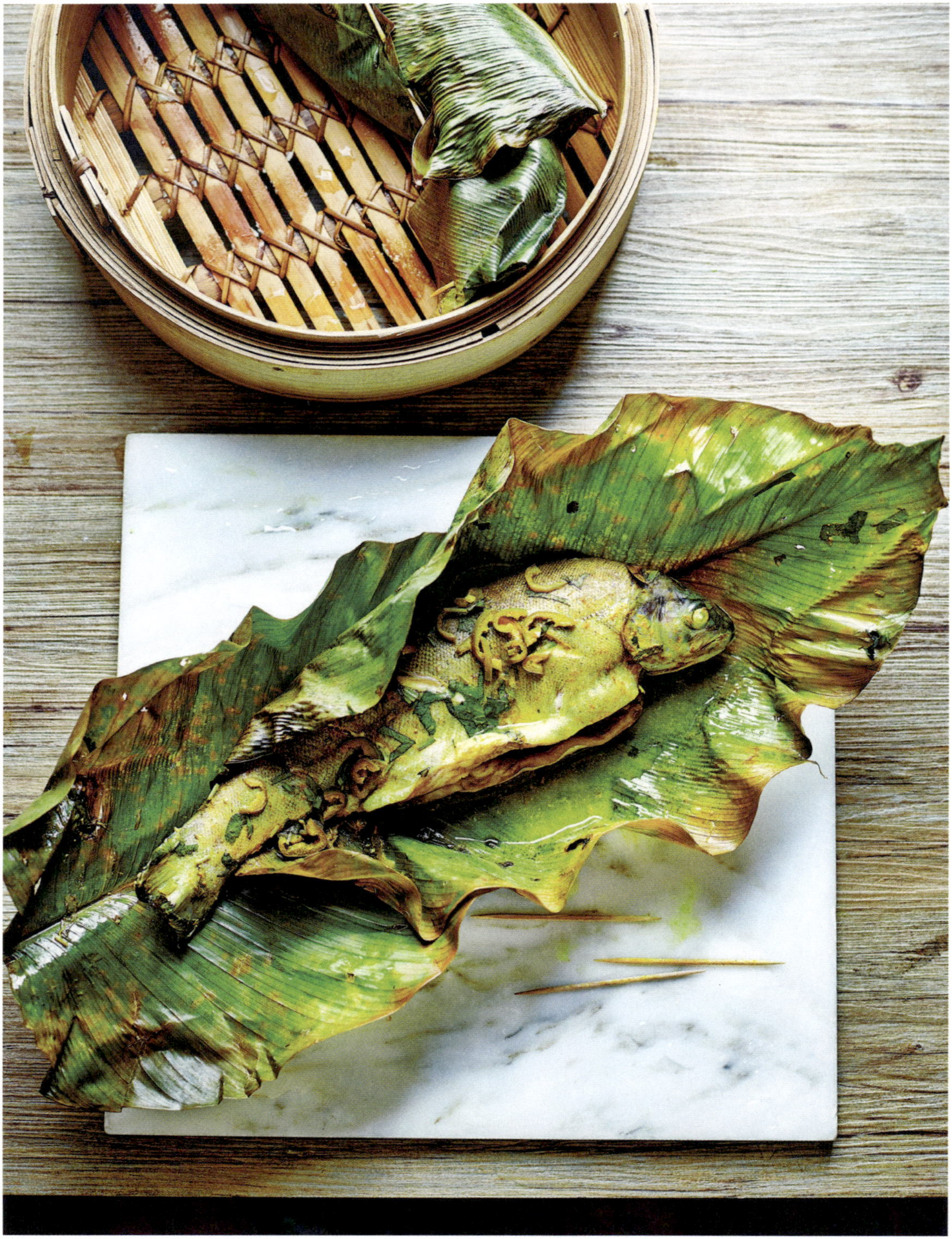

Steamed Bengali trout

Known as *bhapa maach*, this is a very simple dish, beloved in our family. It's the mustard paste and turmeric that take the fish firmly to Indian soil, removing all 'fishiness' and giving sea flesh 'land legs'. You can use tin foil in lieu of banana leaf. It is great on a barbecue with the leaf or foil tents poised over the dying embers. This is superb with any fish and is a great twist on the well-known lemon and olive oil classic.

Prep Time: 10 mins
Cook Time: 20 mins
Serves: 4

- 4 small whole trout, 500 g each, scaled and gutted
- Vegetable oil, 3 tbsp
- English mustard paste, 1 tbsp, loosened with a little water
- 3 large green chillies, deseeded and thinly sliced
- 1 bunch of fresh coriander, leaves roughly chopped, stalks kept
- Ground turmeric, 1 tsp
- Juice of 2 limes
- Salt, 1 tsp
- 4 large banana leaves

Score each trout on both sides, then rub the vegetable oil, mustard paste, green chillies, chopped coriander leaves, ground turmeric, lime juice and salt into the fish. Stuff the belly cavities of the fish with the squeezed lime halves and coriander stalks.

Wrap a banana leaf around each fish to form a loose parcel, then secure the ends with cocktail sticks.

Steam for 15–20 minutes until cooked through. If you haven't got a steamer, roast the fish in a hot oven (fan 180°C/200°C/400°F) or on the barbecue for 10–12 minutes.

Sea bass in fried yoghurt sauce

This is one of the most common sauce bases for fish curry. It is an unusual method of cooking, but a simple one, encouraging the curdling of yoghurt to give a nutty weight and texture. Before they get married, Bengali brides have one day where the family get together and cook all of her favourite dishes for her, and I am yet to go to such a ceremony where this dish did not feature.

Prep Time: 10 mins
Cook Time: 15 mins
Serves: 4

Ground turmeric, ¼ tsp
4 large sea bass fillets, 150 g each
Vegetable oil, 5 tbsp
Nigella seeds, 1½ tsp
1 large green chilli, deseeded and thinly sliced
Chilli powder, ⅛ tsp
White poppy seeds, 3 tbsp, crushed in a pestle and mortar
Natural yoghurt, 6 tbsp
Water, 350 ml
Salt, 1 tsp
Sugar, ½ tsp
English mustard paste, 1 tbsp, loosened with a little water
1 small bunch of fresh coriander, stalks and leaves, roughly chopped
Obligatory backup jug of water, to loosen the dish

Lightly rub the ground turmeric into the fillets of sea bass, then put 2 tablespoons of the vegetable oil in a large non-stick frying pan set over a medium-high heat. When hot, flash fry the sea bass fillets, skin side down, for 1 minute, then set aside.

In a separate large pan, add the remaining 3 tablespoons of vegetable oil and set over a medium-high heat. When hot, add the nigella seeds and green chilli and fry for 30 seconds. Turn the heat down to low and add the chilli powder, white poppy seeds and yoghurt and fry for 3 minutes or until the yoghurt starts to separate, then add the water, salt, sugar and mustard paste and stir everything together.

Add the sea bass fillets and cook gently for 6–8 minutes or until the sea bass is cooked through. Finish by stirring through the fresh coriander just before serving. Add more water if necessary to loosen to your taste.

Aunty Geeta's prawns

Gosh, this is such a precious dish to me. One of my all-time favourite curries, it is best with shell-on prawns and, dare I say it, ones with bellies full of eggs. This adds so much fish stock and flavour to the simmer. Still at my ripe age, aunty Geeta makes this for me and, even now, I hide it from my loved ones behind the pots of detritus in the fridge. I am not proud.

Prep Time: 10 mins
Cook Time: 15 mins
Serves: 4

Vegetable oil, 4 tbsp
Nigella seeds, 1½ tsp
1 large green chilli, deseeded and thinly sliced
Tinned chopped tomatoes, 400 g
Large raw shell-on prawns, 400 g
Ground turmeric, ¼ tsp
Chilli powder, ⅛ tsp
Frozen peas, 80 g
Water, 400 ml
Salt, 1 tsp

Put the vegetable oil in a large non-stick frying pan and set over a medium-high heat. When hot, add the nigella seeds and green chilli and fry for 30 seconds, then add the chopped tomatoes and fry for 5 minutes until the oil starts to split out of the tomatoes.

Add the prawns, ground turmeric and chilli powder and fry for 3 minutes. Then add the frozen peas, water and salt and stir until everything is mixed.

Cover and simmer for 6–8 minutes until the prawns are cooked through.

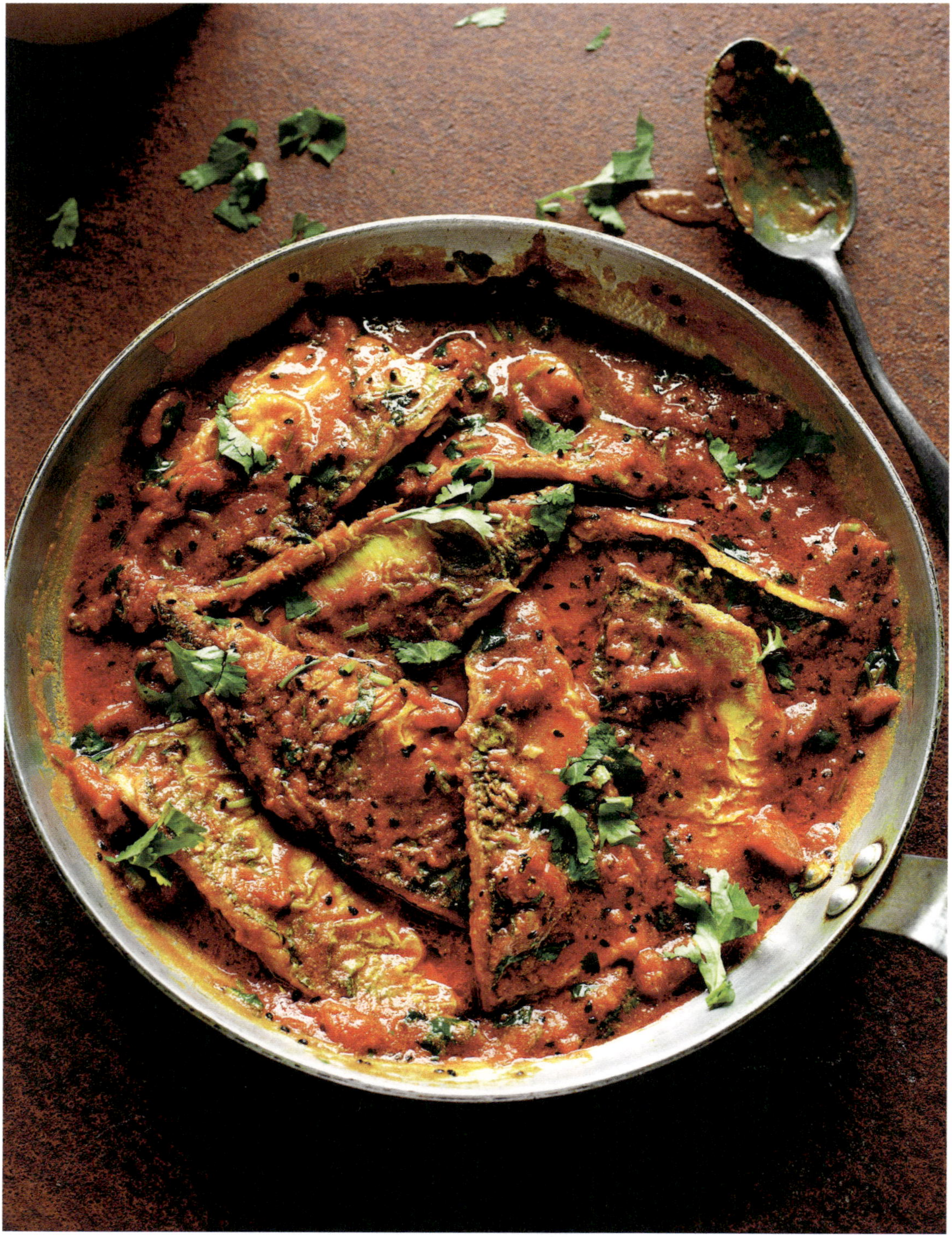

Mackerel with nigella and tomato

Nigella seed is the ultimate fish spice. It has a dusty, earthy undertone that gives particularly 'fishy' species, like mackerel, a pleasant meat-like sweetness. Combined with peaty turmeric, together they work to turn fish into the delicacy of the finest meat.

Prep Time: 10 mins
Cook Time: 15 mins
Serves: 4

Vegetable oil, 4½ tbsp
4 mackerel fillets, 450 g, skin on
Ground turmeric, 2¼ tsp
Nigella seeds, 1½ tsp
3 large green chillies, deseeded and thinly sliced
Tinned chopped tomatoes, 400 g
Chilli powder, ⅛ tsp
Water, 350 ml
Salt, 1 tsp
Sugar, 1½ tsp
English mustard paste, 1 tbsp, loosened with a little water
1 small bunch of fresh coriander, stalks and leaves, roughly chopped

Put 1½ tablespoons of the vegetable oil in a large non-stick frying pan set over a high heat. Rub the fish lightly with 2 teaspoons of the ground turmeric and when the oil is hot, flash fry the fillets, skin side down, for 1 minute, then set aside.

In a separate large pan set over a medium-high heat, add the remaining 3 tablespoons of the vegetable oil. When hot, add the nigella seeds and green chillies and fry for 30 seconds. Then add the chopped tomatoes, the remaining ¼ teaspoon of ground turmeric, the chilli powder, water, salt, sugar and mustard paste and give everything a good mix together.

Add the mackerel fillets and simmer gently, partially covered, for 6–8 minutes until the fish is cooked through. Finish by stirring the fresh coriander through the fish mixture just before serving.

Salmon and cauliflower with panch poron

Prep Time: 10 mins
Cook Time: 30 mins
Serves: 4

Vegetable oil, 4½
2 large green chillies, pierced
Panch poron, 1 tbsp
1 large cauliflower, cut into small florets
Tinned chopped tomatoes, 400 g
Ground turmeric, 2½ tsp
Chilli powder, ⅛ tsp
Water, 450 ml
Coriander powder, 1 tsp
English mustard paste, 1 heaped tbsp, loosened with a little water
Salt, 1 tsp
Sugar, 1 tsp
4 skinless salmon fillets, 650 g, cut into 5 cm chunks
1 small bunch of fresh coriander, stalks and leaves, roughly chopped
Juice of ½ lemon
Obligatory backup jug of water, to loosen the dish to your taste

The spices in this dish are powerful and provocative. They work a treat here, as both salmon and cauliflower can be such quiet, sulking ingredients if left to their own devices. The highly fragrant panch poron provides an intensity that penetrates the muted flesh of the salmon very quickly. This is why I ask you to flash fry the fish, then simply poach the pieces towards the very end. Be careful not to stir them in, otherwise they end up flaking. Instead, make space between the florets of cauliflower and nestle them in. Leave to simmer and then fresh coriander turns the fragrance dial up ten notches.

Put 3½ tablespoons of the vegetable oil in a large heavy-based pan and set over a medium-high heat. When hot, add the green chillies and panch poron and fry until the nuggets of fenugreek begin to turn golden brown and the mustard seeds fizz, pop and turn grey. Turn the heat down to low and add the cauliflower florets, chopped tomatoes, ½ teaspoon of the ground turmeric, the chilli powder and water. Simmer gently for 10–15 minutes or until the cauliflower is tender, then stir in the coriander powder, mustard paste, salt and sugar.

Rub the chunks of salmon lightly with the remaining 2 teaspoons of turmeric powder, then set a large non-stick frying pan over a medium-high heat with the remaining 1 tablespoon of vegetable oil. When hot, add the fish and flash fry for 1 minute, taking care not to burn.

Add the salmon to the cauliflower pan, cover and gently simmer for 6–8 minutes or until the salmon is cooked through. Finish with the fresh coriander and a squeeze of fresh lemon juice. Add more water if necessary to loosen to your taste.

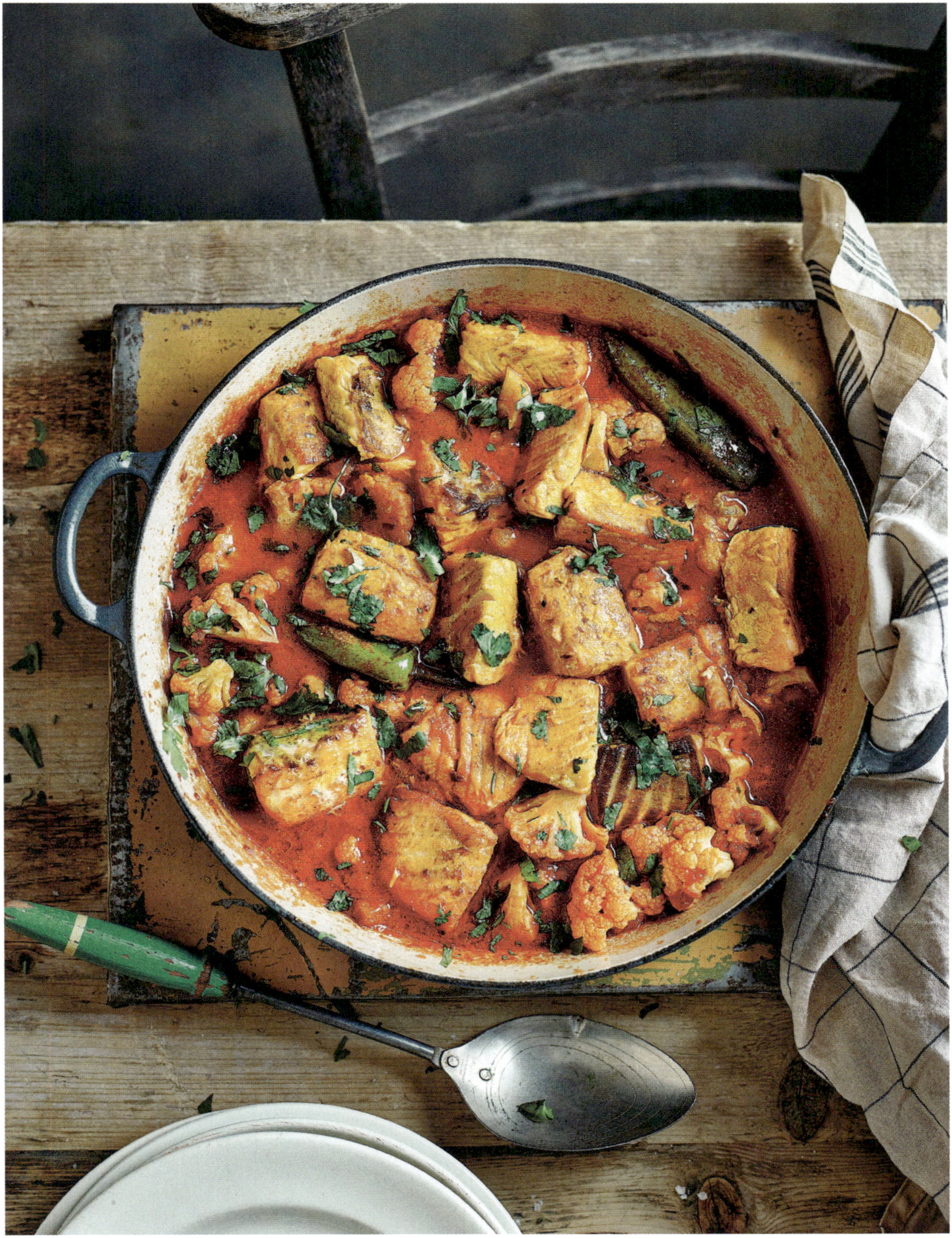

Grandmother's Varanasi crab

Every morning my grandmother used to pray and swim in the Ganges at Varanasi. Her prayers were answered quickest when she found armfuls of crabs amongst the rocks. Her children recall her coming home and cooking this obstacle course of a crab curry; it was the last thing they wanted to eat. Alas, they reminisce, why must the love of crab come so late in life?

Prep Time: 20 mins
Cook Time: 1 hour
Serves: 6–8

FOR THE WHITE CRAB
Vegetable oil, 3 tbsp
Mustard seeds, 1 tsp
1 green chilli, deseeded and thinly sliced
Tinned chopped tomatoes, 150 g
White crab meat, 250 g
Ground turmeric, ¼ tsp
Chilli powder, ⅛ tsp
Water, 300 ml
English mustard paste, 1 heaped tbsp, loosened with a little water
Salt, 1 tsp
Sugar, 1 tsp
5 cm piece of fresh ginger, 20 g, peeled and finely shredded
Coriander powder, 1 tsp
1 small bunch of fresh coriander, stalks and leaves, roughly chopped

For the white crab, put the vegetable oil in a large non-stick frying pan and set over a medium-high heat. When hot, add the mustard seeds and green chilli and fry until the mustard seeds fizz, pop and turn grey, then add the chopped tomatoes and fry for 5 minutes until the oil starts to split out of them.

Turn the heat down to low and add the white crab meat, ground turmeric, chilli powder, water and mustard paste and simmer gently for 20 minutes or until the sauce is thick and rich.

Add the salt, sugar and fresh ginger, then finish by stirring through the coriander powder and fresh coriander just before serving.

For the brown crab, put the vegetable oil in a large non-stick frying pan and set over a medium-high heat. When hot, add the nigella seeds and fry for around 30 seconds until they crackle, then add the onion, ginger and garlic and fry for 8 minutes until the onion is golden brown.

Turn the heat down to medium and add the ground turmeric, chilli powder, brown crab meat, chopped tomatoes and water and simmer gently for 20 minutes or until the sauce is thick and rich.

Finish by stirring through the salt, sugar, garam masala and the fresh lemon juice. The dishes are served as two separate curries.

FOR THE BROWN CRAB
Vegetable oil, 3 tbsp
Nigella seeds, 1 tsp
1 small white onion, cut in half then thinly sliced
5 cm piece of fresh ginger, 20 g, peeled and grated
3 garlic cloves, peeled and grated
Ground turmeric, ½ tsp
Chilli powder, ⅛ tsp
Brown crab meat, 250 g
Tinned chopped tomatoes, 150 g
Water, 350 ml
Salt, 1 tsp
Sugar, 1 tsp
Garam masala, 2 tsp
Juice of ½ lemon

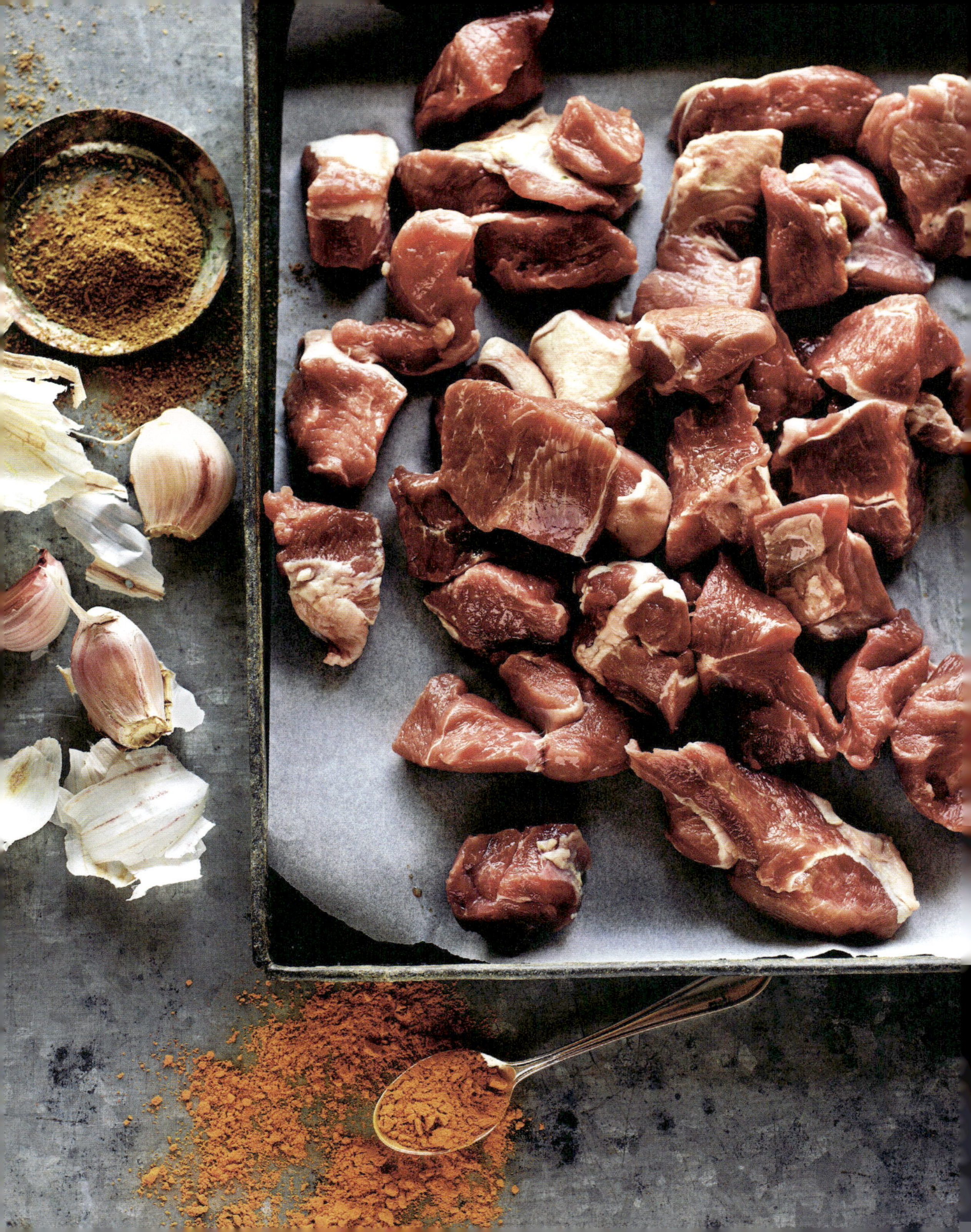

Red Meat, Game and Offal

1

Fry onion, ginger and garlic (the Meat Mantra) – as much as you can be bothered to chop – with a little vegetable oil.

2

Add Garam Masala.

3

If you want more power to your curry, add more Cumin Powder; if you want more of a fragrant curry, add more Coriander Powder.

4

Add your meat to the pan.

5

Now travel up the trunk, adding ground turmeric and chilli powder. Add salt and sugar, to taste.

6

From the leaves, choose one or more of the ingredients to finish your dish. Play around and have fun – this is how you personalise your curry.

KEY

= Onion, Ginger, Garlic

MEAT MANTRA

The North Indian Meat Tree

- Tomato
- Nuts
- Yoghurt
- Fruit & Veg
- Green Chilli
- Coriander Leaf
- Coconut Milk
- Tamarind
- Sugar
- Salt
- Turmeric
- Chilli powder

Want more power? Add Cumin Powder

Want more fragrance? Add Coriander Powder

Garam Masala

Meat Mantra

1

Fry the South Indian Trio in a pan with a drizzle of oil.

2

Add in and fry onion, ginger and garlic (the Meat Mantra) – as much as you can be bothered to chop.

3

Add Garam Masala.

4

For more power, add more Cumin Powder; for a more fragrant curry, add more Coriander Powder.

5

Add your meat to the pan.

6

Now travel up the trunk, adding ground turmeric and chilli powder. Add salt and sugar, to taste.

7

Choose one or more ingredients to finish your dish. Play around and have fun – personalise your curry.

KEY

● **SOUTH INDIAN TRIO** = Mustard Seed, Dried Red Chilli and Curry Leaf

● **MEAT MANTRA** = Onion, Ginger, Garlic

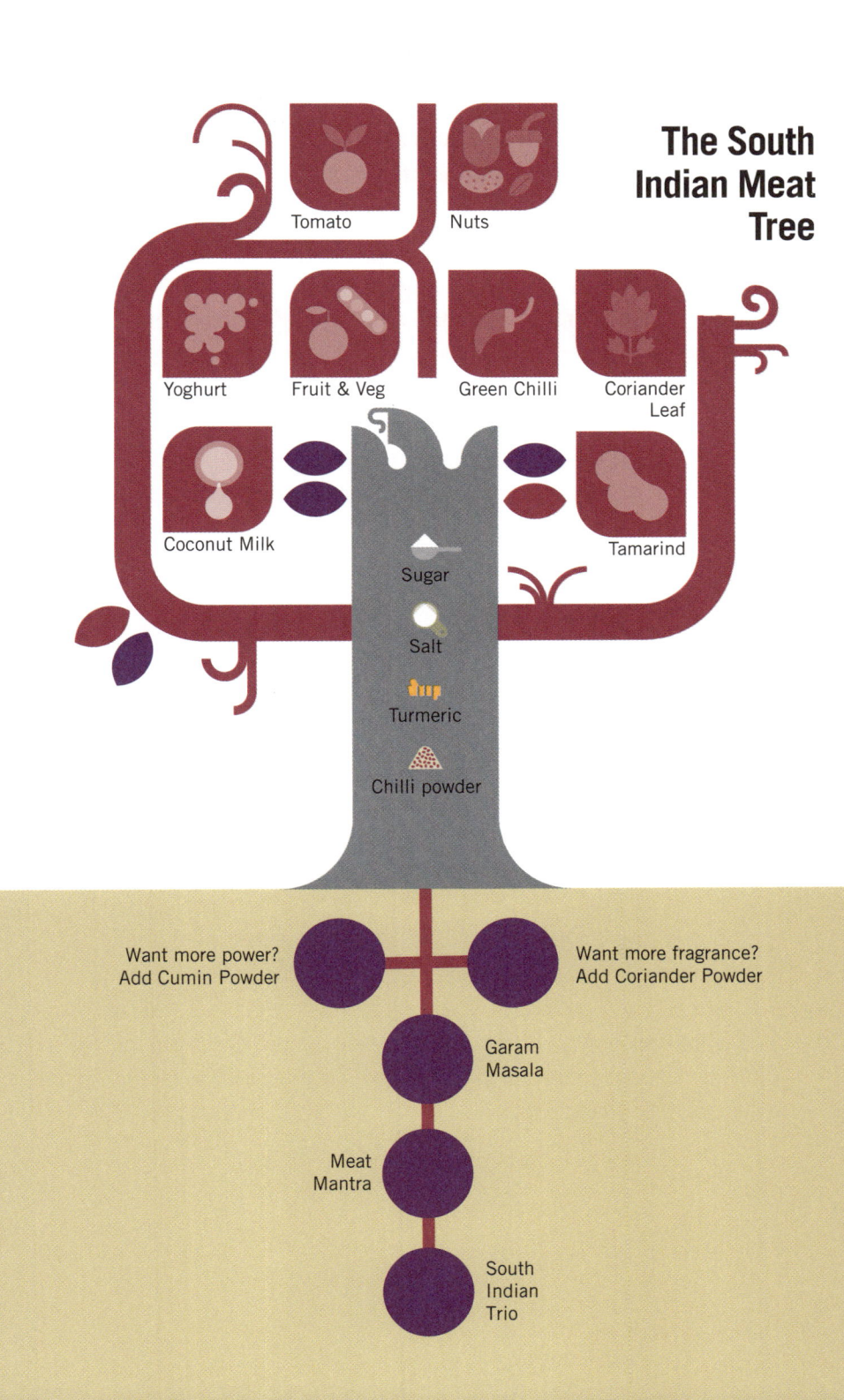

The South Indian Meat Tree

Tomato

Nuts

Yoghurt

Fruit & Veg

Green Chilli

Coriander Leaf

Coconut Milk

Tamarind

Sugar

Salt

Turmeric

Chilli powder

Want more power?
Add Cumin Powder

Want more fragrance?
Add Coriander Powder

Garam Masala

Meat Mantra

South Indian Trio

And so with the fanfare of abandoned caution, we enter the realms of meat cooking. This is the realm of cuisine governed best by the Muslim traditions of cooking. In the way that Hindus are kings of the vegetarian kitchens, none can compare to the Moghul traditions of meat preparation. The Hindu relationship with food is almost a medico-legal one. In meat cooking, outside of Hinduism, one is free to alarm the neighbours with other worldy wafts of onion, ginger and garlic up the driveway.

The theory goes that thousands of years ago, Hindu India was a nation of meat eaters. They believed that herbivores, in eating plants, imbibed the essence and energy of Mother Earth. To eat those empowered herbivores, meant we absorbed a distilled version of the earth's energy. All good one might think, and indeed it was until the Brahmin priests shifted philosophy to pacifism. They decided that energy- or heat-giving ingredients such as meat, but also the heady power of garlic and onion, inspired aggressive tendencies. Energy must be kept to a minimum and channelled into thought and philosophy. Thinking and talking one's way through disputes was better than brute force, the Hindu ascetics believed. To this day, school children in India are offered vegetarian food to keep their energy and minds in gentle focus.

So meat was banned for Hindus. Muslims on the other hand felt that Koranic paradise descriptions with meat-laden banquets were an endorsement of meat eating and they relished the high hedonism of onion, garlic and rich meat curries. So began the two very different strands of cooking methods that still flow through India. (For an explanation of where fish falls, turn to page 182.)

RED MEATS

Indian red meats amount to goat and buffalo, but I know that this will suddenly make real Indian meat curries feel very unachievable and will just downright repulse a good portion of you. For the purposes of this book, goat and lamb are interchangeable, as is buffalo with beef or mutton.

If you imagine woolly sheep against the backdrop of a hot arid, parched Indian landscape it makes no sense. It is no surprise then that Indian sheep are rare. Much more common is goat meat. It is gamier and darker than lamb, with a stringier texture and deep in flavour. Goat is eaten widely. In the West though, Indians eat lamb not goat. Lamb curry is seen as a luxurious treat and is usually the dish we make for guests.

Buffalo is an animal that is loved by Indians. Buffalo are dark, leathery, kindly, lowing tractors. They are found knee-deep in wet mud and manure in pens all around India, city and village. This indignity of habitat means that they did not make the 'holy cow' grade and so, instead, are fair game for the dinner table. Their meat is slightly gamier and richer than beef; it reminds me of good strong mutton but without the air of lanolin. Where I use buffalo, please do feel free to use beef or indeed mutton, and simmer long and low. I can't bring myself to put beef recipes in the book because they just do not feature at all in the Indian kitchens I know.

Beef and pork are not generally eaten in India as Hindus believe the cow to be sacred and it is, therefore, forbidden. It also makes socio-economic sense for cows to remain alive. This way they provide milk and all its ancillary benefits, but also manure, which is used in its dried form as fuel as well as fertiliser.

Pork is forbidden to Muslims and indeed Hindus consider it a dirty meat. In India, you will mainly encounter pigs on rubbish heaps, scavenging and covered in their own muck. Thus, pork is considered a very un-Hindu meat. It sadly sits in the minds of both rather in the same place as vermin.

Pork has an interesting story in Kerala and Goa. The Portuguese converted the Goan Hindus to Catholicism and as part of the pact, they were expected to start eating pork to show that they had truly turned their back on their Hindu ways. Hence dishes like vindaloo were born that were not traditionally Indian at all. The name 'vindaloo' actually comes from the Portuguese words for a garlic and wine sauce, *Vin d'ahlo*, which is why vinegar features even though it is a highly unusual, highly un-Indian finishing flavour.

Wild boar, however, has a preposterous place of privilege in Indian food culture. Hindus do not see it as associated with pork at all. It is seen as a wild, noble and royal meat. It was the favourite of the ancient hunting communities across India, and in Rajasthan it is still seen as one of the main ingredients of royal banquets. Often recipes for wild boar will be ones of roasted flesh, simply rubbed with garam masala spices and garlic. This was the way of eating out in the wilds. Essentially, wild boar has its roots in ancient barbecue fayre.

That wild boar is seen as entirely unrelated to pork leads me on nicely to the unique role of game in Indian culinary traditions.

GAME

Ancient Hindu philosophy proposes that if one eats vegetables one absorbs the spirit and power of the earth. If one eats herbivores then, the distilled earth's energy is even more potent in their meat. The grandeur of game is that those animals have not eaten of tame earth but of the wildest parts of nature. Hence, to eat game is to take on the wild spirit of forests and mountains, and so it was the chosen food of many warrior castes. They felt that there was no greater force to harness for battle than that pure distillation of wild earth that came from eating the flesh of game.

OFFAL

Offal is well loved by Indians because they are hard-working, interesting organs full of flavour and texture. It is the texture that is all important. We add offal to add chew. We don't believe in cooking huge slabs of liver just to pink. No, with all our offal we chop it finely and treat it like red meat, cooking it very well. The resulting toughness is something we embrace.

Offal is cooked like all meat with an onion-ginger-garlic start, but I urge you to chop your onions into fine slices with offal. This produces soft, sweet, caramelised ribbons that weave around the diced bites of offal. The role of finely chopped onions is to thicken the sauce. Sliced onions have a different charm and one that alerts the diner to the fact that a dish is a chewier one.

The key to cooking red meat dishes is a long, long simmer. In days of old this would be on the embers of the fire or stove. The fierce early flames were used to pop the seed spices for vegetable dishes. The long burn was for the evening stewing of meat on the bone, in strong, permeating spices. This slow cooking also helps soften those tougher meats, and for this reason, too, tomatoes are often used as a finishing flavour, as the acidity they provide helps tenderise the flesh.

The beginnings of every red meat dish is the trinity of onion, ginger and garlic. This is the meat mantra one must simply learn and apply every time. These ingredients not only add a huge foundation of sweet, sharp flavour, their high acid content helps tenderise terse red meat. The intense heat of the East does not allow meat to be hung and naturally tenderise before cooking. This is one reason why minced meat is so popular in India, since the process of mincing the meat breaks down the tough fibres. These strong flavours also serve to neutralise any overly animal scent from the flesh, and for the same reason, highly aromatic, perfumed, woody spices full of bullish aromatic oils, are often paired with meats.

The general rule of curry making is 'seed spices in vegetable dishes and ground spices with meat'. Powdered spices (rather than whole) are most often used with meats, as their fine form can infiltrate the tight fibres of red meat more easily. Then their perfumed aromatic oils within can start the process of bullying flavour right the way through the tough grain.

Garam masala is the ground form of a personalised nosegay of family favourite aromatics. If frying onion, ginger and garlic are the foundations of a good meat curry, so garam masala is the cornerstone spice. It is THE meat headnote spice and, frankly, just using garam masala, chilli and turmeric will always get you to a perfectly great home-style red meat curry.

However, within garam masala are the whole range of ground aromatic spices. You can elevate any of them to tailor your dish. So, for instance, if you are a cinnamon fan, use a garam masala base and throw in an extra spoon of cinnamon powder. If you want more of a curry punch to your spice mix, then usually adding cumin powder achieves that. For something more herby and gentle, increase the coriander powder. This simple trial and error method is how Indians make curries 'their own' across India.

If you look at meat recipes in curry cookbooks you will often see a bewildering list of spices required. Now, look again and instead of the list of perfumed woody ingredients read the words 'heaps of garam masala', and then use your own taste to raise the flavours you want to bring out by adding a little more of what you fancy.

Prep Time: 15 mins
Cook Time: 1¾ hours
Serves: 4–6

Vegetable oil, 4½ tbsp
Mustard seeds, 1 tsp
3 fresh curry leaves
2 large white onions, medium diced
5 cm piece of fresh ginger, 20 g, peeled and grated
7 garlic cloves, peeled and grated
2 large green chillies, deseeded and thinly sliced
Garam masala, 2 tbsp
    Plus 1½ tsp more cumin powder and 1¼ tsp coriander powder
Ground turmeric, ½ tsp
Chilli powder, ½ tsp
Ground almonds, 5 tbsp
Diced lamb leg, 750 g
Coconut milk, 200 ml
Natural yoghurt, 300 g
Water, 200 ml
Salt, 1½ tsp
Sugar, 1 tsp
Obligatory backup jug of water, to loosen the dish to your taste

Lamb with yoghurt and almonds

This has all the hallmarks of a royal Mughal dish, emanating deliciously from Lucknow, my father's home town. Even now, Lucknow is the place to go to experience luxurious and complex meat dishes. I use yoghurt because I like the touch of sharpness – or go for something rich and creamy; crème fraîche will work a treat.

Put the vegetable oil in a large heavy-based pan and set over a medium-high heat. When hot, add the mustard seeds and fry until they fizz, pop and then turn grey. Add the curry leaves, onions, ginger, garlic and green chillies and fry for 8 minutes or until the onions have softened and turned golden brown.

Add the garam masala, cumin powder, coriander powder, ground turmeric, chilli powder, ground almonds and the diced lamb and fry until the meat starts to colour, stirring well so that it is mixed fully with the spices.

Add the coconut milk, yoghurt, water, salt and sugar and bring up to the boil, then reduce the heat to low, cover and simmer gently for 1¼–1½ hours or until the lamb is cooked through and tender. Add more water if necessary to loosen to your taste before serving.

Spiced ginger lamb *raan*

This dish was born when, come one stale month of January, I blitzed up my daughters' gingerbread Christmas house with my *raan* mixture of onions, ginger, garlic and garam masala. It could have been destined for the bin but, instead, it was the birth of something beautiful and this is now a regular party mainstay for me. I roast the lamb long and low and it, essentially, pulls into ribbons of sweet, biscuity ooze. *Raan* is the basic technique for slow-roasting large joints of red meat in Indian cooking with blitzed spices, onions, ginger and garlic that tenderise and infuse. You can cook this straight away, but it gets even better if you have the patience to leave the leg to marinate in the gingerbread baste. A tale tells of this dish being the centrepiece of a banquet for Alexander the Great. Works a treat in Birkenhead, too.

Prep Time: 10 mins
Cook Time: 2½–3 hours
Serves: 4–6

4 white onions, peeled
10 cm piece of fresh ginger, 40 g, peeled
8 garlic cloves, peeled
Garam masala, 2 tbsp
   Plus 1½ tbsp more
   cinnamon powder
Nutmeg powder, 1 tsp
Ginger nut biscuits, 450 g
Salt, 1 tbsp
Vegetable oil, 90 ml
2 kg leg of lamb
Water, 250 ml

Preheat the oven to 150°C/300°F. In a food processor, blend together the onions, ginger, garlic, garam masala, cinnamon powder, nutmeg powder, ginger nuts, salt and vegetable oil until it forms a smooth paste.

With a sharp knife, carefully make many deep gashes into the thickest parts of the lamb leg. Pour over the ginger nut paste and rub in a good deep, slathering layer.

Place in a roasting tray, add the water and cover loosely with tin foil, then roast for 2½–3 hours or until the lamb is tender and falling off the bone.

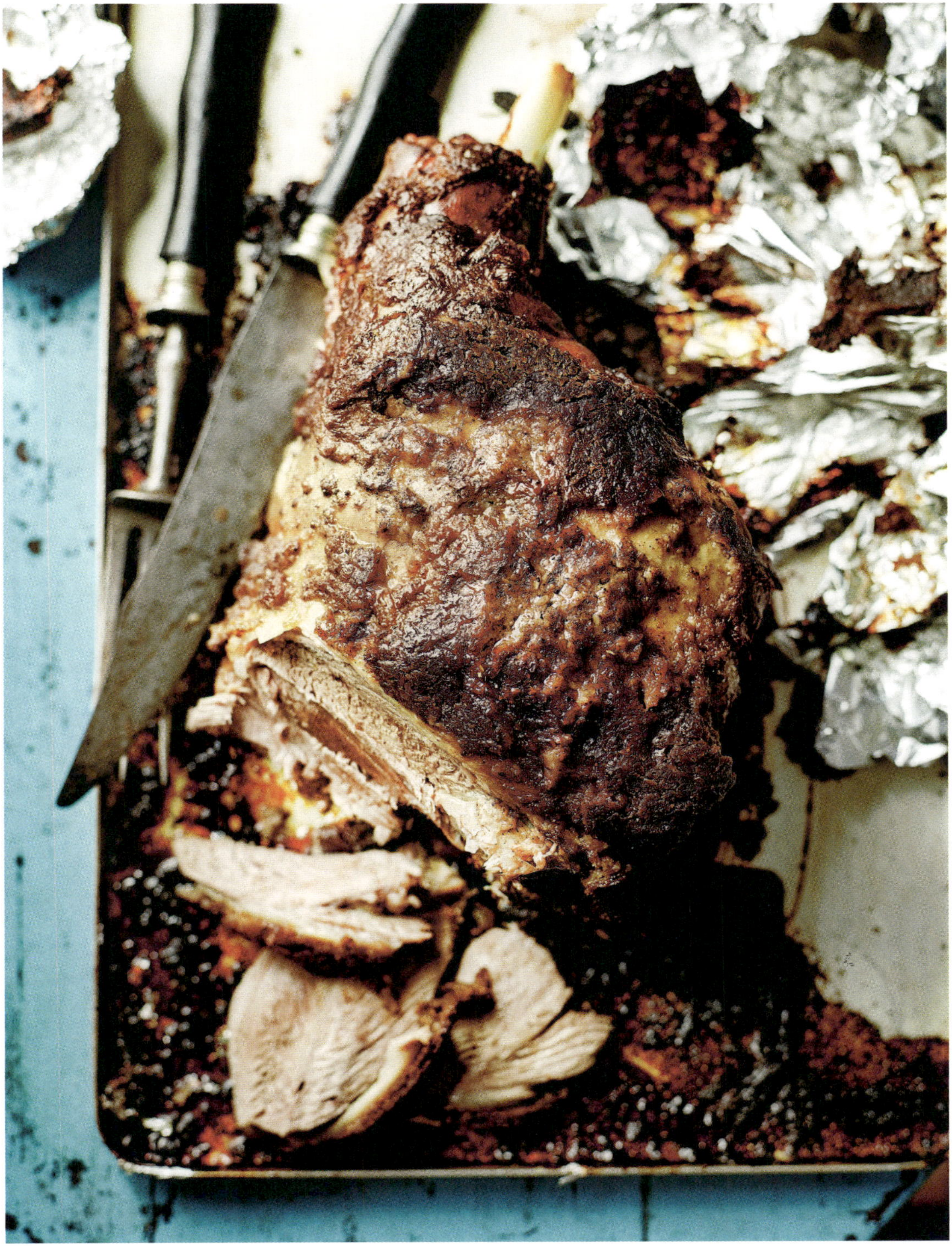

Railway goat curry

If you are offered red meat curry in India, rest assured it will be goat. The woolly lambs of snowy England do not exist in the heat of the East. Rich and gamey, goat is the most common red meat, not an edgy foodie fad. Sometimes served in railway tiffin boxes, these dishes are often the humblest, lowest denominators of Indian cuisine. The blazing flavours in this time-tested standard betray the truth: that simple need not be simpering.

Prep Time: 10 mins
Cook Time: 2¼ hours
Serves: 4–6

Vegetable oil, 80 ml
2 large white onions, medium diced
5 cm piece of fresh ginger, 20 g, peeled and grated
5 garlic cloves, peeled and grated
Garam masala, 2 tbsp
Plus 1 tbsp more cumin powder
Ground turmeric, ½ tsp
Chilli powder, ½ tsp
Diced mutton, 750 g
2 medium potatoes, quartered
Tinned chopped tomatoes, 400 g
Water, 350 ml
Salt, 2 tsp
Sugar, 1 tsp
Obligatory backup jug of water, to loosen the dish to your taste

Put the vegetable oil in a large heavy-based saucepan and set over a medium-high heat. When hot, add the diced onions, ginger and garlic and cook for 8 minutes until the onions have softened and turned golden brown.

Stir in the garam masala, cumin powder, ground turmeric and chilli powder and fry for 30 seconds. Add the diced mutton and fry until it starts to turn brown, stirring well so that it is fully coated with the spices.

Add the quartered potatoes, chopped tomatoes, water, salt and sugar and bring up to the boil, then reduce the heat to low, partially cover and simmer gently for 1½–2 hours or until the mutton is tender and giving. Add more water, if necessary, to loosen to your taste before serving.

Masala lamb chops

Lamb works just brilliantly with garlic and spices, combining so well that their alchemy is beyond the skill of the chef. The best we can do is give them time to marinate. This is a killer barbecue dish. Serve them pink if you dare, but Indians, I have to confess, cook them to a bracing blackened crisp.

Prep Time: 10 mins
Cook Time: 10 mins
Serves: 4

Natural yoghurt, 500 g
Tomato purée, 2 tbsp
Cumin powder, 2 tbsp
Chilli powder, ½ tsp
Juice of 1 lemon
4 garlic cloves, peeled and minced
10 cm piece of fresh ginger, 40 g, peeled and finely grated
Garam masala, 3 tbsp
Salt, 2 tsp
Ground turmeric, 1 tsp
8 lamb chops, each 2.5 cm thick

In a bowl large enough to hold the lamb chops, mix the yoghurt, tomato purée, cumin powder, chilli powder, lemon juice, garlic, ginger, garam masala, salt and ground turmeric, then add the lamb chops and massage the marinade into them, making sure they are fully covered. Cover and leave to marinate in the fridge overnight.

Preheat the grill to its highest setting. Put the chops on a baking tray and grill for 3–4 minutes on each side for a medium-rare chop.

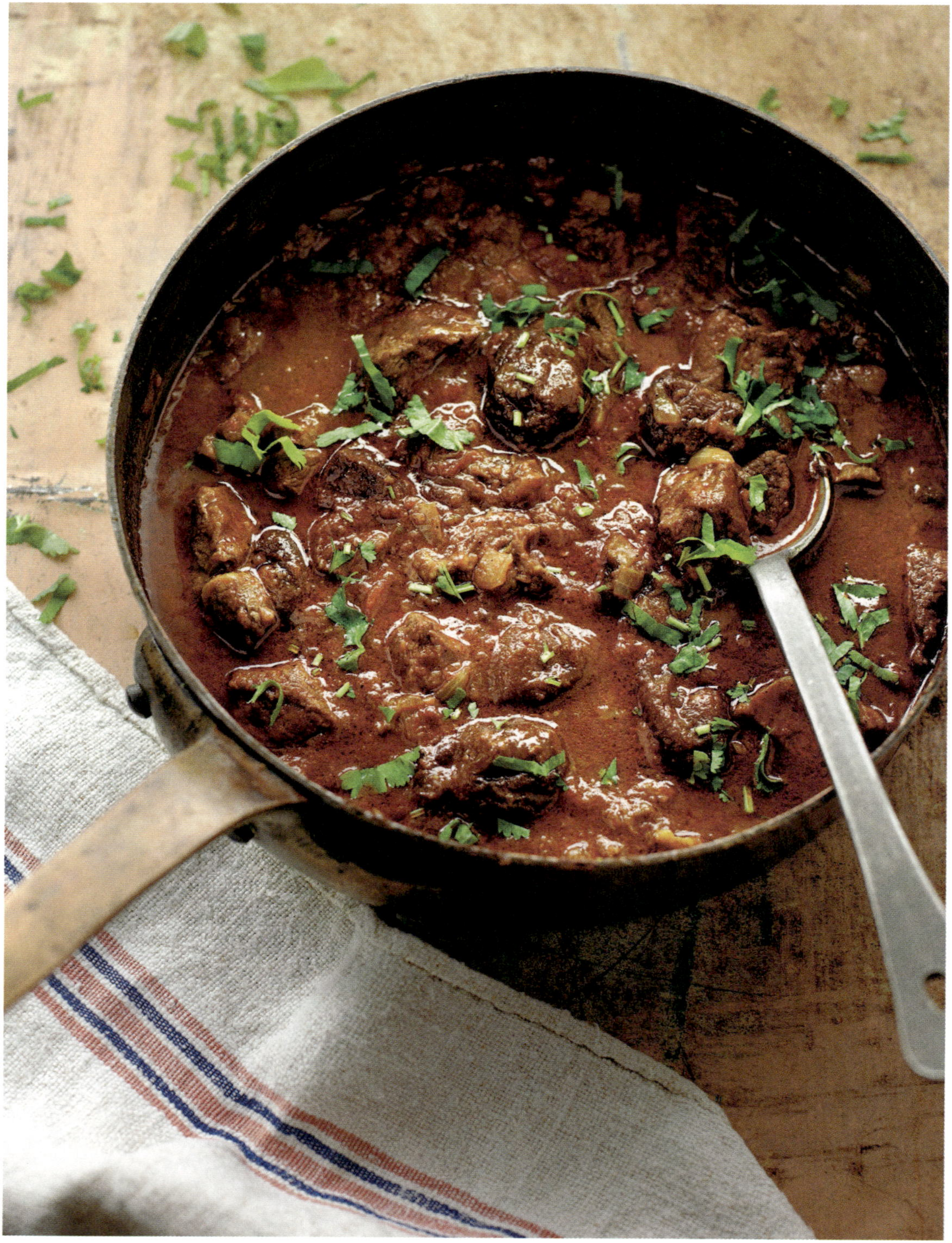

Lamb plum anise curry

I have so many fond memories of watching my father make this dish. Staring longingly into the pan during the long simmer, I would haunt him, 'Mon, is it ready yet? Is it ready yet?' 'Not until the fat sits on the top like a golden mirror,' he would say.

Prep Time: 10 mins
Cook Time: 2¼ hours
Serves: 4–6

Vegetable oil, 4½ tbsp
2 large white onions, medium diced
5 cm piece of fresh ginger, 20 g, peeled and grated
6 garlic cloves, peeled and minced
Garam masala, 2 tbsp Plus 1½ tbsp more cumin powder and 1 tsp more anise powder
Ground turmeric, ½ tsp
Chilli powder, ½ tsp
Diced lamb shoulder, 750 g
Tinned chopped tomatoes, 400 g
Water, 350 ml
Dried plums/prunes or tinned plums, 250 g
Salt, 1 tsp
Sugar, 1 tsp
Obligatory backup jug of water, to loosen the dish to your taste

Put the vegetable oil in a large heavy-based saucepan and set over a medium-high heat. When hot, add the onions, ginger and garlic and fry for 8 minutes until the onions have softened and turned golden brown.

Stir in the garam masala, cumin powder, anise powder, ground turmeric and chilli powder and fry for 30 seconds, then add the diced lamb and fry until it starts to brown, stirring well so it is fully coated with the spices.

Add the chopped tomatoes, water, plums, salt and sugar and bring up to the boil, then partially cover, reduce the heat to low and simmer gently for 1¾–2 hours or until the lamb is tender. Add more water if necessary to loosen to your taste before serving.

Sweet tamarind duck

With the advent of the shooting season, trigger-happy friends bring me their glut of ducks. Tamarind has a fruity sharpness that works so well with dark game meats. Make sure you balance the sweet with plenty of dark sugar or, better still, try a slick of date molasses.

Prep Time: 10 mins
Cook Time: 1 hour 5 mins
Serves: 4

Vegetable oil, 7 tbsp
2 large white onions, cut in half then thinly sliced
5 cm piece of fresh ginger, 20 g, peeled and grated
4 garlic cloves, peeled and grated
2 kg whole duck, cut into 8 joints
Garam masala, 2 tbsp
 Plus 1 tsp more cumin powder
Ground turmeric, ½ tsp
Chilli powder, ½ tsp
Tamarind paste, 1 tbsp
Date molasses, 2 tbsp
Salt, 1 tsp
Water, 350 ml
Mustard seeds, 1 tbsp
Obligatory backup jug of water, to loosen the dish to your taste

Put 5 tablespoons of the vegetable oil in a large heavy-based pan and set over a medium-high heat. When hot, add the onions, ginger and garlic and fry for 8 minutes until the onions have softened and turned golden brown.

Add the duck joints, garam masala, cumin powder, ground turmeric and chilli powder and fry for 5 minutes until the duck has coloured, then add the tamarind paste, date molasses, salt and water and stir everything together. Turn the heat down to low, partially cover with a lid and simmer gently for 45–50 minutes or until the duck is cooked through and tender.

In a separate, small frying pan set over a high heat, add the remaining 2 tablespoons of vegetable oil and when hot, fry the mustard seeds for 30 seconds. Finish by pouring the tempered mustard seeds into the duck pan and mixing well. Add more water if necessary to loosen to your taste.

Buffalo with ginger and nutmeg

Buffalo is known in Bengali as *boror mangsho*, which basically translates as the meat of the 'big animal'. Of course, you can use beef instead – the tougher the cut, the better. I don't have any beef recipes in this book, as it was forbidden by my Hindu Brahmin ancestors. Unusually, though, buffalo is permitted to both Hindus and Muslims. Use the basic meat formula; simmer long and low, and pile up the fresh ginger to cut through the permissive richness.

Prep Time: 15 mins
Cook Time: 1¼ hours
Serves: 4–6

Vegetable oil, 4½ tbsp
2 large white onions, medium diced
5 cm piece of fresh ginger, 20 g, peeled and grated
6 garlic cloves, peeled and minced
Garam masala, 2 tbsp
   Plus 1½ tbsp cumin powder and 1½ tsp more nutmeg powder
Ground turmeric, ½ tsp
Chilli powder, ½ tsp
Diced buffalo, 750 g
Tinned chopped tomatoes, 400 g
Water, 350 ml
Salt, 2 tsp
Sugar, 1 tsp
Obligatory backup jug of water, to loosen the dish to your taste

Put the vegetable oil in a large heavy-based pan and set over a medium-high heat. When hot, add the diced onions, ginger and garlic and cook for 8 minutes until the onions have softened and turned golden brown.

Stir in the garam masala, cumin powder, nutmeg powder, ground turmeric and chilli powder and fry for 30 seconds. Add the diced buffalo and fry until it starts to colour, stirring well so that it is fully coated with the spices.

Add the chopped tomatoes, water, salt and sugar and bring up to the boil, then reduce the heat to low and simmer gently, partially covered, for 45–60 minutes until the buffalo is tender. Add more water if necessary to loosen to your taste before serving.

Mutton *keema* with pine nuts

Keema simply means minced meat. In the heat of the East, where meat cannot naturally hang to tenderise, mechanical mincing is the most popular and sensible way to deal with tougher cuts. My mother's trick was to use this keema as a toasted sandwich filling for a quick samosa fix. Genius.

Prep Time: 10 mins
Cook Time: 2¼ hours
Serves: 4–6

Vegetable oil, 4½ tbsp
2 large white onions, medium diced
5 cm piece of fresh ginger, 20 g, peeled and grated
5 garlic cloves, peeled and minced
Garam masala, 2 tbsp
    Plus 1 tbsp more cumin powder
Ground turmeric, ½ tsp
Chilli powder, ½ tsp
Pine nuts, 3 tbsp
Diced mutton, 1 kg
Tinned chopped tomatoes, 400 g
Water, 350 ml
Salt, 2 tsp
Sugar, 1 tsp
Obligatory backup jug of water, to loosen the dish to your taste

Put the vegetable oil in a large heavy-based saucepan and set over a medium-high heat. When hot, add the diced onions, ginger and garlic and fry for 8 minutes until the onions have softened and turned golden brown.

Stir in the garam masala, cumin powder, ground turmeric, chilli powder and pine nuts and fry for around 30 seconds. Add the diced mutton and stir until it starts to turn brown, mixing well so that it is fully coated with the spices.

Add the chopped tomatoes, water, salt and sugar and bring up to the boil, then partially cover, reduce the heat to low and simmer gently for 1½–2 hours or until the mutton is tender and the sauce is thick and rich. Add more water if necessary to loosen to your taste.

Pheasant with cinnamon and apricots

Fruit tends not to feature often in meat dishes, but game seems to sit in a more liberal corner of the Indian kitchen and so here its earthy flavours pair well with sweet apricots. From the wild it came, with the windfall it may pass.

Prep Time: 15 mins
Cook Time: 1 hour
Serves: 4

Vegetable oil, 7 tbsp
2 pheasants, cut into 8 joints each, bone in
2 white onions, finely diced
5 cm piece of fresh ginger, 20 g, peeled and grated
4 garlic cloves, peeled and minced
Ground turmeric, ¼ tsp
Chilli powder, ½ tsp
Garam masala, 2 tbsp
  Plus 1 tsp cinnamon powder
Water, 400 ml
Dried apricots, 100 g, soaked in warm water for 1 hour, then drained
Salt, 1 tsp
Obligatory backup jug of water, to loosen the dish to your taste

In a large non-stick frying pan set over a medium-high heat, add 3½ tablespoons of the vegetable oil and, when hot, add the pheasant joints in batches, frying until golden brown and then setting aside.

Put the remaining 3½ tablespoons of vegetable oil in a large heavy-based pan and set over a medium-high heat. When hot, add the onions, ginger and garlic and cook for 8 minutes until the onions have softened and turned golden brown.

Add the ground turmeric, chilli powder, garam masala and cinnamon powder and fry for 2 minutes. Add the water, soaked apricots, browned pheasant joints and salt and mix everything together.

Reduce the heat to low, partially cover and simmer gently for 35 minutes or until the pheasant is cooked through and tender. Add more water if necessary to loosen to your taste.

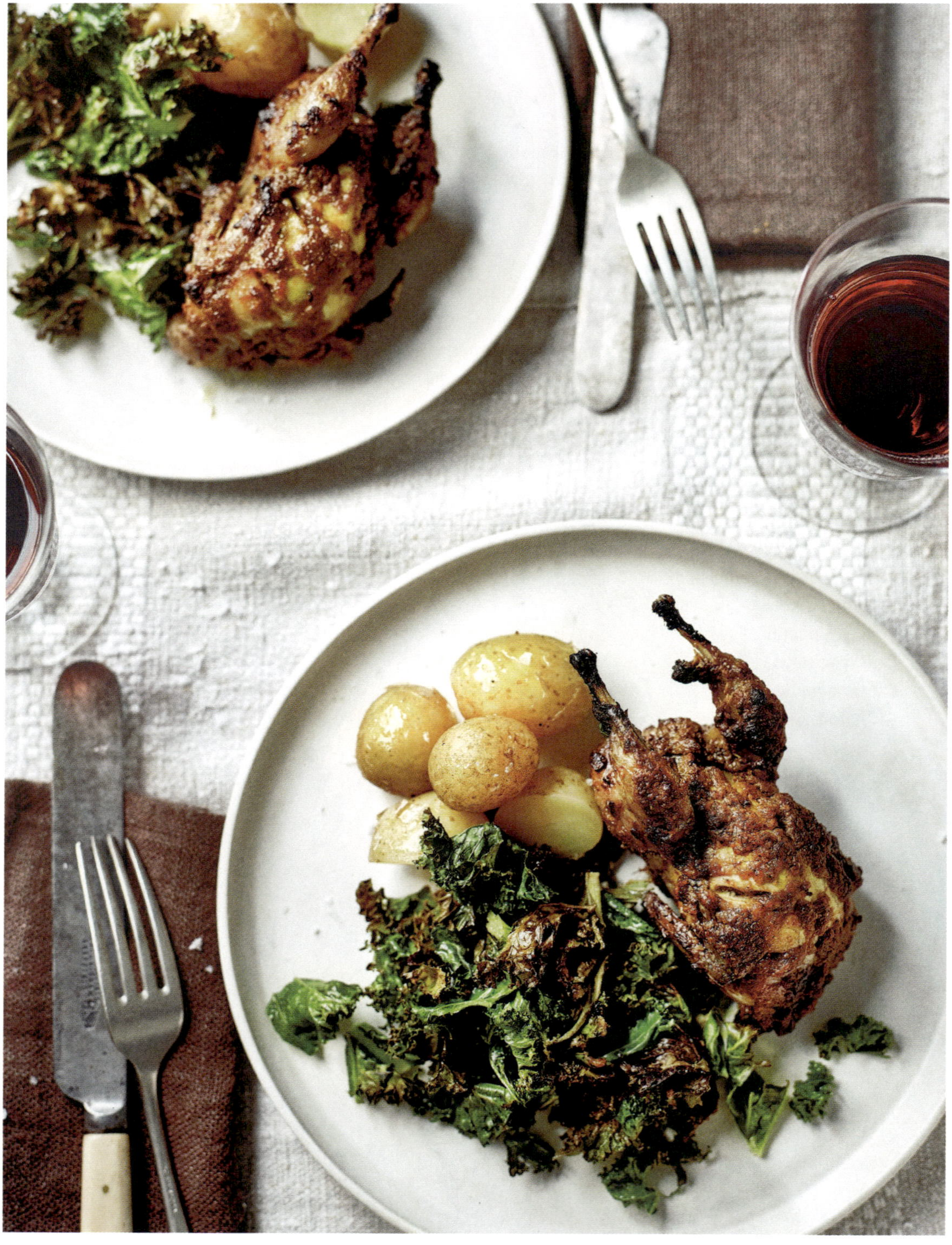

Masala roasted quail with kale

Quail are so loved in India that they are now rarely seen – they run wild and are hunted voraciously. To dine on them is to imbibe the energy of the wild: such was the belief of the ancient Indian warriors. Roasting meat over open fires in villages is rare as meat is usually preferred safely stewed in a bracing pot of curry. Small quail, however, are rubbed with spiced oil and 'fired' to an aromatic crisp, and these quail are baked on a bed of zinging kale. There are few ingredients that cook at the fast pace of these tiny delicacies, so baste aplenty. The dark luxury of the leaves sets off beautifully the sweet heat of the spiced birds.

Prep Time: 10 mins
Cook Time: 30 mins
Serves: 2

Vegetable oil, 5 tbsp
4 garlic cloves, peeled
5 cm piece of fresh ginger, 20 g, peeled
Garam masala, 1½ tbsp
Soft brown sugar, 2 tbsp
Salt, 1 tsp
Kale, 250 g, leaves washed and chopped
English mustard paste, 1 heaped tbsp, loosened with juice of ½ lemon
2 oven-ready quail, strings removed
Water, 200 ml

Preheat the oven to 200°C/400°F. In a food processor, blend 2½ tablespoons of the vegetable oil with the garlic, ginger, garam masala, brown sugar and salt to a smooth paste.

Mix the kale with the mustard paste and the remaining 2½ tablespoons of the vegetable oil and place in a shallow roasting tray.

With a sharp knife, carefully make a deep incision into each quail breast, then rub the paste into the incisions and over the quail and place them on top of the kale. Add the water into the bottom of the roasting tray.

Roast the quail for 25–30 minutes or until coloured nicely and cooked through.

Oxtail curry

This is the ultimate comfort curry. Oxtail is the most unctuous cut of meat there is in my view, and it is the slow, low simmer that brings out the very best of the flavour from the bones and the hard-working muscle. Because it's a long simmer, oxtail is always cooked on a tomato base; the acids in the sauce do much of the work of tenderisation.

Prep Time: 15 mins
Cook Time: 4¼ hours
Serves: 4–6

Vegetable oil, 4½ tbsp
2 large white onions, medium diced
5 cm piece of fresh ginger, 20 g, peeled and grated
5 garlic cloves, peeled and grated
Garam masala, 2 tbsp
  Plus 1½ tsp more
cinnamon powder
Ground turmeric, ½ tsp
Chilli powder, ½ tsp
Oxtail, 1 kg, chopped into large chunks (ask your butcher to do this)
2 medium potatoes, quartered
Tinned chopped tomatoes, 400 g
Water, 350 ml
Salt, 2 tsp
Soft brown sugar, 2 tbsp
Obligatory backup jug of water, to loosen the dish
1 handful of coriander leaves, chopped

Put the vegetable oil in a large heavy-based pan and set over a medium-high heat. When hot, add the diced onions, ginger and garlic and cook for 8 minutes until the onions have softened and turned golden brown.

Stir in the garam masala, cinnamon powder, ground turmeric and chilli powder and fry for 30 seconds. Add the oxtail and fry until it starts to turn brown, stirring well so that it is fully coated with the spices.

Add the quartered potatoes, chopped tomatoes, water, salt and brown sugar and bring up to the boil, then reduce the heat to low, partially cover, and simmer gently for 3½–4 hours until the oxtail is tender and falling off the bone. Add more water, if necessary, to loosen to your taste before serving.

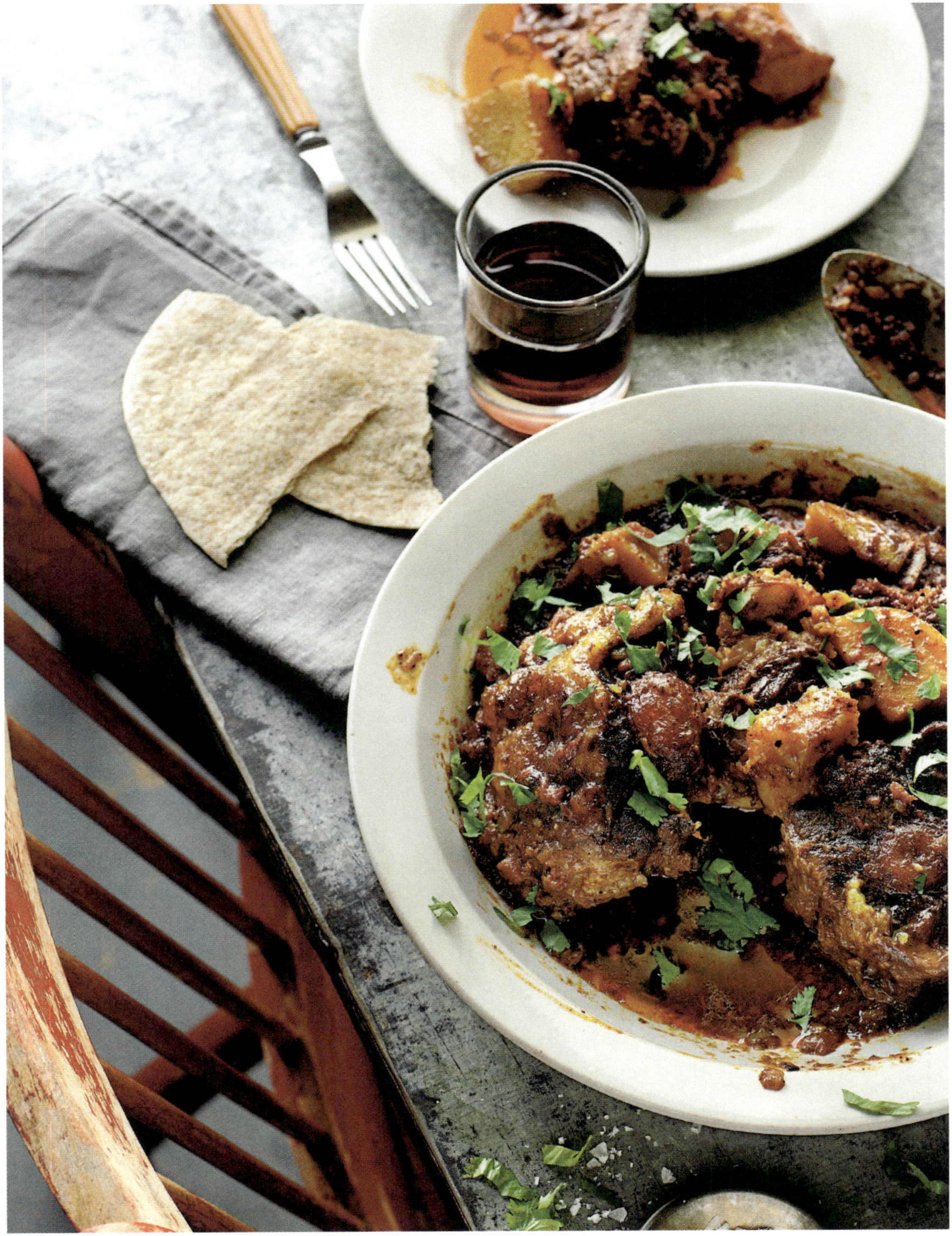

Guinea fowl with raisins, cumin and green chilli

Raisin curry is beloved festival food in south India. Raisin curry is essentially a vegetable curry with meat added in as an adulterant. And being from the south, we, of course, use the headnotes of curry leaf and mustard seed. In this dish, the Gujrati influence dictates we use cumin seed, too. Remember, where we use mustard seed, we also use dried red chilli; where there is cumin seed, there is fresh green chilli. This is a fascinating method: it's a meat curry, cooked only with the fresh headnote spices of the vegetable kitchen.

Prep Time: 10 mins
Cook Time: 50 mins
Serves: 4

Vegetable oil, 5½ tbsp
1 guinea fowl, cut into 8 joints
Raisins, 60 g, soaked in warm water for 1 hour, drained
Mustard seeds, 1 tsp
Cumin seeds, 1 tsp
3 large fresh curry leaves
1 large dried red chilli
1 large green chilli, deseeded and thinly sliced
Chilli powder, ¼ tsp
Ground turmeric, ¼ tsp
Water, 350 ml
Juice of ½ lemon
Salt, 1 tsp
Obligatory backup jug of water, to loosen the dish to your taste

Put 2½ tablespoons of the vegetable oil in a large heavy-based pan and set over a medium-high heat. When hot, add the guinea fowl joints and fry until they turn golden brown, then set aside.

Mash the soaked raisins with a fork. Put the remaining 3 tablespoons of vegetable oil in a large non-stick frying pan and set over a medium-high heat. When hot, add the mustard and cumin seeds and fry until the mustard seeds fizz, pop and turn grey and the cumin seeds turn a dark brown, then add the curry leaves, dried red chilli, green chilli, mashed raisins, chilli powder, ground turmeric, water, lemon juice, salt and the browned guinea fowl joints.

Turn the heat down to low and partially cover the pan. Simmer gently for 30–35 minutes until the guinea fowl is tender and giving. Add more water if necessary to loosen to your taste.

Indian liver and onions

Unlike our modern British tastes for eating pink flesh, in India, liver is enjoyed very well cooked and quite heavily spiced. The concept of pink meat has not managed to stick in a nation where health requires meat to be practically cremated. My paternal grandmother used to fool me into eating liver by calling it 'cheese meat' and I found it charming once my mouth was looking for the texture and flavour of strong cheese. Onions seem to be the universal pairing to the Cheddar-like intensity of cooked liver.

Prep Time: 10 mins
Cook Time: 25 mins
Serves: 4

Vegetable oil, 4½ tbsp
2 large white onions, cut in half then thinly sliced
5 cm piece of fresh ginger, 20 g, peeled and grated
3 garlic cloves, peeled and grated
Garam masala, 1½ tbsp Plus ½ tsp more cumin powder and ½ tsp more black pepper
Chicken livers, 600 g, cut into large chunks
Ground turmeric, ½ tsp
Chilli powder, ½ tsp
Double cream, 200 ml
Water, 200 ml
Obligatory backup jug of water, to loosen the dish to your taste

Put the vegetable oil in a large non-stick frying pan over a medium-high heat. When hot, add the onions, ginger and garlic and fry for 8 minutes until the onions are a golden tangle. Add the garam masala, cumin powder, black pepper and chicken livers and fry for 4 minutes until the livers have changed colour.

Add the ground turmeric, chilli powder, double cream and water and bring up to the boil. Turn the heat down to low, cover and simmer gently for 10 minutes or until the chicken livers are cooked through. Add more water if necessary to loosen to your taste.

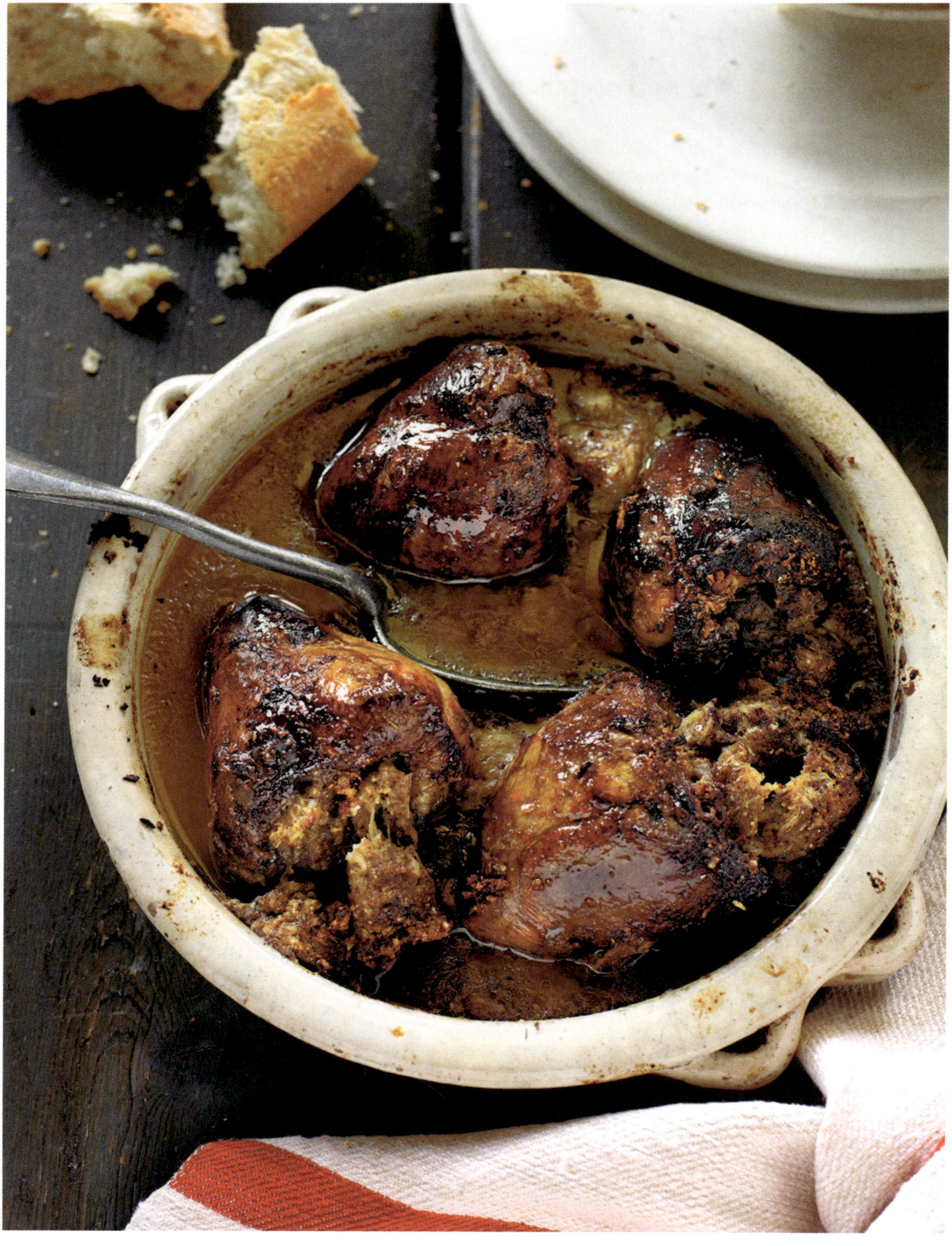

Spiced stuffed lamb's hearts

My Liverpool friends tell me mouthwatering tales of their 'Nanna's heart' – stuffed lamb's hearts were a favourite in many a Scouse grandmother's kitchen, alongside Scouse stew and dishing out life advice. I once made these for Bobsey, my Everton sister from another mother, and they filled her with nostalgia. I make them whenever I can get hearts. Asian butchers have racks and racks of them, which is a testimony to how well loved this dish is in the Indian kitchen.

Prep Time: 20 mins
Cook Time: 1 hour 10 mins
Serves: 4

Vegetable oil, 4 tbsp
4 lamb's hearts, trimmed of any fat, gristle and tubes removed
Soft brown sugar, 2 tbsp
1 large white onion, 100 g, peeled
4 garlic cloves, peeled
2–3 cm piece of fresh ginger, peeled
100 g raisins
3 pieces of stale white bread
Garam masala, 2 tbsp
  Plus 1½ tsp more cumin powder
Water, 250 ml

Preheat the oven to fan 160°C/180°C/350°F. Put the vegetable oil in a large non-stick frying pan and set over a medium heat. When hot, add the lamb's hearts and brown sugar and fry on all sides until the hearts are golden brown, basting carefully with the sauce in the pan, then remove from the heat and set aside to cool.

In a food processor, blend the onion, garlic, ginger, raisins, bread, garam masala and cumin powder together until it forms a rough stuffing-like mix.

When the lamb's hearts are cool, take them and fill the cavities with the stuffing, then place in an ovenproof roasting dish just big enough to hold them. Add the water to the bottom of the dish, cover with tin foil and roast for 50–60 minutes or until the hearts are tender and have a crunchy brown outside.

Allow to cool slightly for 5 minutes before serving.

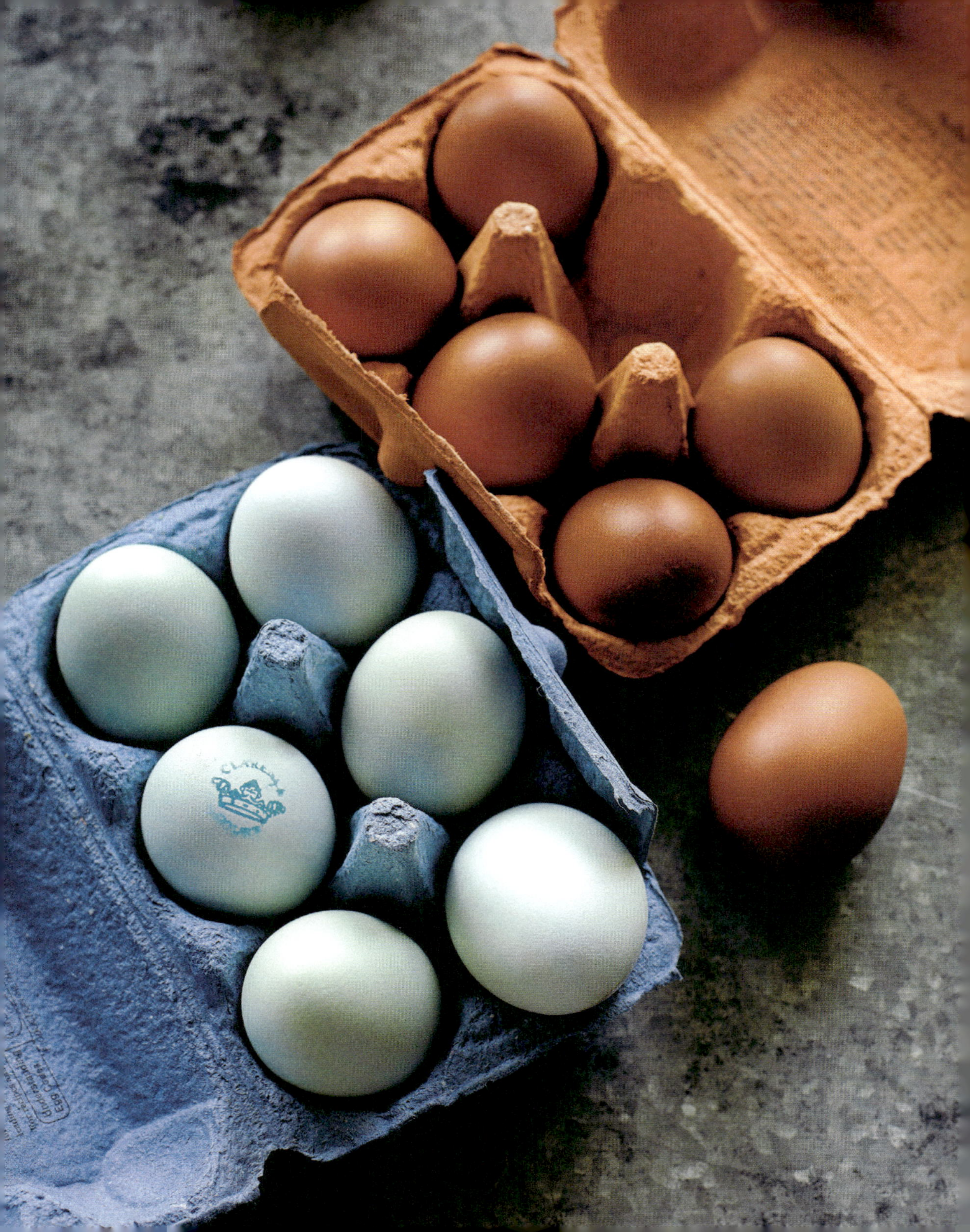

The Chicken and the Egg

Chicken is the entry level white meat in India. And when I say chicken, I mean chicken on the bone. The way it works in India is one goes to the market. One selects a live chicken. It is slaughtered then and there in front of you, and the carcass is carved in a certain way. It is 'cut for curry', which means that every piece of meat will combine both meat and bone. Boneless meat, for the majority of the world's population outside of the West, is for the toothless and the infirm. Bone-in meat curries in the East are eaten with the hand. Each mouthful is pressed and formed with spice-seeking fingers.

Shopping for chicken may sound like a traumatic experience and believe me it is. In India, I become completely vegetarian. The chickens are almost pigeon-like in size. We may baulk, but the truth is they are wiry because they are busy, free-range birds, who have been busy accumulating flavour miles through their un-GM, antibiotic- and hormone-free lives. Out of respect for the life they gave, Indians cherish every part of the bird. The gizzards, the liver, the hearts; the bits we bin in the West are the bits we fight over at the dining table.

And now to the egg. Unlike their meat-eating Muslim counterparts, Hindus in India are actually strictly primarily vegetarian, if not vegan. I come from a lineage of Hindu Brahmin priests and to such strict Hindus, even eggs are considered to be 'meat'. And because of this, they are cooked according to meat principles on an onion-ginger-garlic basis. But like the heavy pulses, the pan is started with a fried headnote seed spice, as a nod to the fact that eggs are really at heart, vegetarian.

The strength of feeling goes further: for Brahmin Hindus, hens' eggs are considered to be unclean and they would always prefer to buy ducks' eggs. My mother has memories of being hurried past hens' eggs with a tut of disdain.

Every home has its own way of cooking their chicken curry, but all chicken dishes work in accordance with the general meat formula. The names of the dishes that are given by British curry houses do not exist in India (see page 38). In an Indian home, a chicken dish will start with the general spice formula for meat: onion, ginger, garlic and garam masala, and from there the chef will make it their own.

After your meat mantra of onion, ginger and garlic have been fried to a caramelised brown, a good next move would be to add in a strong amount of garam masala as your meat headnote spice – and then the rest of the trinity of spices: turmeric and chilli. Now, think long and hard about which garam masala spice you like the flavour of the most and add some more. Cinnamon? Nutmeg? Cloves? Conduct your garam masala orchestra by elevating the flavours you like best. Generally, Indians cook meat with tomato as a finishing flavour, as this makes for the easiest, lightest, tangiest sauce and the tomatoes' acidity helps tenderise the flesh. There are three general colours in the spectrum of chicken curries: the brown ones, the cream ones and the tikka-masala orange ones.

If you add tomato as your finishing flavour, then you will get that whole 'brown' range of curries. If you are venturing this way, know that your curry house dopiaza simply translates as 'double the onion', so make sure you start with heaps. To get a jalfrezi, add green capsicums as well as tomato. For a fiery vindaloo, add extra chilli and a splash of vinegar as the traditional Portuguese roots of this dish demand.

To add natural yoghurt, cream or coconut milk, you will be going down the korma cream-coloured route. These dishes are sweet, so make sure you season with enough sugar. This style of curry is also one of the rare examples of when it actually works to add fruit and nuts. Play around and find your tailor-made favourite. I make a banana and cashew korma that makes my mother weep with shame. I love it.

That whole range of orange-through-red tikka masala-type curries achieve that creamy texture and colour by combining tomato AND dairy. My Butter chicken on page 242 follows these rules.

So, you see, now you can create any of those curry house dishes by just knowing which finishing flavour to use. Most importantly, play around with different combinations, permutations and additions like fruit, nuts, vegetables, and make it your own. This is what Indians do. Simply stick to the permitted parameters of the garam masala spice family and the finishing flavours of tomato and/or dairy, and your experiments will then all be entirely authentic. It is in this way that each cook in each household becomes an artist and adjusts their dishes to their own tastes.

Prep Time: 10 mins
Cook Time: 55 mins
Serves: 4–6

Vegetable oil, 4½ tbsp
2 large white onions, medium diced
5 cm piece of fresh ginger, 20 g, peeled and grated
6 garlic cloves, peeled and grated
2 large green chillies, deseeded and thinly sliced
Garam masala, 2 tbsp
  Plus 1½ tsp more cumin powder and 1½ tsp more cinnamon powder
Ground turmeric, ½ tsp
Chilli powder, ¼ tsp
Diced chicken thighs, bone in, 750 g
Tinned chopped tomatoes, 400 g
Water, 350 ml
Salt, 1 tsp
Sugar, 1 tsp
Baby spinach, 200 g
1 small bunch of fresh coriander, stalks and leaves, roughly chopped
Obligatory backup jug of water, to loosen the dish to your taste

Agra ginger chicken

My parents met at Agra medical college in 1957 and this was one of the doctors' mess hall dishes that captured both of their attentions. Pouring into the canteen after long hard days, with even longer, harder evenings ahead of them, this chicken dish was all things to all students. Meat simmered on the bone in a rich, tomato-based sauce, but with the added wake up of a fragrant ginger bite. This was the irreverent, go get 'em twist of the university chefs.

Put the vegetable oil in a large heavy-based pan and set over a medium-high heat. When hot, add the diced onions, ginger, garlic and green chillies and fry for 8 minutes until the onions have softened and turned a deep golden brown.

Add the garam masala, cumin powder, cinnamon powder, ground turmeric, chilli powder and the diced chicken thighs and fry for 3–5 minutes until the chicken starts to brown, stirring well so it is coated with the spices.

Add the chopped tomatoes, water, salt and sugar and bring up to the boil, then reduce the heat to low and simmer gently for 35–40 minutes, partially covered, or until the chicken is cooked through and tender.

Finish by adding the baby spinach to the curry and when wilted, stir through the chopped coriander. Add more water if necessary to loosen to your taste before serving.

Hyderabadi coconut and almond chicken

Prep Time: 15 mins
Cook Time: 55 mins
Serves: 4–6

Vegetable oil, 4½ tbsp
Mustard seeds, 1 tsp
3 fresh curry leaves
1 dried red chilli
2 large white onions, medium diced
5 cm piece of fresh ginger, 20 g, peeled and grated
6 garlic cloves, peeled and grated
2 large green chillies, deseeded and thinly sliced
Garam masala, 2 tbsp
   Plus 1½ tsp cumin powder and 1¼ tsp coriander powder
Ground turmeric, ½ tsp
Chilli powder, ¼ tsp
Ground almonds, 4 tbsp
Diced chicken thighs, bone in, 750 g
Coconut milk, 200 ml
Natural yoghurt, 200 g
Water, 200 ml
Salt, 1 tsp
Sugar, 1 tsp
Obligatory backup jug of water, to loosen the dish to your taste

This recipe comes from my mother's private recipe notes. They are hidden in her kitchen at the back of the cracker-and-peanut-butter cupboard. She has hidden them there since she found a friend of hers fingering her hand-writtens looking for this recipe. 'A compliment, surely?' I suggested. 'Theft,' she replied. Blood, however, is thicker than water, so it's now all mine, and so all yours.

Put the vegetable oil in a large heavy-based pan and set over a medium-high heat. When hot, add the mustard seeds and fry until they fizz, pop and turn grey. Add the curry leaves, dried red chilli, onions, ginger, garlic and green chillies and fry for 8 minutes or until the onions have softened and turned golden brown.

Add the garam masala, cumin powder, coriander powder, ground turmeric, chilli powder, ground almonds and the diced chicken thighs and fry for 3–5 minutes until the chicken starts to colour, stirring well so that it is mixed with the spices.

Add the coconut milk, yoghurt, water, salt and sugar and bring up to the boil, then reduce the heat to low, cover and simmer gently for 35–40 minutes or until the chicken is cooked through and tender. Add more water if necessary to loosen to your taste before serving.

Prep Time: 10 mins
Cook Time: 55 mins
Serves: 4–6

Vegetable oil, 4½ tbsp
2 large white onions, medium diced
5 cm piece of fresh ginger, 20 g, peeled and grated
6 garlic cloves, peeled and grated
Garam masala, 2 tbsp
  Plus 1½ tsp more cumin powder, 1½ tsp more coriander powder and 1 tsp more cinnamon powder
Ground turmeric, ½ tsp
Chilli powder, ¼ tsp
Diced chicken thighs, bone in, 750 g
Tinned chopped tomatoes, 400 g
Water, 200 ml
Salt, 1 tsp
Sugar, 1 tsp
Obligatory backup jug of water, to loosen the dish to your taste

Home-style chicken

Every Indian home will have a variation of this beloved dish. It is the ultimate chicken carte blanche to play with and make your own. Fundamentals are bone-in chicken, a tomato base, and then you elevate the bits of the garam masala you fancy the most. Use this entry-level curry to develop the flavour of your own hand.

Put the vegetable oil in a large heavy-based pan and set over a medium-high heat. When hot, add the diced onions, ginger and garlic and fry for 8 minutes until the onions have softened and turned golden brown.

Add the garam masala, cumin, coriander and cinnamon powders, the ground turmeric, chilli powder and diced chicken thighs and fry for 3–5 minutes until the chicken starts to brown at the edges, stirring well so that it is coated with the spices.

Add the chopped tomatoes, water, salt and sugar and bring up to the boil, then reduce the heat to low and simmer gently for 35–40 minutes, partially covered, or until the chicken is cooked through. Add more water if necessary to loosen to your taste before serving.

Pictured overleaf

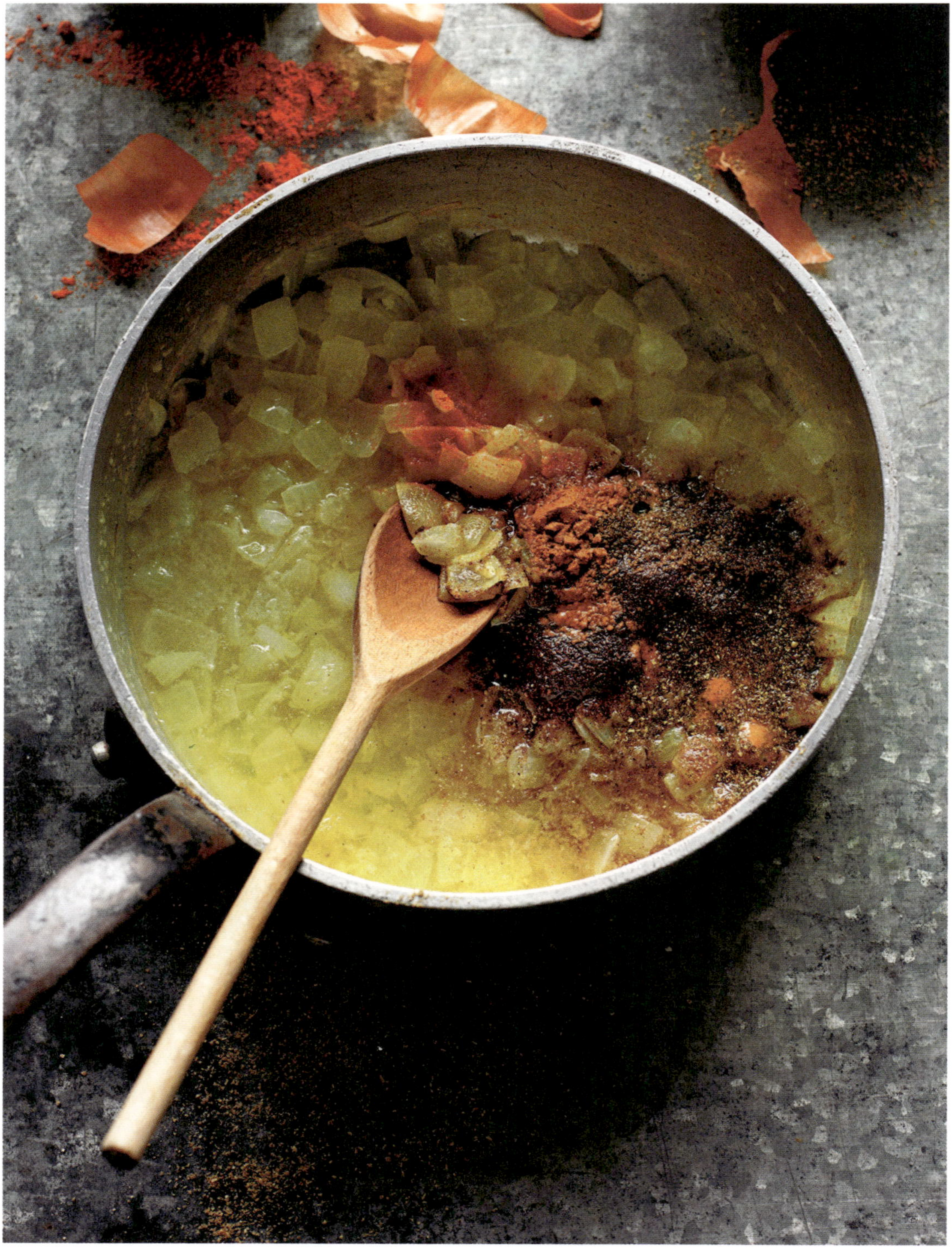

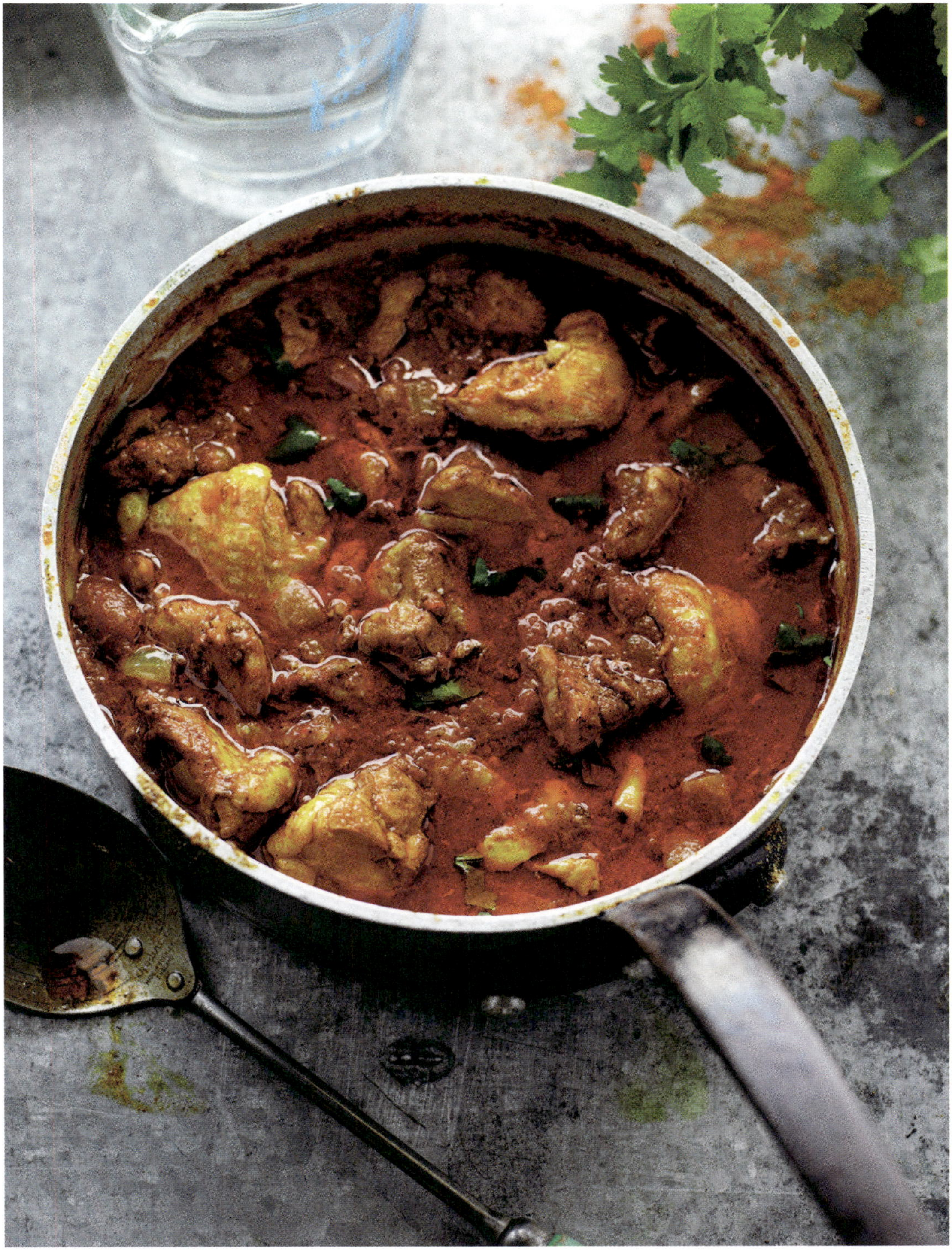

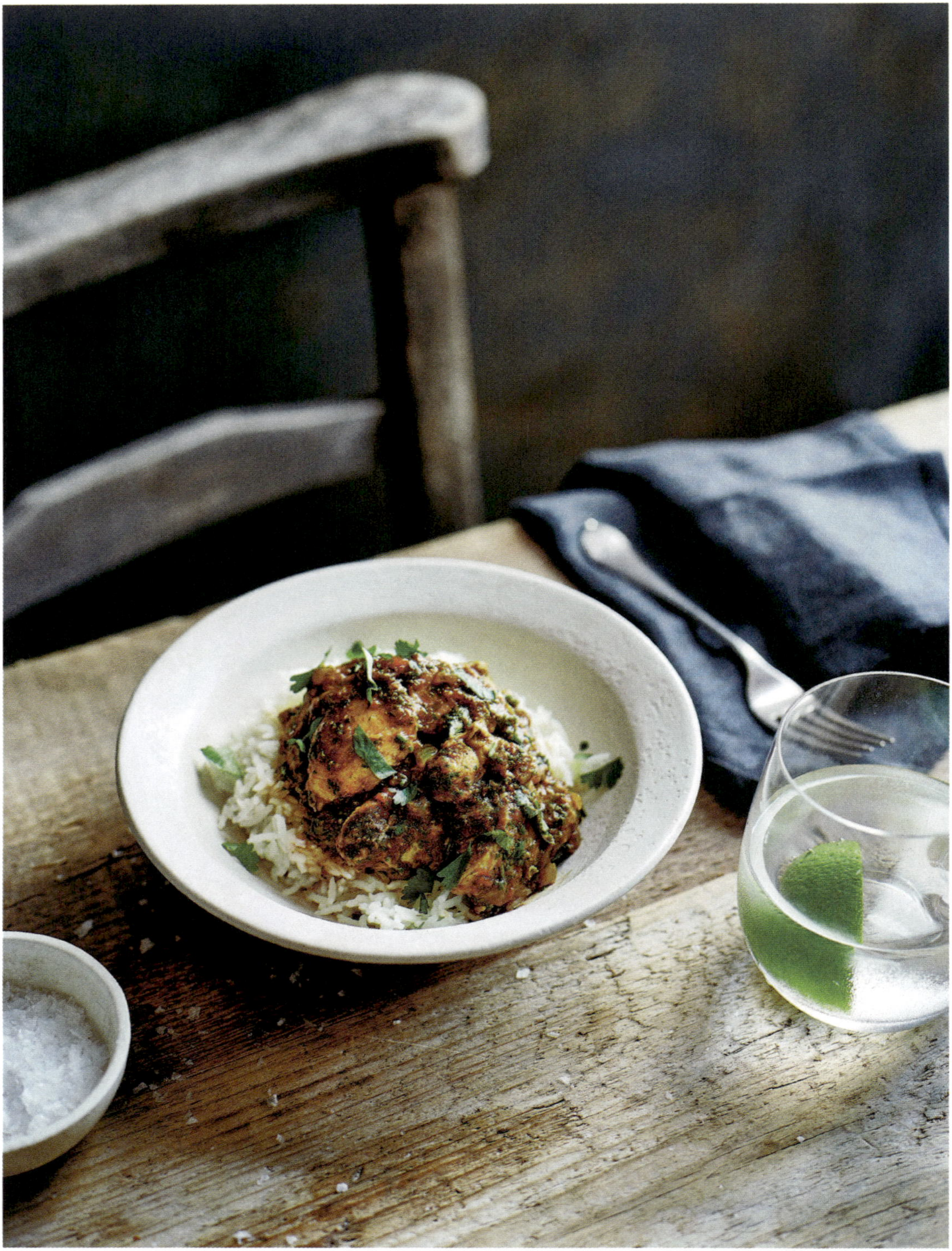

Chicken with spinach and fenugreek

Prep Time: 10 mins
Cook Time: 55 mins
Serves: 4–6

Vegetable oil, 80 ml
2 large white onions, medium diced
5 cm piece of fresh ginger, 20 g, peeled and grated
6 garlic cloves, peeled and grated
Garam masala, 2 tbsp
  Plus 1½ tsp more nutmeg powder and 1 tbsp more cumin powder
Dried fenugreek leaves, 2 tsp
Ground turmeric, ½ tsp
Chilli powder, ¼ tsp
Diced chicken thighs, bone in, 750 g
Tinned chopped tomatoes, 400 g
Fresh spinach leaves, 400g, washed and blended or fresh baby spinach leaves, 400 g
Water, 350 ml
Salt, 1 tsp
Sugar, 1 tsp
1 small bunch of fresh coriander, stalks and leaves, roughly chopped
Obligatory backup jug of water, to loosen the dish to your taste

Chicken in spinach has a very deep, iron-bound umami hit. It's not usual in my home kitchen to combine green veg with chicken in curries, but in this dish, the spinach and fenugreek meld to provide a thick, earthy, velvety sauce. It looks so inviting and has the added benefit of being so wonderfully good for you. You can go one of two ways: unblended fresh spinach leaves and you will end up with a clean common or garden chicken curry; blending the spinach gives you the lawn-like luxury of green silk.

Put the vegetable oil in a large heavy-based saucepan and set over a medium-high heat. When hot, add the diced onions, ginger and garlic and fry for 8 minutes until the onions have softened and turned golden brown.

Add the garam masala, nutmeg powder, cumin powder, fenugreek leaves, ground turmeric, chilli powder and diced chicken thighs and fry for 3–5 minutes until the chicken starts to colour, stirring so it's well coated with the spices.

Add the chopped tomatoes, spinach purée (if using), water, salt and sugar and bring up to the boil. Reduce the heat to low, cover and simmer gently for 35–40 minutes or until the chicken is cooked through.

Finish by stirring through the fresh coriander and baby spinach leaves (if using). Add more water if necessary to loosen to your taste before serving.

Butter chicken

Prep Time: 15 mins
Cook Time: 50 mins
Serves: 4–6

Vegetable oil, 5 tbsp
2 large white onions, medium diced
5 cm piece of fresh ginger, 20 g, peeled and grated
6 garlic cloves, peeled and grated
Garam masala, 2 tbsp
   Plus 1 tbsp more cumin powder and
   1½ tsp coriander powder
Dried fenugreek leaves, 1 tbsp
Ground turmeric, ½ tsp
Chilli powder, ¼ tsp
Tomato purée, 2 tbsp
Tinned chopped tomatoes, 400 g
Natural yoghurt, 5 tbsp
Tandoori masala, 2 tbsp
Diced chicken thighs, 750 g
Salt, 1½ tsp
Sugar, 1–2 tbsp, to taste
Butter, 40 g
Obligatory backup jug of water, to loosen the dish to your taste

Chicken tikka masala was invented in Glasgow but this is the closest you might get to it in an Indian home kitchen. Fenugreek leaf is the nuclear headnote spice in this dish. It gives you that instant 'curry' hit that is powerful and hypnotic. It sweeps through the brain, but also your soft furnishings.

Put 1½ tablespoons of the vegetable oil in a large heavy-based pan and set over a medium-high heat. When hot, add the diced onions, ginger and garlic and fry for 8 minutes or until the onions have softened and turned golden brown.

Turn the heat down to low and add the garam masala, cumin powder, coriander powder, fenugreek leaves, ground turmeric, chilli powder, tomato purée, chopped tomatoes and yoghurt, stir well and cook for a further 5 minutes. Add water to loosen and blend the mixture with a stick blender until it turns into a smooth sauce, then set aside.

Rub the tandoori masala into the diced chicken, then heat a separate large non-stick frying pan with the remaining 3½ tablespoons of oil over a medium-high heat, add the chicken and fry for 6 minutes or until the chicken starts to change colour and brown at the edges.

Add the browned chicken to the blended sauce. Return to a low heat, cover and simmer gently for 30 minutes or until the chicken is cooked through.

Add the salt and sugar and finish by stirring the butter through to create a thick and creamy sauce. Finally, don't be afraid to add more water to loosen the sauce to your taste.

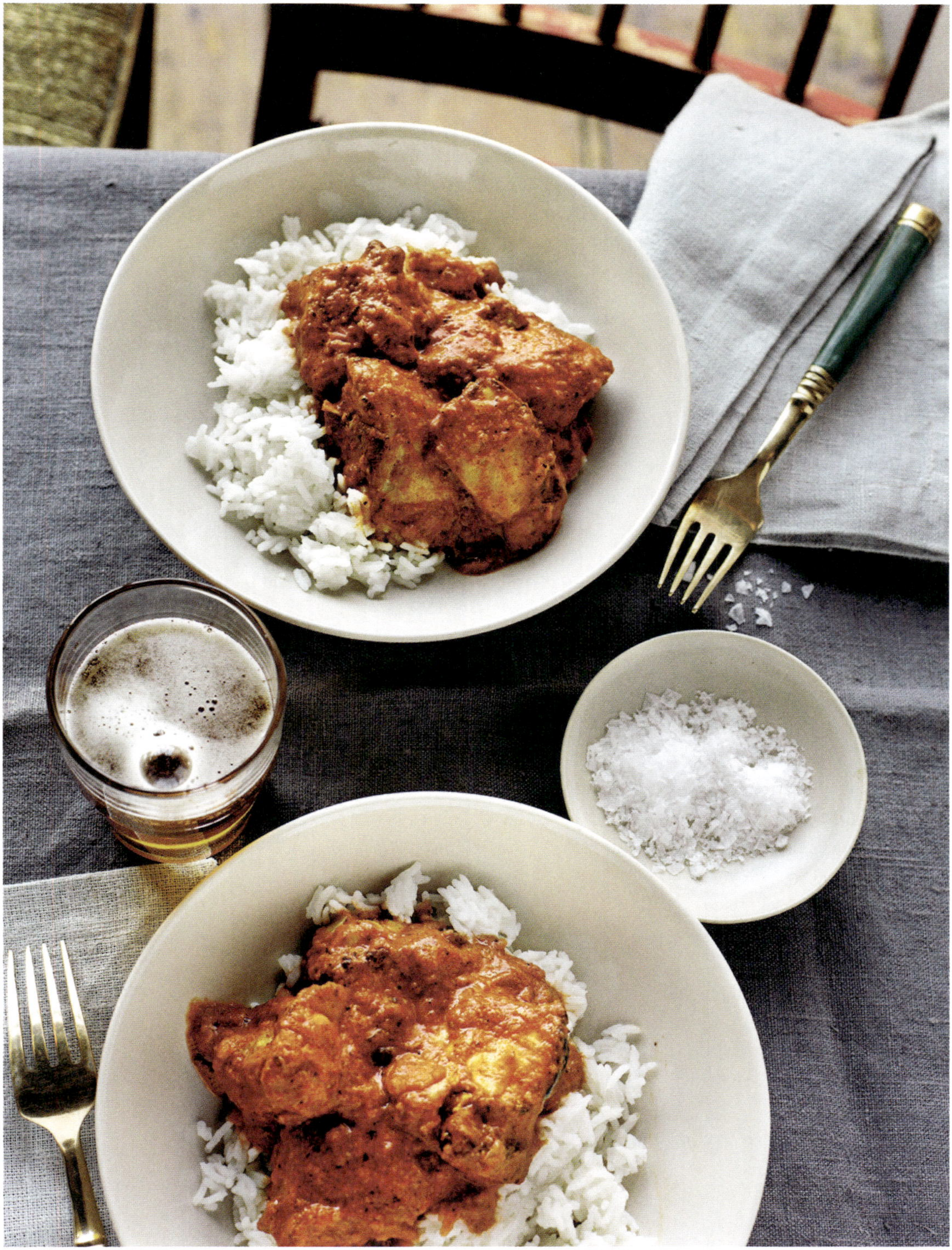

Gizzard and heart jalfrezi

If you visit an Asian butcher, you will see trays of gizzards next to jewel-like chicken hearts. They are often cooked in with meat curries or simply spiced together in a relatively dry base; bear in mind, we Indians love the fight of tough cuts. I remember asking my Bangladeshi butcher how he tenderised gizzards in his curries. 'What's the point in that,' he said. 'The dish would lose all its fun.'

Prep Time: 10 mins
Cook Time: 45 mins
Serves: 4

Vegetable oil, 3 tbsp
2 white onions, finely diced
5 cm piece of fresh ginger, 20 g, peeled and grated
4 garlic cloves, peeled and minced
Chicken gizzards, 400 g
Chicken hearts, 400 g
Garam masala, 2 tbsp
  Plus 1 tsp more cumin powder
Ground turmeric, ½ tsp
Chilli powder, ¼ tsp
Tinned chopped tomatoes, 400 g
Water, 200 ml
Salt, 1 tsp
2 large green capsicums, deseeded and roughly chopped
1 large banana chilli, deseeded and thinly sliced

Put the vegetable oil in a large heavy-based pan and set over a medium-high heat. When hot, add the onions, ginger and garlic and cook for 8 minutes until the onions have softened and turned golden brown. Add the gizzards and hearts and fry until they have coloured.

Add the garam masala, cumin powder, ground turmeric and chilli powder and fry for 2 minutes, then add the chopped tomatoes, water, salt, green capsicums and chilli. Give everything a good stir together, then turn the heat down to low, cover and simmer gently for 30 minutes or until the meat is cooked through and tender.

Chicken with green papaya

Prep Time: 15 mins
Cook Time: 1 hour
Serves: 4–6

Vegetable oil, 80 ml
2 large white onions, medium diced
5 cm piece of fresh ginger, 20 g, peeled and grated
5 garlic cloves, peeled and grated
1 fresh papaya, 200 g, peeled, deseeded and cut into large chunks
3 large green chillies, deseeded and thinly sliced
1 small bunch of fresh coriander, stalks and leaves, roughly chopped
Garam masala, 2 tbsp
   Plus ½ tsp more cumin powder and 1 tbsp more coriander powder
Ground turmeric, ½ tsp
Chilli powder, ¼ tsp
Diced chicken thighs, bone in, 750 g
Tinned chopped tomatoes, 200 g
Water, 350 ml
Salt, 1 tsp
Sugar, 1 tsp
Juice of ½ lemon
Obligatory backup jug of water, to loosen the dish

Tart green papaya is used across the East for its magical ability to tenderise meat. It has a subtle flavour and I think grated into this dish, it gives a fragrant, almost apple edge. You are looking to use the coriander, green chilli and lemon to coax the green notes out of the papaya and into the simmering chicken.

Put the vegetable oil in a large heavy-based pan and set over a medium-high heat. When hot, add the diced onions, ginger and garlic and fry for 8 minutes or until the onions have softened and turned golden brown.

Put the papaya, green chillies and fresh coriander into a food processor and blend until it forms a smooth paste.

In the pan with the onions, add the garam masala, cumin powder, coriander powder, ground turmeric, chilli powder and diced chicken thighs and fry for 4 minutes until the chicken starts to colour and is coated fully in the spices.

Add the papaya paste, chopped tomatoes, water, salt and sugar and bring up to the boil, then reduce the heat to low, cover and simmer gently for 40–45 minutes or until the chicken is cooked through.

Finish with the fresh lemon juice. Add more water if necessary to loosen to your taste before serving.

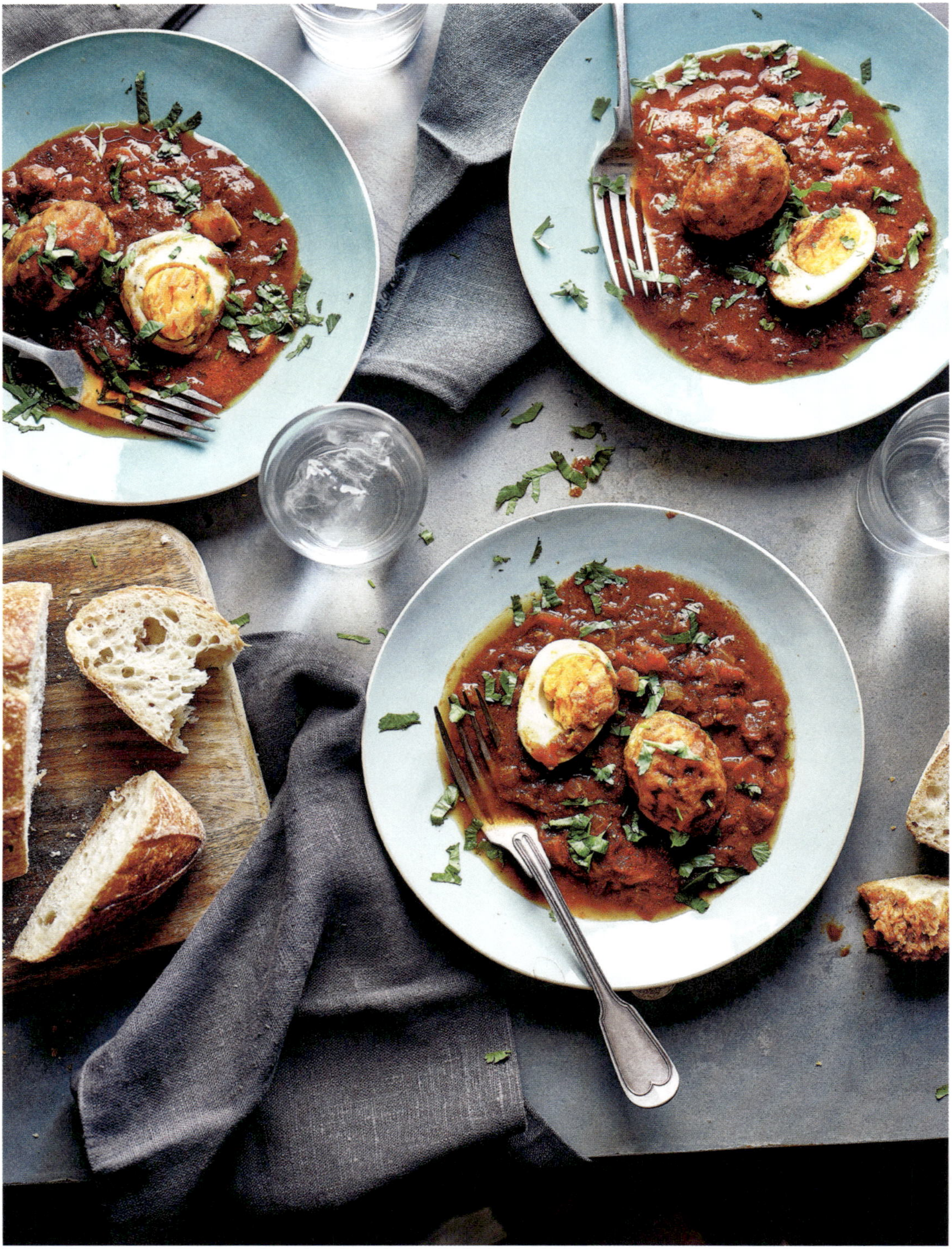

Egg curry

Growing up, this was a dish of luxury. We would only have meat once a week, as is often the case in Indian Hindu households, but these spiced, gnarly eggs were easily as good as a meat hit, mashed into rice and eaten with the fingers. Eggs represent that fascinating intersection between meat and non-meat. Strict Hindus are not allowed them, as for many they rank as a 'non veg' and are prohibited. Eggs are cooked with meat spices, the famous onion-ginger-garlic and garam masala base, but as a nod to the vegetarian method of cooking, they are started with a fried seed spice. The frying and gnarling of the egg whites adds a certain bite that almost emulates the fibres of meat.

Prep Time: 15 mins
Cook Time: 30 mins
Serves: 4

Vegetable oil, 4½ tbsp
Cumin seeds, 1 tsp
2 large white onions, medium diced
5 cm piece of fresh ginger, 20 g, peeled and grated
6 garlic cloves, peeled and grated
Garam masala, 2 tbsp
Plus 1½ tsp more cumin powder and 1½ tsp more coriander powder
Ground turmeric, 1 tsp
Chilli powder, ¼ tsp
Tinned chopped tomatoes, 400 g
Water, 350 ml
Salt, 1 tsp
Sugar, 2 tsp
8 large eggs
Obligatory jug of water, to loosen the dish

Put 3 tablespoons of the vegetable oil in a large heavy-based pan and set over a medium-high heat. When hot, add the cumin seeds and wait for them to turn brown and fragrant. Now add the diced onions, ginger and garlic and fry for 8 minutes or until the onions have softened and turned golden brown.

Add the garam masala, cumin powder, coriander powder, ground turmeric and chilli powder and stir until everything is mixed, then add the chopped tomatoes, water, salt and sugar. Bring up to the boil, then reduce the heat to low and simmer gently for 10 minutes, partially covered.

While the sauce is simmering, boil the eggs in a large pan of water for 8 minutes, then run under cold water and peel off their shells.

Put the remaining 1½ tablespoons of vegetable oil in a large non-stick frying pan and set over a medium-high heat. When hot, add the boiled eggs and fry until they become gnarled, cracked and brown all over. You can leave the eggs whole and add to the curry in bobbing, golden glory or halve to allow some of the yolk to melt into the sauce. Add the eggs to the curry sauce and bring back up to the boil, then simmer for a further 6–8 minutes, partially covered. Add more water if necessary to loosen to your taste before serving.

Note: page numbers in **bold** refer to main entries for individual spices in the spice rack.

A

ajwain **40**
almond
 Hyderabadi coconut and almond chicken 236
 lamb with yoghurt and almonds 211
aloo ghobi 61–2, 68–9
amchoor (dried green mango) 32, **40**, 46, 108, 120–1, 124, 132
 courgette and potato with Panch Poron and amchoor 121
Ancient Alliances of Flavour 18, 56, 74, 94, 114, 138, 180
anise 49, 217
 lamb plum anise curry 216–17
apricot and cinnamon with pheasant 221
asafoetida 27, 28, **40–1**, 50
 and brassicas 56, 66
 and fish and shellfish 180
 and green vegetables 74
 and heavy pulses and grains 158, 175
 and light lentils and dahl 138, 142, 148–9, 152
 and root vegetables 94, 98, 105, 109
 spinach and asafoetida yellow split dahl 152
 and squash 114, 116, 117, 120, 122, 124
 see also Gujrati Quartet; Nuclear Duo
aubergine 119–20, 133
 aubergine with nigella and poppy seed 130–1
 funeral aubergine and potato 129

B

balti 38
bay leaf 28, **41**, 47
 braised red cabbage with mustard and bay 70
 and brassicas 64, 70
 and heavy pulses and grains 165, 169, 171, 174, 176
 and light lentils and dahls 154
 and root vegetables 97
 and squash 132
beef 207
beetroot 99
 sweet-and-sour beetroot and carrot with Panch Poron 100–1
beetroot tops 78
 beetroot tops with mustard and lemon 86
Bengali dishes 28
bhel 162
black peppercorn 36–8, **41**, 47
black salt **41–2**
brassicas 55–71
broccoli 58, 61
 broccoli with mustard and lemon 71
Brussels sprouts 58, 59
 pan-fried sprouts with mustard, lemon and cashew nuts 63
buffalo 207
 buffalo with ginger and nutmeg 219
butter chicken 242–3
butternut squash 117
 butternut curry 132

C

cabbage 58–9, 60
 basic white 60, 64–5
 braised red cabbage with mustard and bay 70
 red 60, 70
 Savoy 60–1
 white cabbage with cumin and tomato 64–5
capsicum (pepper) 79, 244
 capsicum curry 87
cardamom 47
cardamom, black/pods **42**
 and heavy pulses and grains 165, 172, 176
 Puy lentils and chard with cardamom and garam masala 176
cardamom, green/ground **42**, 49, 169
carom *see* ajwain
carrot 97, 161
 carrot and green chilli pickle 105–7
 sweet-and-sour beetroot and carrot with Panch Poron 100–1
cauliflower 58, 61–2
 aloo ghobi 68–9
 cauliflower stalk yellow split dahl 149
 salmon and cauliflower 196–7
chard and Puy lentils with cardamom and garam masala 176
chicken 231–45
 Agra ginger chicken 235
 butter chicken 242–3
 chicken with green papaya 245
 chicken with spinach and fenugreek 240–1
 gizzard and heart jalfrezi 244
 home-style chicken 237–9
 Hyderabadi coconut and almond chicken 236
chickpea(s) 161
 roasted chickpeas 170
 tea-steeped chickpeas 171
 see also gram flour
chilli 17, 24, 26–7, 96, 184, 210
chilli, dried red 28, **42–4**, 51
 and brassicas 63, 66, 67, 70, 71
 and chicken 236
 and green vegetables 74–5, 84, 86, 88, 90
 and heavy pulses and grains 166, 175
 and light lentils and dahls 148

and red meat, game and offal
  226
and root vegetables 100, 105,
  109, 111
and squash 120, 124–5, 133
see also Gujrati Quartet;
  Mustard Seed & Dried Red
  Chilli; South Indian Trio
chilli, fresh green 28, 32, 35–6,
  44, 51
  and brassicas 66, 69
  carrot and green chilli pickle
    105–7
  and chicken 235, 236, 245
  and fish and shellfish 184,
    187, 189, 192–3, 195–6, 198
  green chilli and mango channa
    dahl 150–1, 154
  and green vegetables 83, 84, 85
  guinea fowl with raisins, cumin
    and green chilli 226
  and heavy pulses and grains
    174, 176
  hot sweet potatoes with chilli
    and tomato 110
  and light lentils and dahl 142,
    146–54
  masala spice paste 166, 169
  and red meat, game and offal
    211, 226
  and root vegetables 103
  and squash 128, 130, 132, 134
  see also Nigella Seed with
    Green Chilli
chilli powder 16, 27, 29, 31
  and brassicas 63, 64, 66, 67,
    69, 70, 71
  and chicken 235, 236, 237,
    241, 242, 244, 245
  and fish and shellfish 180,
    187–8, 192–3, 195–6, 198–9
  and green vegetables 74, 80,
    83–8, 90–1
  and heavy pulses and grains
    158, 165, 169–71, 174–6
  hot sweet potatoes with chilli
    and tomato 110
  and light lentils and dahls 138,

146–9, 151–4
and red meat, game and
  offal 202, 204, 211, 214–15,
  217–21, 224, 226–7
and root vegetables 94, 97,
  100, 103, 111
and squash 114, 121–2,
  124–5, 128–30, 132–4
chips, Indian 104
cinnamon 24, **44**, 47, 49
  and chicken 235, 237
  and garam masala 210
  and heavy pulses and grains
    165, 169
  pheasant with cinnamon and
    apricots 221
  and red meat, game and offal
    210, 212, 221, 224
clam 185–6
clove(s) **44–5**, 47, 49, 172
cockle(s) 186
coconut flakes, coconut and
  raisin channa dahl 154–5
coconut milk 32, 35, 36, 165,
  187, 211
  Hyderabadi coconut and
    almond chicken 236
coriander 24, 47
coriander leaf 32, 35–6, **45**
  and brassicas 69
  and chicken 235, 236, 241, 245
  and fish and shellfish 187,
    188, 192, 195, 196, 198
  and green vegetables 85
  and heavy pulses and grains
    165–6, 169, 171, 174–5
  and light lentils and dahls 142,
    146–9, 151–3
  and red meat, game and offal
    224
  and root vegetables 103, 109
  and squash 134
coriander powder 32, **45**, 49, 247
  and brassicas 64, 66
  and chicken 237, 242, 245
  and fish and shellfish 196, 198
  green beans with Panch Poron
    and coriander 91

and green vegetables 87, 90, 91
and heavy pulses and grains
  160, 170, 176
and red meat, game and offal
  202–5, 210, 221
and root vegetables 96–7,
  108–9
and squash 129
courgette 79, 117–18
  courgette and potato with
    Panch Poron and amchoor
    121
  courgette stalks and leaves 133
  fried courgette flowers 134–5
crab 185–6
  grandmother's Varanasi crab
    198–9
cumin 24, 47, 50, 51
cumin powder **46**, 247
  and chicken 235–7, 241–2,
    244–5
  crunchy okra with cumin 82–3
  green beans with cumin, honey
    and pecans 80–1
  and green vegetables 80–3
  and heavy pulses and grains
    160, 165, 170, 171, 176
  and red meat, game and offal
    202–5, 211, 214–15,
    217–20, 226–7, 229
  and root vegetables 98
  and squash 134
cumin powder, roasted **46**
cumin seed 27, 28, 29, **45–6**,
  247
  and brassicas 56, 57, 59,
    64–6, 69
  and fish and shellfish 180,
    181, 183
  green beans with cumin, honey
    and pecans 80–1
  and green vegetables 74–6,
    84–5, 87
  guinea fowl with raisins, cumin
    and green chilli 226
  and heavy pulses and grains
    158–9, 165–6, 169, 171,
    174

and light lentils and dahls 138–9, 146, 148–9, 151–4
and root vegetables 94–8, 108–9
and squash 114, 132
white cabbage with cumin and tomato 64–5
see also Gujrati Quartet
curry leaf 27, 28, **46**
and fish and shellfish 186, 187
and heavy pulses and grains 166, 175
and light lentils and dahls 148
and red meat, game and offal 211, 226
and root vegetables 98
and squash 120
see also South Indian Trio
curry names 38

D

dahl 39
cauliflower stalk yellow split dahl 149
channa dahl 124, 143, 150–1, 154–5
coconut and raisin channa dahl 154–5
garam masala black dahl 168–9
gooseberry dahl 146
green chilli and mango channa dahl 150–1
green dahl with rhubarb and ginger 174
light dahls 137–55
spinach and asafoetida yellow split dahl 152
and squashes 117, 118
tamarind, okra and radish red dahl 148
toor dahl 143
white onion and nigella seed red dahl 147
yellow moong dahl 143
dopiaza 233
dried fruit 35, 36
duck, sweet tamarind 218

E

egg 232–3
egg curry 246–7
English mustard paste 25, 28, 32, **50**
and brassicas 63, 67
and fish and shellfish 189, 192, 195–6, 198
and green vegetables 84–8, 90–1
and red meat, game and offal 223
and root vegetables 111
and squash 130, 133

F

fennel 24, 47, 51
fenugreek 27, 51
fenugreek leaf (dried) **47**, 124, 165, 242
chicken with spinach and fenugreek 240–1
fenugreek leaf (fresh) **47**
fenugreek powder **47**
fenugreek seed **47**
and root vegetables 94, 105
and squash 114, 116, 120, 122, 129, 133
see also Nuclear Duo
finishing flavours 31–6
fish and shellfish 14–16, 25–6, 28–9, 35, 39, 179–99
Aunty Geeta's prawns 193
Goan fish curry with tamarind 188–9
grandmother's Varanasi crab 198–9
mackerel with nigella and tomato 194–5
salmon and cauliflower 196–7
sea bass in fried yoghurt sauce 192
South Indian monkfish 187
steamed Bengali trout 190–1
foraged greens 78–9
fruit 32, 35
dried 35, 36

G

game see red meat, game and offal
garam masala 24, 27–8, 32, 38–9, **47–9**, 248
and brassicas 64
and chicken 233, 235–7, 241–2, 245
and fish and shellfish 199
garam masala black dahl 168–9
and heavy pulses and grains 160–2, 165, 171, 176
individual spices of 41–2, 44–5, 47, 50–1
Puy lentils and chard with cardamom and garam masala 176
and red meat, game and offal 202–5, 210–12, 214–15, 217–21, 223–4, 227, 229
and root vegetables 98, 99
and squash 122, 132
garlic 28, 32, 35, 39, 247
and brassicas 59–61, 63, 67
and chicken 233, 235–7, 241–2, 244–5
and fish and shellfish 180, 184, 187, 188, 199
and green vegetables 76
and heavy pulses and grains 158, 160, 162, 165, 171, 174
kale with mustard and garlic 67
and masala spice paste 166, 169
and red meat, game and offal 202, 204, 209–12, 214–15, 217–20, 223–4, 227, 229
and root vegetables 98
and squash 129, 134
see also Meat Mantra; Meat-Veg Marriage
ghee **49**, 64
and light lentils and dahls 146–9, 151–4
ginger, fresh 28, 35, 39, **50**, 247
Agra ginger chicken 235
and brassicas 59, 60, 64

buffalo with ginger and nutmeg 219
and chicken 233, 235–7, 241–2, 244–5
and fish and shellfish 180, 184, 187–8, 198–9
green dahl with rhubarb and ginger 174
and heavy pulses and grains 158, 160, 162, 165–6, 169, 171, 174, 176
and masala spice paste 166
pumpkin and ginger curry 122–3
and red meat, game and offal 202, 204, 209–15, 217–21, 223–4, 227, 229
and root vegetables 96–8, 109
spiced ginger lamb *raan* 212–13
see also Meat Mantra; Meat-Veg Marriage
gizzard and heart jalfrezi 244
Goan fish curry with tamarind 188–9
goat 207
  railway goat curry 214
gooseberry dahl 146
gourds 118–19
  hot bitter gourds 128
grains, heavy 157–76
gram flour 161, 175
green bean 78
  green beans with cumin, honey and pecans 80–1
  green beans with Panch Poron and coriander 91
green vegetables 73–91
guinea fowl with raisins, cumin and green chilli 226
Gujrat 36, 41
Gujrati dishes 28, 66, 109
Gujrati Quartet 17, 31
  and brassicas 56, 57
  and green vegetables 74–5
  and heavy pulses and grains 158, 159
  and light lentils and dahl 138, 139
  and root vegetables 94, 95

and squash 114, 115

H

headnote spices 27–31, 35, 50
  and brassicas 56, 59
  and chicken 233
  and fish and shellfish 180, 182, 183–4, 186
  and green vegetables 74
  and heavy pulses and grains 158, 160–2
  and light lentils and dahl 138
  and red meat, game and offal 202, 204, 210
  and root vegetables 94, 96, 97, 98, 99
  and squash 114, 119, 120
Hindu tradition 20, 182, 206, 207–8, 232–3
Hyderabadi coconut and almond chicken 236

J

jalfrezi 233
  gizzard and heart jalfrezi 244

K

kale 58, 60
  kale with mustard and garlic 67
  masala roasted quail with kale 222–3
karhi 161, 175
kedgeree 25, 183
kidney bean(s) 162, 165
king fish 185
kitchuri 183
kohlrabi 58, 60
  Gujrati kohlrabi 66
Koi 185
korma 234

L

lamb 207
  lamb plum anise curry 216–17
  lamb with yoghurt and almonds 211
  masala lamb chops 215
  spiced ginger lamb *raan* 212–13

spiced stuffed lambs hearts 228–9
see also mutton
lau, milk 125–7
lemon 32, 35
  beetroot tops with mustard and lemon 86
  and brassicas 59, 61, 63, 67, 70–1
  broccoli with mustard and lemon 71
  and chicken 245
  and fish and shellfish 196, 199
  and green vegetables 80, 84–6
  and heavy pulses and grains 166, 169, 174, 176
  and light lentils and dahl 146–9, 151–4
  pan-fried sprouts with mustard, lemon and cashew nuts 63
  and red meat, game and offal 215, 226
  and root vegetables 96, 100, 105, 109–10
  and squash 120–2, 128
lentil(s) 32–5, 39
  black lentils 162, 169
  green bean and cumin red dahl 153
  light (red/yellow) lentils 137–55
  okra and radish red dahl 148
  Puy lentils and chard with cardamom and garam masala 176
  white onion and nigella seed red dahl 147
liver, Indian liver with onions 227
lobster 185

M

mace 47, **50**
mackerel 185
  mackerel with nigella and tomato 194–5
mange tout and potato with Panch Poron 90
mango
  green chilli and mango channa

251

dahl 150–1
see also amchoor
marrow 78, 117–18
  Mona's nutty marrow 124
masala lamb chops 215
masala roasted quail with kale 222–3
masala spice paste 166
Meat Mantra 18, 31, 202, 204, 205
Meat-Veg Marriage 18, 31, 181
milk lau 125–7
millet 162–3
molluscs 185–6
monkfish 185
  South Indian monkfish 187
mooli 62, 86, 133
Muslim tradition 206, 207
  mustard paste
  and brassicas 59, 61
  and green vegetables 77
  and root vegetables 96, 99
  and squash 119, 125
  see also English mustard paste
mustard seed 24, 26–8, **50–1**
  beetroot tops with mustard and lemon 86
  braised red cabbage with mustard and bay 70
  and brassicas 56, 59, 61, 63, 66, 70–1
  broccoli with mustard and lemon 71
  and chicken 236
  and fish and shellfish 180, 183–4, 186, 187, 198
  and green vegetables 74–5, 76, 84, 86, 88–9
  and heavy pulses and grains 158, 166, 175
  kale with mustard and garlic 67
  and light lentils and dahl 138, 146, 148
  mustardy pea shoots and potatoes 88–9
  pan-fried sprouts with mustard, lemon and cashew nuts 63
  popped mustard radish pods 84
  and red meat, game and offal 204, 211, 218, 226
  and root vegetables 94, 98, 105, 109
  and squash 114, 119–20, 125, 133
  see also Gujrati Quartet; Mustard Seed & Dried Red Chilli; South Indian Trio
Mustard Seed & Dried Red Chilli 18
  for brassicas 56, 57
  for fish and shellfish 180, 181
  for light lentils and dahl 138, 139
  for root vegetables 94, 95
  for squash 114, 115
mutton 207
  mutton *keema* with pine nuts 220
  railway goat curry 214
  see also lamb

N

nigella seed 26, 27, 28, **51**
  aubergine with nigella and poppy seed 130–1
  and fish and shellfish 180, 183–4, 192–3, 195, 199
  and green vegetables 76
  and light lentils 138, 147
  mackerel with nigella and tomato 194–5
  potato with nigella, onion and poppy seed 102–3
  and root vegetables 94, 110
  and squash 128
  white onion and nigella seed red dahl 147
  see also Nigella Seed with Green Chilli
Nigella Seed with Green Chilli 18, 94–5, 138–9, 180–1
Nuclear Duo 17, 29, 59, 95, 114, 115
nutmeg 47, 169, 212, 241
  buffalo with ginger and nutmeg 219
nuts 32, 35, 36, 80–1
  Mona's nutty marrow 124

O

offal *see* red meat, game and offal
okra 79, 119
  crunchy okra with cumin 82–3
  okra curry 85
  tamarind, okra and radish red dahl 148
onion 28, 35, 39, 247
  and brassicas 59
  and chicken 233, 235–7, 241–2, 244–5
  and fish and shellfish 180, 184, 187, 188, 199
  and green vegetables 76, 83, 85, 87, 90, 91
  and heavy pulses and grains 158, 160, 162, 165, 169, 171, 174, 176
  Indian liver with onions 227
  and light lentils and dahl 147
  potato with nigella, onion and poppy seed 102–3
  and red meat, game and offal 202, 204, 209–12, 214, 217–21, 224, 227, 229
  and root vegetables 98, 100, 103, 111
  and squash 121, 128, 129, 132
  white onion and nigella seed red dahl 147
  see also Meat Mantra; Meat-Veg Marriage
oxtail curry 224–5

P

Panch Poron seed 27, 28, **51**
  and brassicas 56, 57, 59
  courgette and potato with Panch Poron and amchoor 121
  and fish and shellfish 180, 181, 188, 196
  green beans with Panch Poron and coriander 91

and green vegetables 74–5, 76, 78, 90–1
and light lentils and dahl 138, 139
mange tout and potato with Panch Poron 90
picnic potatoes with radish and Panch Poron 111
and root vegetables 94–5, 97, 99–101, 111
and squash 114, 115
sweet-and-sour beetroot and carrot with Panch Poron 100–1
papaya, chicken with green papaya 245
parsnip with potato, Gujrati 109
pea shoots 79
  mustardy pea shoots and potatoes 88–9
peanut and potato *powa* 166–7
pepper see capsicum
pheasant with cinnamon and apricots 221
pickle, carrot and green chilli 105–7
pine nut 35
  mutton *keema* with pine nuts 220
pippali 38, **41**
plum anise lamb curry 216–17
pomfret 185
poppy seed 119, 120
  aubergine with nigella and poppy seed 130–1
  potato with nigella, onion and poppy seed 102–3
  see also white poppy seed
pork 207–8
Portuguese tradition 208
potato 29, 96–7
  aloo ghobi 68–9
  beetroot tops with mustard and lemon 86
  capsicum curry 87
  courgette and potato with Panch Poron and amchoor 121
  courgette stalks and leaves 133

funeral aubergine and potato 129
Gujrati kohlrabi 66
Gujrati potato with parsnip 109
Indian chips 104
mange tout and potato with Panch Poron 90
mustardy pea shoots and potatoes 88–9
oxtail curry 224
peanut and potato *powa* 166–7
picnic potatoes with radish and Panch Poron 111
potato with nigella, onion and poppy seed 102–3
railway goat curry 214
white cabbage with cumin and tomato 64
powa 162–3
  peanut and potato powa 166–7
prawn 185
  Aunty Geeta's prawns 193
pressure cookers 143–4
pulses 14–16, 28–9, 32–5, 39
  heavy 157–76
pumpkin 116–17
  pumpkin and ginger curry 122–3
pumpkin-type squashes 116–17
Puy lentil and chard with cardamom and garam masala 176

Q

quail, masala roasted quail with kale 222–3

R

radish
  picnic potatoes with radish and Panch Poron 111
  popped mustard radish pods 84
  tamarind, okra and radish red dahl 148
raisin 229
  coconut and raisin channa dahl 154–5
  guinea fowl with raisins, cumin and green chilli 226

rajasic ingredients 140–1
rajma curry 165
red meat, game and offal 14–16, 28–9, 35–6, 39, 201–29
rhubarb and ginger with green dahl 174
rice 162–3
  boiled rice 164
  family fried rice 172–3
  fried rice 163
root vegetables 93–111
roti breads 39

S

salmon and cauliflower 196–7
salt, black **41–2**
satvic ingredients 140–1
sea bass in fried yoghurt sauce 192
seasoning 36–8
sesame seed, white 166
South Indian dishes 28
South Indian Trio 17, 29
  for brassicas 56, 57
  for fish and shellfish 180, 181
  for green vegetables 74–5
  for heavy pulses and grains 158, 159
  for light lentils and dahl 138, 139
  for red meat, game and offal 204, 205
  for root vegetables 94, 95
  for squash 114, 115
spice kit 24
spice rack 40–52
spice traditions 24–6
spice treatment 38–9
spice trinity 26–7
spinach 110, 171, 235
  chicken with spinach and fenugreek 240–1
  spinach and asafoetida yellow split dahl 152
squash 60, 113–35
squid 185
star anise **51**
starter balls 16–17

for brassicas 56
for fish and shellfish 180
for green vegetables 74
for heavy pulses and grains 158
for light lentils and dahl 138
for red meat, game and offal 204
for root vegetables 94
for squash 114
starter buttons 29
swede 161
sweet potato 98–9
   hot sweet potatoes with chilli and tomato 110
sweet-and-sour beetroot and carrot with Panch Poron 100–1
Swiss chard and Puy lentil with cardamom and garam masala 176

T

tamarind paste 32, 35, 36, 184
   Goan fish curry with tamarind 188–9
   sweet tamarind duck 218
   tamarind, okra and radish red dahl 148
Tandoori Masala **52**, 242
tea-steeped chickpeas 171
Tenderstem broccoli with mustard and lemon 71
tikka masala 38
tomato 32, 35, 36
   and chicken 235, 237, 241–2, 244–5
   and egg curry 247
   and fish and shellfish 188, 193–6, 198–9
   and green vegetables 76, 85, 87, 91
   and heavy pulses and grains 161–2, 165, 169, 171, 174
   hot sweet potatoes with chilli and tomato 110
   and light lentils and dahls 147, 148, 151, 153–4
   mackerel with nigella and tomato 194–5
   and red meat, game and offal 214, 217, 219–20, 224
   and root vegetables 96–7, 109–11
   and squash 121, 130
   white cabbage with cumin and tomato 64–5
   white onion and nigella seed red dahl 147
trout, steamed Bengali 190–1
turmeric, ground 16–17, 24, 26, 29, 31, 39, **52**, 247
   and brassicas 63–4, 66–7, 69–71
   and chicken 235–7, 241–2, 244–5
   and fish and shellfish 180, 183, 187–9, 192–3, 195–6, 198–9
   and green vegetables 74, 80, 83–8, 90–1
   and heavy pulses and grains 158, 165–6, 169–71, 174–6
   and light lentils and dahls 138, 146–9, 151–4
   and red meat, game and offal 202, 204, 210–11, 214–15, 217–21, 224, 226–7
   and root vegetables 94, 96–7, 100, 103–4, 108–11
   and squash 114, 119, 121–2, 124–5, 128–30, 132–4
turnip 70
village turnip 108

V

vegetables 14–16, 25, 28–9, 32, 36, 39
   see also green vegetables; root vegetables; *specific vegetables*
vindaloo 208, 233

W

white poppy seed 32, **52**, 103, 192
   aubergine with nigella and poppy seed 130–1

wild boar 208

Y

yam 98
yellow split pea 143, 146
   cauliflower stalk yellow split dahl 149
   spinach and asafoetida yellow split dahl 152
yin and yang 140–1
yogurt, natural 32, 35, 36
   and chicken 234, 236, 242
   and fish and shellfish 187, 192
   and heavy pulses and grains 162, 175
   lamb with yoghurt and almonds 211
   and red meat, game and offal 211, 215
   sea bass in fried yoghurt sauce 192

ACKNOWLEDGEMENTS

Thank you to Jan and Borra my agents at DML for their patient support always. Speaking of patience, Laura Higginson at Ebury fluctuated between saint, friend, sister and counsel with grace and gravity. I could not have asked for a better publishing experience Laura, thank you.

Thanks also go to the superb team behind the production, editing, proofreading, photography and design in its myriad complexity: Chris Hegarty, Lucy Harrison, Peter Grundy, David and Two Associates, Toby Clarke, Kay Delves, Martin Poole, James Murphy and Anne Shelby.

Writing a book takes up every ounce of ones being. During those long years, months and weeks, my family stood by and doffed their caps to a mythical tome that only existed in my mind. Nothing was tangible to them, apart from a laptop and a wife/mother/daughter utterly absorbed. Throughout, Zoltan, India, Tia and Maa remained enthusiastic and patient and kind. And they are the ones who will be the first to greet *The Spice Tree* with the joy of a proud sibling. I would have no appetite for food, no appetite for writing, no appetite for very much without them.

3 5 7 9 10 8 6 4 2

Ebury Press, an imprint of Ebury Publishing,
20 Vauxhall Bridge Road,
London, SW1V 2SA

Ebury Press is part of the Penguin Random House group of companies whose addresses can be found at global.penguinrandomhouse.com

Penguin
Random House
UK

Copyright © Nisha Katona 2017
Photography © James Murphy 2017
Photography on pages 4, 81, 103, 106, 107, 178, 190,
197, 213, 220, 240, 246 © Martin Poole 2017
Spice Tree Illustrations © Peter Grundy

Nisha Katona has asserted her right to be identified as the author of this Work in accordance with the Copyright, Designs and Patents Act 1988

First published by Ebury Press in 2017
This edition published in 2018

www.penguin.co.uk

A CIP catalogue record for this book is available from the British Library

Designed by Two Associates

ISBN: 9781529102994

Colour origination by Altaimage, London
Printed and bound in Italy by L.E.G.O. S.p.A

Penguin Random House is committed to a sustainable future for our business, our readers and our planet. This book is made from Forest Stewardship Council® certified paper.

MIX
Paper from responsible sources
FSC® C018179